The Incarnation

AN ANTHOLOGY

The Incarnation
AN ANTHOLOGY

THOMAS NELSON PUBLISHERS
Nashville

Library of Congress Cataloging-in-Publication Data is available.

Published in Nashville, Tennessee by Thomas Nelson, Inc.

Printed in the United States of America
1 2 3 4 5 — 06 05 04 03 02

Table of Contents

Preface .... *xiii*

CHAPTER ONE: *The Betrothal* *1*
- "Joseph Was an Old Man"
- "Joseph's Prayer," *Max Lucado*
- "Joseph," *G. K. Chesterton*
- "As Joseph Was a-Walking"
- "Joseph Son of David," *Charles L. Allen and Charles L. Wallis*
- "The Man Joseph," *Sally Meyer*
- "The Vigil of Joseph," *Elsa Barker*
- "While the World Awaited," *R. Michael Cullinan*
- "Joseph's Suspicion," *Rainer Maria Rilke, Trans. by J. B. Leishman*
- "The Betrothal," *Beth Moore*

CHAPTER TWO: *The Annunciation* *16*
- "Gabriel's Questions," *Max Lucado*
- "The Annunciation," *Samuel Menashe*
- "Annunciation," *John Donne*
- "Annunciation," *Kathleen Norris*
- "Mary and Gabriel," *Rupert Brooke*
- Excerpt from *The Divine Comedy, Dante*
- "Putting Christ Back Into Christmas," *John Hagee*
- "I Sing of a Maiden"
- "A New Carol of Our Lady"
- "The Holy Mother," *Romano Guardini*
- "Advent," *Christina Rosetti*
- "Annunciation," *Penelope Stokes*

- "From East to West, From Shore to Shore"
- "The Annunciation," *Stephen Mitchell*
- "The Angelic Encounter: Mary and Gabriel," *Beth Moore*
- "I Know of a Name," *Jean Perry*
- "Good Tidings of Great Joy," *Jackie McCullough*
- "The Second Nun's Tale," *Geoffrey Chaucer*
- "Annunciation," *David Craig*
- "Annunciation to Mary," *Rainer Maria Rilke, Trans. by J. B. Leishman*

CHAPTER THREE: *Mary's Song* 52
- "Mary's Song," *Luci Shaw*
- "The Wondrous Soul," *Martin Luther*
- "The Blessed Virgin Compared to the Air We Breathe," *Gerard Manley Hopkins*
- "The Angel Assured Mary That Nothing Is Impossible with God," *Jack Hayford*
- "A Virgin Most Pure"
- "Mary's Visitation," *Rainer Maria Rilke, Trans. by J. B. Leishman*
- "Be Compassionate," *Warren Wiersbe*
- "A Great and Mighty Wonder," *St. Germanus*
- "Mother Mary," *Sally Meyer*
- "Bethlehem"
- "On the Favored One, the Virgin Mary," *Harold John Ockenga*
- "Gentle Mary Laid Her Child," *Joseph Simpson Cook*
- "The Virgin Mary," *John Donne*
- "The Mary Model," *Creflo A. Dollar*
- "Vermeer," *Stephen Mitchell*
- "Sleep, My Little Jesus," *William C. Gannett*
- "On the Purity of Conception," *Ulrich Zwingli*
- "The Love That I Bear," *Michael Card and Scott Brasher*
- "The Mother of God," *W. B. Yeats*
- "Virgin Birth," *Frederick Buechner*
- "On the Mystery of God's Ways," *Dietrich Bonhoeffer*

CHAPTER FOUR: *No Room in the Inn* **77**
- "Room for Jesus," *Billy Graham*
- "The Nativity," *C. S. Lewis*
- "New Prince, New Pomp," *Robert Southwell*
- "Open My Heart," *Rosalyn Hart Finch*
- "The Maid-Servant at the Inn," *Dorothy Parker*
- "No Room at the Inn," *Max Lucado*
- "Room in the Inn," *Sally Meyer*
- "Away in a Manger"
- "The Nativity," *G. K. Chesterton*
- "No Room in the Inn," *A. L. Skilton*
- "Child in the Manger," *Mary M. Macdonald, Trans. by Lachlan Macbean*
- "Nativity," *John Donne*
- "Prayer at the Manger"
- "The Oxen," *Thomas Hardy*
- "Visiting Bethlehem," *Annie Dillard*
- "Now Yield We Thanks and Praise," *Howard C. Robbins*
- "The Nativity," *Henry Vaughn*
- "The Friendly Beasts"
- "Upon Christ His Birth," *Sir John Suckling*
- "Christmas Day Prayer"
- "Once in Royal David's City," *Cecil F. Alexander*
- "On the Morning of Christ's Nativity," *John Milton*
- "Cradled in a Manger, Meanly," *George Stringer Rowe*
- "There Came a Little Child to Earth," *Emily E. Elliott*
- "Infant Holy, Infant Lowly," *Trans. by Edith M. Reed*
- "A Christmas Carol," *Christina Rossetti*
- "O Jesus Christ, Thy Manger Is," *Paul Gerhardt*
- "Christmas I," *George Herbert*
- "A Small Cathedral," *Max Lucado*

CHAPTER FIVE: *The Incarnation* **114**
- "A Hymn on the Nativity of My Saviour," *Ben Jonson*
- "On the Incarnation of the Word," *Athanasius*
- "A Word," *G. K. Chesterton*

- "When Came in Flesh the Incarnate Word," *Joseph Anstice*
- "Where God Enters," *Meister Eckhart*
- "Satan Legend," *Chuck Swindoll*
- "On the Incarnation," *Karl Barth*
- "The Birth of Christ," *Alfred Lord Tennyson*
- "Jesus Is an Esteemed Name," *David Jeremiah*
- "Born of Woman," *Wislawa Szymborska*
- "Come, Thou Redeemer of the Earth," *Ambrose of Milan*
- "The Burning Babe," *Robert Southwell*
- "Christmas Is a Simple Story," *Charles L. Allen and Charles L. Wallis*
- "John 1:14 (1964)," *Jorge Luis Borges*
- "What Child Is This?"
- "The Name of a King," *Ron Phillips*
- "Lauda Sion Salvatorem," *St. Thomas Aquinas*
- "In Excelsis Gloria"
- "The Divine Dawning," *Karl Rahner*
- "The Lamb," *William Blake*
- "On the Incarnation," *Dietrich Bonhoeffer*
- "The Incarnation Is No Compromise," *A. W. Tozer*
- "O Come Redeemer of Mankind," *Ambrose of Milan*
- "Incarnation," *Frederick Buechner*
- "Made Flesh," *Luci Shaw*

CHAPTER SIX: *The Gifts of the Magi* *145*
- "Moonless Darkness," *Gerard Manley Hopkins*
- "The Adoration of Kings," *William Carlos Williams*
- "The Jealousy of King Herod," *Charles Dickens*
- "Hymn," *Sydney Godolphin*
- "Journey of the Magi," *T. S. Eliot*
- "The Wise Men," *G. K. Chesterton*
- "Star Song," *Luci Shaw*
- "The Three Kings of Cologne," *Sir Thomas Browne*
- "The First Noel"
- "The Three Holy Kings (Legend)," *Rainer Maria Rilke*

- "There Came Wise Men from the East," *Charles L. Allen and Charles L. Wallis*
- "The Three Kings," *Henry Wadsworth Longfellow*
- "The Star Still Guides," *Tommy Barnett*
- "Wise Men," *Sally Meyer*
- "The Star," *George Herbert*
- "They Saw His Star," *Charles L. Allen and Charles L. Wallis*
- "The Adoration of the Wise Men," *Cecil Frances Alexander*
- "Words for the Magi," *Elizabeth Jennings*
- "The Other Wise Man (Abridged)," *Henry Van Dyke*
- "A Song of Gifts to God," *G. K. Chesterton*
- "The Star in the East," *Charles L. Allen and Charles L. Wallis*
- "The Magi," *W. B. Yeats*
- "Christmas Memories," *James Dobson*
- "From the Eastern Mountains," *Godfrey Thring*
- "The Gift," *William Carlos Williams*
- "The Gift of the Magi," *O. Henry*

CHAPTER SEVEN: *As Shepherds Watched Their Flocks by Night* *200*
- "As Shepherds Watched Their Flocks," *Charles Dickens*
- "Shepherds, Rejoice! Lift Up Your Eyes," *Isaac Watts*
- "Annunciation to the Shepherds from Above," *Rainer Maria Rilke, Trans. by J. B. Leishman*
- "Rise Up, Shepherd, and Follow"
- "Shepherds at the Grange," *Henry Wadsworth Longfellow*
- "Angels We Have Heard on High," *Trans. by James Chadwick*
- "A Christmas Carol," *Samuel Coleridge*
- "From Far Away"
- "The Three Poor Shepherds," *Sir Thomas Browne*
- "The Shepherd's Hymn," *Richard Crashaw*
- "In the Lonely Midnight," *Theodore C. Williams*
- "Dawning Fair, Morning Wonderful"
- "There Were Shepherds," *Charles L. Allen and Charles L. Wallis*
- "Peaceful the Wondrous Night," *Eliza E. Hewitt*

- "The Shepherds Had an Angel," *Christina Rossetti*
- "Shepherd," *Sally Meyer*
- "Come, All Ye Shepherds," *Trans. by Mari Ruef Hofer*
- "We Have Christmas in Our Neighbor," *Martin Luther*
- "Christians Awake, Salute the Happy Morn," *John Byrom*
- "Hark! The Herald Angels Sing," *Charles Wesley*
- "Christmas (II)," *George Herbert*
- "Go Tell It on the Mountain," *John W. Work, Jr.*
- "A Christmas Prayer," *Robert Louis Stevenson*
- "The Child and the Shepherd," *Frank Sewall*
- "The Truce of Christmas," *G. K. Chesterton*
- "While Shepherds Watched Their Flocks," *Nahum Tate*

CHAPTER EIGHT: *Flight to Egypt and the Massacre of the Innocents* 227
- "All Hail, Ye Little Martyr Flowers," *Aurelius Prudentius, Trans. by John A. L. Riley*
- "The Massacre of the Innocents," *Jose Saramago*
- "The Carnal and the Crane"
- "Who Can Forget—Never To Be Forgot"
- "Coventry Carol"
- "On the Flight into Egypt and the Massacre of the Innocents" *Frederic Farrar*
- "The Murder of the Innocents," *Charles Dickens*
- "Glory to Thee, O Lord," *Emma L. Toke*
- "Wassailing Song"
- "Night Flight into Egypt," *Penelope Stokes*
- "Flight by Night," *Charles L. Allen* and *Charles L. Wallis*
- "Rest on the Flight into Egypt," *Rainer Maria Rilke, Trans. by J. B. Leishman*
- "The Suffering Servant," *Billy Graham*

CHAPTER NINE: *The Home in Nazareth* 258
- "Twelfth Night," *Elinor Wylie*
- "The Visited Planet," *Philip Yancey*

- "Where Shall We Find Him," *Charles L. Allen and Charles L. Wallis*
- "Making a Home in Nazareth," *Charles Dickens*

CHAPTER TEN: *Simeon and Anna Await the Christ* 268
- "A Song for Simeon," *T. S. Eliot*
- "The Ancients," *Penelope Stokes*
- "Narrative of the Story in Luke: Simeon and Anna Retold," *Stormie Omartian*
- "Advent," *Jane T. Clement*
- "The Presentation in the Temple," *Michael Bruce*
- "Hymn on Simeon," *Peter Cornelius, Trans. by Emily Ezust*
- "On the Character of Simeon," *Paul D. Gardner*
- "On the Character of Anna," *Paul D. Gardner*
- "O Zion Open Wide Your Gates"
- "Simeon: God Hears," *Jack Miles*
- "Our Days, Alas! Our Mortal Days," *Isaac Watts*
- "The Story of Anna," *Ivan J. Kauffman*
- "On Simeon and Anna," *Beth Moore*
- "O Come, O Come Emmanuel"
- "The Wait"
- "Words from an Old Spanish Carol"
- "Name of Jesus," *Max Lucado*

Acknowledgments 297

Index of Authors 301

Index of Titles 303

Preface

If you are a lover of good literature, from Longfellow to Lucado, then you will enjoy the pages that follow. If you are seeking meditative pieces for personal devotion during the Advent season, then you will treasure these chapters. And, if you have a family that celebrates Christmas with stories and songs, then this is the book for your home. *Thomas Nelson Reference and Electronic Publishing* is proud to present our first book in Nelson's Anthology Series. *The Incarnation* provides you and your family with a collection of the best classic and contemporary literature about the joyous event of the birth of Christ!

Within this collection, we have included both secular and Christian writers to provide you with multiple perspectives, understandings, and experiences that surround the glorious nativity scene. For this reason, we have compiled poems, short stories, hymns, quotations, and more from authors in many different languages, cultures, and epochs. With all these different writings, there are variant spellings throughout the book. From German to Italian to Old English, we have included, in some cases, the original language of the piece in which it was written. For this reason, be aware that we may have purposely chosen to adhere to the spelling of that time and language. With these diverse selections, we hope that you will come to understand the gospel stories with a renewed sense of vigor as you identify with the writers of different times and cultures.

To highlight some of the special authors and pieces, we have provided brief biographies and trivia that we think you will find fascinating. These side notes will offer a bit more depth and background to the

writers and writings so that you might have a greater appreciation of their inclusion in this collection!

Take time to treasure these writings about the humble birth of Jesus Christ. From the story of the Betrothal to the rejoicing of Simeon and Anna, we hope you will come to know the hearts of Mary, Joseph, the Shepherds, and the Wise Men in a unique and intimate way. We have carefully placed the chapters in chronological order according to their event as recorded in the gospels. With this event order, you can develop your own personal devotion during the Advent season. Experience the joys and sorrows of these writers as they delineate both the rejoicing and the suffering that surrounds this blessed story of our Savior's Birth!

> _"Behold, I bring you good tidings of great joy which will be to all people. For there is born to you this day, in the city of David, a Savior, who is Christ the Lord . . . Glory to God in the highest, And on earth, peace, goodwill toward men!"_ (Luke 2:10–14).

The Betrothal of Joseph and Mary

MATTHEW 1:18–25

[18]*"Now the birth of Jesus Christ was as follows: After His mother Mary was betrothed to Joseph, before they came together, she was found with child of the Holy Spirit.* [19]*Then Joseph her husband, being a just* man, *and not wanting to make her a public example, was minded to put her away secretly.* [20]*But while he thought about these things, behold, an angel of the Lord appeared to him in a dream, saying, "Joseph, son of David, do not be afraid to take to you Mary your wife, for that which is conceived in her is of the Holy Spirit.* [21]*"And she will bring forth a Son, and you shall call His name JESUS, for He will save His people from their sins."* [22]*So all this was done that it might be fulfilled which was spoken by the Lord through the prophet, saying:* [23]*"Behold, the virgin shall be with child, and bear a Son, and they shall call His name Immanuel," which is translated, "God with us."* [24]*Then Joseph, being aroused from sleep, did as the angel of the Lord commanded him and took to him his wife,* [25]*and did not know her till she had brought forth her firstborn Son. And he called His name JESUS."*

Joseph Was An Old Man
(or The Cherry Tree Carol)

Joseph was an old man,
And an old man was he,
When he wedded Mary
In the land of Galilee.

Joseph and Mary walked
Through an orchard good,
Where was cherries and berries
So red as any blood.

Joseph and Mary walked
Through an orchard green,
Where was berries and cherries
As thick as might be seen.

O then bespoke Mary,
So meek and so mild,
Pluck me one cherry, Joseph,
For I am with child.

"Joseph was an Old Man" was originally known as *The Cherry Tree Carol.* This carol is a standard hymn sung in the Appalachian highlands and is reportedly taken from the apocryphal book of pseudo-Matthew. From this book, tradition holds that Joseph was an older man when he betrothed Mary. Though the author of this title is unknown, Sir Arthur Thomas Quiller-Couch (1863–1944) chose and edited it for the *Oxford Book of Ballads,* published in 1910.

Joseph's Prayer

Joseph . . . did what the Lord's angel had told him to do.
—MATTHEW 1:24

The white space between Bible verses is fertile soil for questions. One can hardly read Scripture without whispering, "I wonder . . ."

"I wonder if Eve ever ate any more fruit."

"I wonder if Noah slept well during storms."

"I wonder if Jonah liked fish or if Jeremiah had friends."

"Did Moses avoid bushes? Did Jesus tell jokes? Did Peter ever try water-walking again?"

"Would any woman have married Paul had he asked?"

The Bible is a fence full of knotholes through which we can peek but not see the whole picture. It's a scrapbook of snapshots capturing people in encounters with God, but not always recording the result. So we wonder:

When the woman caught in adultery went home, what did she say to her husband?

After the demoniac was delivered, what did he do for a living?

After Jairus's daughter was raised from the dead, did she ever regret it?

Knotholes and snapshots and "I wonders." You'll find them in every chapter about every person. But nothing stirs so many questions as does the birth of Christ. Characters appear and disappear before we can ask them anything. The innkeeper too busy to welcome God—did he ever learn who he turned away? The shepherds—did they ever hum the song the angels sang? The wise men who followed the star—what was it like to worship a toddler? And Joseph, especially Joseph. I've got questions for Joseph.

Did you and Jesus arm wrestle? Did he ever let you win?

Did you ever look up from your prayers and see Jesus listening?

How do you say "Jesus" in Egyptian?

What ever happened to the wise men?

What ever happened to you?

We don't know what happened to Joseph. His role in Act I is so crucial that we expect to see him in the rest of the dramas—but with the exception of a short scene with twelve-year-old Jesus in Jerusalem, he never reappears. The rest of his life is left to speculation, and we are left with our questions.

But of all my questions, my first would be about Bethlehem. I'd like to know about the night in the stable. I can picture Joseph there. Moonlit pastures. Stars twinkle above. Bethlehem sparkles in the distance. There he is, pacing outside the stable.

What was he thinking while Jesus was being born? What was on his mind while Mary was giving birth? He'd done all he could do—heated the water, prepared a place for Mary to lie. He'd made Mary as comfortable as she could be in a barn and then he stepped out. She's asked to be alone, and Joseph has never felt more so.

In that eternity between his wife's dismissal and Jesus' arrival, what was he thinking? He walked into the night and looked into the stars. Did he pray?

For some reason, I don't see him silent; I see Joseph animated, pacing. Head shaking one minute, fist shaking the next. This isn't what he had in mind. I wonder what he said . . .

This isn't the way I *planned* it, God. Not at all. My child being born in a stable? This isn't the way I thought it would be. A cave with sheep and donkeys, hay and straw? My wife giving birth with only the stars to hear her pain?

This isn't at all what I imagined. No, I imagined family. I imagined grandmothers. I imagined neighbors clustered outside the door and friends standing at my side. I imagined the house erupting with the first cry of the infant. Slaps on the back. Loud laughter. Jubilation.

> *Any minute now Mary will give birth. Not to a child, but to the Messiah.*

That's how I thought it would be.

The midwife would hand me my child and all the people would applaud. Mary would rest and we would celebrate. All of Nazareth would celebrate.

But now. Now look. Nazareth is five days' journey away. And here we are in a . . . in a sheep pasture. Who will celebrate with us? The sheep? The shepherds? The stars?

This doesn't seem right. What kind of husband am I? I provide no midwife to aid my wife. No bed to rest her back. Her pillow is a blanket from my donkey. My house for her is a shed of hay and straw.

The smell is bad, the animals are loud. Why, I even smell like a shepherd myself.

Did I *miss* something? Did I, God?

When you sent the angel and spoke of the son being born—this isn't what I pictured. I envisioned Jerusalem, the temple, the priests, and the people gathered to watch. A pageant perhaps. A parade. A banquet at least. I mean, this is the Messiah!

Or, if not born in Jerusalem, how about Nazareth? Wouldn't Nazareth have been better? At least there I have my house and my business. Out here, what do I have? A weary mule, a stack of firewood, and a pot of warm water. This is not the way I wanted it to be! This is not the way I wanted my son.

Oh my, I did it again. I did it again didn't I, Father? I don't mean to do that; it's just that I forget. He's not my son . . . he's yours.

The child is yours. The plan is yours. The idea is yours. And forgive me for asking but . . . Is this how God enters the world? The coming of the angel, I've accepted. The questions people asked about the pregnancy, I can tolerate. The trip to Bethlehem, fine. But why a birth in a stable, God?

Any minute now Mary will give birth. Not to a child, but to the Messiah. Not to an infant, but to God. That's what the angel said. That's what Mary believes. And, God, my God, that's what I want to believe. But surely you can understand; it's not easy. It seems so . . . so . . . so . . . bizarre.

I'm unaccustomed to such strangeness, God. I'm a carpenter. I make things fit. I square off the edges. I follow the plumb line. I measure twice before I cut once. Surprises are not the friend of a builder. I like to know the plan. I like to see the plan before I begin.

But this time I'm not the builder, am I? This time I'm a tool. A hammer in your grip. A nail between your fingers. A chisel in your hands. This project is yours, not mine.

I guess it's foolish of me to question you. Forgive my struggling. Trust doesn't come easy to me, God. But you never said it would be easy, did you?

One final thing, Father. The angel you sent? Any chance you could send another? If not an angel, maybe a person? I don't know anyone around here and some company would be nice. Maybe the innkeeper or a traveler? Even a shepherd would do.

I wonder. Did Joseph ever pray such a prayer? Perhaps he did. Perhaps he didn't.

But you probably have.

You've stood where Joseph stood. Caught between what God says and what makes sense. You've done what he told you to do only to wonder if it was him speaking in the first place. You've stared into a sky blackened with doubt. And you've asked what Joseph asked.

You've asked if you're still on the right road. You've asked if you were supposed to turn left when you turned right. And you've asked if there is a plan behind this scheme. Things haven't turned out like you thought they would.

Each of us knows what it's like to search the night for light. Not outside a stable, but perhaps outside an emergency room. On the gravel of a roadside. On the manicured grass of a cemetery. We've asked our questions. We've questioned God's plan. And we've wondered why God does what he does.

The Bethlehem sky is not the first to hear the pleadings of a confused pilgrim.

If you are asking what Joseph asked, let me urge you to do what Joseph did. Obey. That's what he did. He obeyed. He obeyed when the angel called. He obeyed when Mary explained. He obeyed when God sent.

> *Each of us knows what it's like to search the night for light.*

He was obedient to God.

He was obedient when the sky was bright.

He was obedient when the sky was dark.

He didn't let his confusion disrupt his obedience. He didn't know everything. But he did what he knew. He shut down his business, packed up his family, and went to another country. Why? Because that's what God said to do.

What about you? Just like Joseph, you can't see the whole picture. Just like Joseph your task is to see that Jesus is brought into your part of your world. And just like Joseph you have a choice: to obey or disobey. Because Joseph obeyed, God used him to change the world.

Can he do the same with you?

God still looks for Josephs today. Men and women who believe that God is not through with this world. Common people who serve an uncommon God.

Will you be that kind of person? Will you serve . . . even when you don't understand?

No, the Bethlehem sky is not the first to hear the pleadings of an honest heart, nor the last. And perhaps God didn't answer every question for Joseph. But he answered the most important one. "Are you still with me, God?" And through the first cries of the God-child the answer came.

"Yes. Yes, Joseph. I'm with you."

There are many questions about the Bible that we won't be able to answer until we get home. Many knotholes and snapshots. Many times we will muse, "I wonder . . ."

But in our wonderings, there is one question we never need to ask. Does God care? Do we matter to God? Does he still love his children?

Through the small face of the stable-born baby, he says yes.

Yes, your sins are forgiven.

Yes, your name is written in heaven.

Yes, death has been defeated.

And yes, God has entered your world.

Immanuel. God is with us.

—MAX LUCADO
from *He Still Moves Stones*

MAX LUCADO—Using his signature storytelling style, Max Lucado has sold over 15 million books. Currently, he is the pastor of Oak Hills Church of Christ in San Antonio, TX. He holds degrees from Abilene Christian University in Abilene, TX including a Master of Biblical Studies. His engaging and captivating writings include three books that have won the Gold Medallion Christian Book of the Year Award. Lucado is one of the best-loved Christian authors of our day.

Joseph

If the stars fell, night's nameless dreams
    Of bliss and blasphemy came true,
If skies were green and snow were gold,
    And you loved me as I love you;

O long light hands and curled brown hair,
   And eyes where sits a naked soul;
Dare I even then draw near and burn
   My fingers in the aureole?

Yes, in the one wise foolish hour
   God gives this strange strength to a man.
He can demand, though not deserve,
   Where ask he cannot, seize he can.

But once the blood's wild wedding o'er,
   Were not dread his, half dark desire,
To see the Christ-child in the cot,
   The Virgin Mary by the fire?

—G. K. CHESTERTON

As Joseph Was A-Walking

As Joseph was a-walking,
He heard an angel sing,
"This night shall be the birth-time
Of Christ, the heavenly king.

"He neither shall be born
In housen nor in hall,
Nor in the place of Paradise,
But in an ox's stall.

"He neither shall be clothed
In purple, nor in pall,
But in the fair white linen
That usen babies all.

"He neither shall be rocked
In silver nor in gold,
But in a wooden manger
That resteth on the mould."

As Joseph was a-walking,
There did an angel sing,
And Mary's child at midnight
Was born to be our King.

Then be ye glad, good people,
This night for all the year,
And light ye up your candles,
For His star it shineth clear.

—Traditional English Carol

Joseph, Son of David

Little is known about Joseph of Nazareth. He is spoken of briefly in the Gospels of Matthew, Luke, and John, but he is mentioned nowhere else in the Scriptures. Matthew calls him a just man.

In a deep sleep he heard the voice of a messenger from the Lord who said to him: "Joseph, son of David, do not fear to take Mary as your wife, for that which is conceived in her is of the Holy Spirit; she will bear a son, and you shall call his name Jesus, for he will save his people from their sins." And Joseph ". . . did as the angel of the Lord commanded him . . ." (Matthew 1:20, 21, 24).

Joseph was descended from King David and his family home was Bethlehem. What mighty wonders of old are mirrored in him—but none so wondrous as God's purpose for him at this later hour. He apparently had migrated to Nazareth where he established himself in the trade of carpentry and where in time he was engaged to Mary, a maiden of that community. He was at Mary's side when Jesus was born. . . .

When the wrath of Herod was kindled against Jesus, Joseph took

Mary and the Child and together they sought safety in Egypt. Later the three returned to Nazareth, and the hand of Joseph protected and provided for the growing Boy. When Jesus was twelve years old, the devout father journeyed with Mary and Jesus to the Temple in Jerusalem.

Nothing more is given in the Bible by which we may complete the tapestry of Joseph's life, although tradition says that he was considerably older than Mary and that he died during Jesus' childhood. Soon, however, Jesus assumed the responsibility of the household and probably also followed the carpenter's trade. His family obligations may account for the fact that Jesus delayed His public ministry until the age of thirty.

A few biblical references and a scattered account from tradition are all we can know of Joseph. But are there not some details which our imaginations may add?

Joseph was, first of all, a God-fearing man who was loyal to the God of his fathers and faithful to their religious practices. Jesus, in His formative years, learned from Joseph the great lessons of faith and morality, of love toward man and God, of service and sacrifice.

> *On the first Christmas Joseph stood at the side of Mary as the Lord had bidden him.*

Everything we know of Joseph suggests that he was a loving and devoted husband. The teachings of Jesus concerning love for family and neighbor reflect His home training and discipline. The highest compliment which we can pay to Joseph is found in Jesus' teaching that men should call God their heavenly Father. Would this image have come from the lips of Jesus if He had not already known the love and care, the protection and concern of an earthly father?

A little boy, who had been cast in the role of Joseph in a Christmas play, complained that he did not have a "speaking part." Joseph had a silent, though very important role in the drama of salvation. Do not "They also serve who only stand and wait"? On the first Christmas Joseph, silent and stalwart, stood at the side of Mary. When God called upon him, he did as the Lord had bidden him.

—CHARLES L. ALLEN and CHARLES L. WALLIS
from *Christmas in Our Hearts*

The Man Joseph

With sturdy frame and callused hands, how overlooked, this
gentle man.

With hammer and peg and saw and plane, he cut the wood
and smoothed the grain.

Trusted by the Father of all to raise His Son, an awesome
call.

He never doubted Mary's word, though others claimed it
was absurd.

We know he loved the Lord his God, as on to Bethlehem
they trod.

With stars so dim his only guide, he walked along by
Mary's side.

A crowded town forced them to stay in a tiny stable filled
with hay.

He held her close as she winced with pain and squeezed
her hand with every strain.

I'm sure he wept a father's tear as the glorious birth grew
ever near.

He wiped the drops from off her face, brought straw to
soften the birthing place.

And when the infant came at length, he stayed right there
to lend her strength.

He welcomed those who traveled far to see the babe
beneath the star.

From lowly shepherds to mighty kings all knew they'd
witnessed sacred things.

He stood aside, no want for fame, with callused hands and
sturdy frame.

—SALLY MEYER

The Vigil of Joseph

After the Wise Men went, and the strange star
Had faded out, Joseph the father sat
Watching the sleeping Mother and the Babe,
And thinking stern, sweet thoughts the long night
    through.

"Ah, what am I, that God has chosen me
  To bear this blessed burden, to endure
  Daily the presence of this loveliness,
  To guide this Glory that shall guide the world?

"Brawny these arms to win Him bread, and broad
  This bosom to sustain her. But my heart
  Quivers in lonely pain before the Beauty
  It loves—and serves—and cannot understand!"

—Elsa Barker
from *Christmas in Our Hearts*

While the World Awaited

While the world awaited God's redeeming love—
Came to Joseph, dreaming, Gabriel from above:
"God would have you take this virgin as your wife,
For the Child within her is the Lord of Life!"

Lo! The weary Family travels on its way
To the Holy City for the night to stay.
Called for an accounting unto Bethlehem—
There would the Messiah bloom from Jesse's stem.

Since there was no place for them to settle down—
They, with beasts of burden, rested on the ground.
And in David's City early that next morn,
Clothed in human vesture, Word of God was born.

Jesus Christ, our Savior—born upon this day:
Ox and ass surrounded Your bed of golden hay.
In the humble stable, manger for Your rest—
Sleep now, infant Jesus, as the world is blest!

                  —R. MICHAEL CULLINAN

Joseph's Suspicion

And the angel, taking some pains, told
  Considerately the man who clenched his fists:
"But can't you see in her robe's every fold
  That she is cool as the Lord's morning mists?"

But the other murmured, looking sinister:
"What is it that has wrought this change in her?"
  Then cried the angel to him: "Carpenter,
  Can't you see yet that God is acting here?"

"Because you plane the planks, of your pride could
  You really make the Lord God answerable,
  Who unpretentiously from the same wood
  Makes the leaves burst forth, the young buds swell?"

He understood that. And then as he raised
  His frightened glance toward the angel who
  Had gone away . . . slowly the man drew
  Off his heavy cap. Then in song he praised.

          —RAINER MARIA RILKE
          Translated by J. B. Leishman
          from *Selected Works of R. M. Rilke: Poetry, Vol. II*

RAINER MARIA RILKE (1875–1926)—Born in the city of Prague, Rilke's parents sent him to military school as a young boy. Luckily, his uncle realized that Rilke was quite gifted and had him sent to a preparatory school. By the time he had reached his undergraduate studies, he was steadily publishing poetry while pursuing studies in literature. After his studies, Rilke traveled to Germany, Italy, Russia, and France. In these countries, he befriended such thinkers as Tolstoy and Rodin. Paris served as the geographic center of his life, where he first began to develop a new style of lyrical poetry, influenced by the visual arts. He lived the last few years of his life in Switzerland during and after WWI, where he died of leukemia. Widely read by scholars, he was virtually unknown to the general public. Today, however, he is hailed as a master of verse.

The Betrothal: A Commitment Remembered

. . . Miles and decades separated an expectant senior adult, Elizabeth, from her kid-cousin up north, Mary. Jewish families were close-knit, but these women, presumably related by marriage, inhabited very different cultures. A few constants would have permeated their family lives, however. The practices of the ancient Jewish betrothal were consistent.

Luke 1:27 tells us that Mary, a virgin, was "pledged to be married to a man named Joseph." *Pledged* or *betrothed* are the English translations from the Greek root word *mnesteuomai*, meaning "to remember." What a perfect expression of betrothal! When God instructed the Israelites to build the altar of sacrifice in the tabernacle courtyard so that He could "meet" with them, He used no ordinary word (Ex. 29:42–43). The Hebrew word for *meet* (see Ex. 25:22) is *ya'ad*, which means to "betroth" (*Strong's*). Believer, you can rest assured that God remembers. He longs for us to act as if we do, too.

Betrothal compares more to our idea of marriage than engagement. The difference was the matter of physical intimacy, but the relationship was legally binding. Betrothal began with a contract drawn up by the parents or by a friend of the groom. Then at a meeting between the two families, in the presence of witnesses, the groom would present the bride with jewelry. The groom announced his intentions to firmly observe the contract. Then he would sip from a cup of wine and offer

the cup to the bride. If she sipped from the same cup, she was in effect entering covenant with him.

The next step was the payment of the *mohar* or dowry by the groom. This occurred at a ceremony, ordinarily involving a priest. Other traditions were also practiced, but these were the most basic and consistent. By the time a couple reached this step, their betrothal was binding, though a marriage ceremony and physical intimacy had not taken place. An actual divorce would be necessary to break the covenant. Furthermore, if the prospective groom died, the bride-to-be was considered a widow.

> *Betrothal compares more to our idea of marriage than engagement.*

Betrothal traditionally occurred soon after the onset of adolescence, so we are probably accurate to imagine Mary around the age of 13 at the time of the announcement. Remember, in that culture a 13- or 14-year-old was commonly preparing for marriage.

—BETH MOORE
from *Jesus, the One and Only*

CHAPTER TWO

The Annunciation

LUKE 1:26–38
²⁶*Now in the sixth month the angel Gabriel was sent by God to a city of Galilee named Nazareth,* ²⁷*to a virgin betrothed to a man whose name was Joseph, of the house of David. The virgin's name was Mary.* ²⁸*And having come in, the angel said to her, "Rejoice, highly favored one, the Lord is with you; blessed are you among women!"* ²⁹*But when she saw him, she was troubled at his saying, and considered what manner of greeting this was.* ³⁰*Then the angel said to her, "Do not be afraid, Mary, for you have found favor with God.* ³¹*"And behold, you will conceive in your womb and bring forth a Son, and shall call His name JESUS.* ³²*"He will be great, and will be called the Son of the Highest; and the Lord God will give Him the throne of His father David.* ³³*"And He will reign over the house of Jacob forever, and of His kingdom there will be no end."* ³⁴*Then Mary said to the angel, "How can this be, since I do not know a man?"* ³⁵*And the angel answered and said to her, "The Holy Spirit will come upon you, and the power of the Highest will overshadow you; therefore, also, that Holy One who is to be born will be called the Son of God.* ³⁶*"Now indeed, Elizabeth your relative has also conceived a son in her old age; and this is now the sixth month for her who was called barren.* ³⁷*"For with God nothing will be impossible."* ³⁸*Then Mary said, "Behold the maidservant of the Lord! Let it be to me according to your word." And the angel departed from her.*

Gabriel's Questions

Gabriel must have scratched his head at this one.

He wasn't one to question his God-given missions. Sending fire and dividing seas were all in an eternity's work for this angel. When God sent, Gabriel went.

And when word got out that God was to become man, Gabriel was enthused. He could envision the moment:

The Messiah in a blazing chariot.

The King descending on a fiery cloud.

An explosion of light from which the Messiah would emerge.

That's what he expected. What he never expected, however, was what he got: a slip of paper with a Nazarene address. "God will become a baby," it read. "Tell the mother to name the child Jesus. And tell her not to be afraid."

Gabriel was never one to question, but this time he had to wonder.

God will become a baby? Gabriel had seen babies before. He had been platoon leader on the bulrush operation. He remembered what little Moses looked like.

That's okay for humans, he thought to himself. *But God?*

> *Mary was a Jewish peasant who'd barely outgrown her acne and had a crush on a guy named Joe.*

The heavens can't contain him; how could a body? Besides, have you seen what comes out of those babies? Hardly befitting for the Creator of the universe. Babies must be carried and fed, bounced and bathed. To imagine some mother burping God on her shoulder—why, that was beyond what even an angel could imagine.

And what of this name—what was it—*Jesus?* Such a common name. There's a Jesus in every cul-de-sac. Come on, even *Gabriel* has more punch to it than *Jesus.* Call the baby *Eminence* or *Majesty* or *Heaven-sent.* Anything but *Jesus.*

So Gabriel scratched his head. What happened to the good ol' days? The Sodom and Gomorrah stuff. Flooding the globe. Flaming swords. That's the action he liked.

But Gabriel had his orders. Take the message to Mary. *Must be a special girl,* he assumed as he traveled. But Gabriel was in for another shock. One peek told him Mary was no queen. The mother-to-be of God was not regal. She was a Jewish peasant who'd barely outgrown her acne and had a crush on a guy named Joe.

And speaking of Joe—what does this fellow know? Might as well

be a weaver in Spain or a cobbler in Greece. He's a carpenter. Look at him over there, sawdust in his beard and nail apron around his waist. You're telling me God is going to have dinner every night with him? You're telling me the source of wisdom is going to call this guy "Dad"? You're telling me a common laborer is going to be charged with giving food to God?

What if he gets laid off?

What if he gets cranky?

What if he decides to run off with a pretty young girl from down the street? Then where will we be?

It was all Gabriel could do to keep from turning back. "This is a peculiar idea you have, God," he must have muttered to himself.

Are God's guardians given to such musings?

Are we? Are we still stunned by God's coming? Still staggered by the event? Does Christmas still spawn the same speechless wonder it did two thousand years ago?

I've been asking that question lately—to myself. As I write, Christmas is only days away and something just happened that has me concerned that the pace of the holidays may be overshadowing the purpose of the holidays.

I saw a manger in a mall. Correct that. I *barely* saw a manger in a mall. I almost didn't see it. I was in a hurry. Guests coming. Santa dropping in. Sermons to be prepared. Services to be planned. Presents to be purchased.

The crush of things was so great that the creche of Christ was almost ignored. I nearly missed it. And had it not been for the child and his father, I would have.

But out of the corner of my eye, I saw them. The little boy, three, maybe four years old, in jeans and high-tops staring at the manger's infant. The father, in baseball hat and work clothes, looking over his son's shoulder, gesturing first at Joseph, then Mary, then the baby. He was telling the little fellow the story.

And oh, the twinkle in the boy's eyes. The wonder on his little face. He didn't speak. He just listened. And I didn't move. I just

watched. What questions were filling the little boy's head? Could they have been the same as Gabriel's? What sparked the amazement on his face? Was it the magic?

And why is it that out of a hundred or so of God's children, only two paused to consider his son? What is this December demon that steals our eyes and stills our tongues? Isn't this the season to pause and pose Gabriel's questions?

The tragedy is not that we can't answer them, but that we are too busy to ask them.

Only heaven knows how long Gabriel fluttered unseen above Mary before he took a breath and broke the news. But he did. He told her the name. He told her the plan. He told her not to be afraid. And when he announced, "With God nothing is impossible!" he said it as much for himself as for her.

For even though he couldn't answer the questions, he knew who could, and that was enough. And even though we can't answer them all, taking time to ask a few would be a good start.

—MAX LUCADO
from *When God Whispers Your Name*

The Annunciation

She bows her head
Submissive, yet
Her downcast glance
Asks the angel, "Why,
For this romance,
Do I qualify?"

—SAMUEL MENASHE
from *Collected Poems*

Annunciation

Salvation to all that will is nigh;
That All, which always is all everywhere,
Which cannot sin, and yet all sins must bear,
Which cannot die, yet cannot choose but die,
Lo faithful Virgin, yields Himself to lie
In prison, in thy womb; and though He there
Can take no sin, nor thou give, yet He'll wear,
Taken from thence, flesh, which death's force may try.
Ere by the spheres time was created thou
Wast in His mind, who is thy Son, and Brother;
Whom thou conceivest, conceived; yea, thou art now
Thy Maker's maker, and thy Father's mother.
Thou hast light in dark, and shutt'st in little room,
Immensity, cloister'd in thy dear womb.

—JOHN DONNE

Annunciation

"Annunciation" means "the announcement." It would not be a scary word at all, except that as one of the Christian mysteries, it is part of a language of story, poetry, image, and symbol that the Christian tradition has employed for centuries to convey the central tenets of the faith. The Annunciation, Incarnation, Transfiguration, Resurrection. A Dominican friend defines the mysteries simply as "events in the life of Christ celebrated as stories in the gospels, and meant to be lived by believers." But modern believers tend to trust in therapy more than in mystery, a fact that tends to manifest itself in worship that employs the bland speech of pop psychology and self-help rather than language resonant with poetic meaning—for example, a call to worship that begins: "Use this hour, Lord, to get our perspectives straight again." Rather than express awe, let alone those negative feelings, fear and

trembling, as we come into the presence of God, crying "Holy, Holy, Holy," we focus totally on ourselves, and arrogantly issue an imperative to God. Use this hour, because we're busy later; just send us a bill, as any therapist would, and we'll zip off a check in the mail. But the mystery of worship, which is God's presence and our response to it, does not work that way.

The profound skepticism of our age, the mistrust of all that has been handed to us by our grandfathers and grandmothers as tradition, has led to a curious failure of the imagination, manifested in language that is thoroughly comfortable, and satisfyingly unchallenging. A hymn whose name I have forgotten cheerfully asks God to "make our goals your own." A so-called prayer of confession confesses nothing but whines to God "that we have hindered your will and way for us by keeping portions of our lives apart from your influence." To my ear, such language reflects an idolatry of ourselves, that is, the notion that the measure of what we can understand, what

> *The mystery of worship, which is God's presence and our response to it, does not work that way.*

is readily comprehensible and acceptable to us, is also the measure of God. It leads all too many clerics to simply trounce on mystery and in the process say remarkably foolish things. The Annunciation is as good as any place to start. I once heard a Protestant clergywoman say to an ecumenical assembly, "We all know there was no Virgin Birth. Mary was just an unwed, pregnant teenager, and God told her it was okay. That's the message we need to give girls today, that God loves them, and forget all this nonsense about a Virgin Birth." A gasp went up; people shook their heads. This was the first (and only) gratuitously offensive remark made at the convention marked by great theological diversity. When it came, I happened to be sitting between some Russian Orthodox, who were offended theologically, and black Baptists, whose sense of theological affront was mixed with social concern. They were not at all pleased to hear a well-educated, middle-class white woman say that what we need to tell pregnant teenagers is, "It's okay."

I realized that my own anger at the woman's arrogance had deep personal roots. I was taken back to my teenage years, when the

"de-mythologizing" of Christianity that I had encountered in a misguided study of modern theology had led me to conclude that there was little in religion for me. In the classroom, at least, it seemed that anything in the Bible that didn't stand up to reason, that we couldn't explain, was primitive, infantile, and ripe for discarding. So I took all my longing for the sacred, for mystery, into the realm of poetry, and found a place for myself there. Now, more than thirty years later, I sat in a room full of Christians and thought, *My God, they're still at it, still trying to leach every bit of mystery out of this religion, still substituting the most trite language imaginable. You're okay, the boy you screwed when you were both too drunk to stand is okay, all God chooses to say about it is, it's okay.*

The job of any preacher, it seems to me, is not to dismiss the Annunciation because it doesn't appeal to modern prejudices but to remind congregations of why it might still be an important story. I once heard a Benedictine friend who is an Assiniboine Indian preach on the Annunciation to an Indian congregation. "The first thing Gabriel does when he encounters Mary," he said, "is to give her a new name: 'Most favored one.' It's a naming ceremony," he emphasized, making a connection that excited and delighted his listeners. When I brood on the story of the Annunciation, I like to think about what it means to be "overshadowed" by the Holy Spirit; I wonder if a kind of overshadowing isn't what every young woman pregnant for the first time might feel, caught up in something so much larger than herself. I think of James Wright's little poem "Trouble," and the wonder of his pregnant milltown girl. The butt of jokes, the taunt of gossips, she is amazed to carry such power within herself. "Sixteen years, and / all that time, she thought she was nothing / but skin and bones." Wright's poem does, it seems to me, what the clergywoman talks about doing, but without resorting to the ideology or the false assurance that "it's okay." Told all her life that she is "nothing," the girl discovers in herself another, deeper reality. A mystery; something holy, with a potential for salvation. The poem has challenged me for years to wonder what such a radically new sense of oneself would entail. Could it be a form of virgin birth?

Wondering at the many things that the story of the Annunciation might mean, I take refuge in the fact that for centuries so many poets and painters have found it worthy of consideration. European art would

not have been enriched had Fra Angelico, or Dante Gabriel Rossetti for that matter, simply realized that the Annunciation was a form of negative thinking, moralistic nonsense that only a modern mindset—resolutely intellectual, professional, therapeutic—could have straightened out for them. I am glad also that many artists and poets are still willing to explore the metaphor (and by that I mean the truth) of the Virgin Birth. The contemporary poet Laurie Sheck, in her poem "The Annunciation," respects the "honest grace" that Mary shows by not attempting to hide her fear in the presence of the angel, her fear of the changes within her body. I suspect that Mary's "yes" to her new identity, to the immense and wondrous possibilities of her new and holy name, may provide an excellent means of conveying to girls that

> *The first thing Gabriel does when he encounters Mary is to give her a new name: "Most favored one."*

there is something in them that no man can touch; that belongs only to them, and to God.

When I hear remarks like the one made by the pastor at that conference, I am struck mainly by how narrow and impoverished a concept of virginity it reveals. It's in the monastic world that I find a broader and also more relevant grasp of what it could mean to be a virgin. Thomas Merton, in *Conjectures of a Guilty Bystander*, describes the true identity that he seeks in contemplative prayer as a "point vierge" at the center of his being, "a point untouched by illusion, a point of pure truth . . . which belongs entirely to God, which is inaccessible to the fantasies of our own mind or the brutalities of our own will. This little point . . . of absolute poverty," he wrote, "is the pure glory of God in us."

It is only when we stop idolizing the illusion of our control over the events of life and recognize our poverty that we become virgin in the sense that Merton means. Adolescents tend to be better at this than grown-ups, because they are continually told that they don't know enough, and they lack the means to hide behind professional credentials. The whole world confirms to them that they are indeed poor, regrettably laboring through what is called "the awkward age." It is no wonder that teenagers like to run in packs, that they surround themselves with

people as gawky and unformed as themselves. But it is in adolescence that the fully formed adult self begins to emerge, and if a person has been fortunate, allowed to develop at his or her own pace, this self is a liberating force, and it is virgin. That is, it is one-in-itself, better able to cope with peer pressure, as it can more readily measure what is true to one's self, and what would violate it. Even adolescent self-absorption recedes as one's capacity for the mystery of hospitality grows: it is only as one is at home in oneself that one may be truly hospitable to others—welcoming, but not overbearing, affably pliant but not subject to crass manipulation. This difficult balance is maintained only as one remains virgin, cognizant of oneself as valuable, unique, and undiminishable at core . . .

> *We all need to be told that God loves us.*

We all need to be told that God loves us, and the mystery of the Annunciation reveals an aspect of that love. But it also suggests that our response to this love is critical. A few verses before the angel appears to Mary in the first chapter of Luke's Gospel, another annunciation occurs; an angel announces to an old man, Zechariah, that his equally aged wife is to bear a son who will "make ready a people prepared for the Lord." The couple is to name him John; he is known to us as John the Baptist. Zechariah says to the angel, "How will I know that this is so?" which is a radically different response from the one Mary makes. She says, "How can this be?"

I interpret this to mean that while Zechariah is seeking knowledge and information, Mary contents herself with wisdom, with pondering a state of being. God's response to Zechariah is to strike him dumb during the entire term of his son's gestation, giving him a pregnancy of his own. He does not speak again until after the child is born, and he has written on a tablet what the angel has said to him: "His name is John." This confounds his relatives, who had expected that the child would be named after his father. I read Zechariah's punishment as a grace, in that he could not say anything to further compound his initial arrogance when confronted with mystery. When he does speak again, it is to praise God; he's had nine months to think it over.

Mary's "How can this be?" is a simpler response than Zechariah's,

and also more profound. She does not lose her voice but finds it. Like any of the prophets, she asserts herself before God saying, "Here am I." There is no arrogance, however, but only holy fear and wonder. Mary proceeds—as we must do in life—making her commitment without knowing much about what it will entail or where it will lead. I treasure the story because it forces me to ask: When the mystery of God's love breaks through into my consciousness, do I run from it? Do I ask of it what it cannot answer? Shrugging, do I retreat into facile cliches, the popular but false wisdom of what "we all know"? Or am I virgin enough to respond from my deepest, truest self, and say something new, a "yes" that will change me forever?

—KATHLEEN NORRIS
from *Amazing Grace*

KATHLEEN NORRIS (1947–) is an author, poet, and one of the most comtemplative writers of our time. Her works, *Dakota: A Spiritual Geography, The Cloister Walk, Amazing Grace,* and *The Virgin of Bennington,* are deeply contemplative pieces of everyday life and theological concepts. Norris explores the difficulty, the complexity, and the depths of life itself. For her meditative works, she has received critical acclaim and praise. Alongside her writings, she has also served as the minister of a Presbyterian church for a short time.

Mary and Gabriel

Young Mary, loitering once her garden way,
Felt a warm splendour grow in the April day,
As wine that blushes water through. And soon,
Out of the gold air of the afternoon,
One knelt before her: hair he had, or fire,
Bound back above his ears with golden wire,
Baring the eager marble of his face.
Not man's nor woman's was the immortal grace
Rounding the limbs beneath that robe of white,
And lighting the proud eyes with changeless light,
Incurious. Calm as his wings, and fair,

That presence filled the garden.

        She stood there,
Saying, 'What would you, Sir?'

        He told his word,
'Blessed art thou of women!' Half she heard,
Hands folded and face bowed, half long had known,
The message of that clear and holy tone,
That fluttered hot sweet sobs about her heart;
Such serene tidings moved such human smart.
Her breath came quick as little flakes of snow.
Her hands crept up her breast. She did but know
It was not hers. She felt a trembling stir
Within her body, a will too strong for her
That held and filled and mastered all. With eyes
Closed, and a thousand soft short broken sighs,
She gave submission; fearful, meek and glad . . .

 She wished to speak. Under her breasts she had
Such multitudinous burnings, to and fro,
And throbs not understood; she did not know
If they were hurt or joy for her; but only
That she was grown strange to herself, half lonely,
All wonderful, filled full of pains to come
And thoughts she dare not think, swift thoughts and
  dumb,
Human, and quaint, her own, yet very far,
Divine, dear, terrible, familiar . . .
Her heart was faint for telling; to relate
Her limbs' sweet treachery, her strange high estate,
Over and over, whispering, half revealing,
Weeping; and so find kindness to her healing,
'Twixt tears and laughter, panic hurrying her,
She raised her eyes to that fair messenger.
He knelt unmoved, immortal; with his eyes
Gazing beyond her, calm to the calm skies;
Radiant, untroubled in his wisdom, kind.
His sheaf of lilies stirred not in the wind.

How should she, pitiful with mortality,
Try the wide peace of that felicity
With ripples of her perplexed shaken heart,
And hints of human ecstasy, human smart,
And whispers of the lonely weight she bore,
And how her womb within was hers no more
And at length hers?
        Being tired, she bowed her head;
And said, 'So be it!'
        The great wings were spread,
Showering glory on the fields, and fire.
The whole air, singing, bore him up, and higher,
Unswerving, unreluctant. Soon he shone
A gold speck in the gold skies; then was gone.

The air was colder, and grey. She stood alone.

      —RUPERT BROOKE, Autumn 1912
      from *Poems of Rupert Brooke*

Excerpt from the *Divine Comedy*

Vergine Madre, figlia del tuo figlio,
   umile e alta piu che creatura,
   termine fisso d'etterno consiglio,

tu se' colei che l'umana natura
   nobilitasti si che il suo fattore
   non disdegno di farsi sua fattura.

Nel ventre tuo si raccese l'amore,
   per lo cui caldo ne l'etterna pace
   cosi e germinato questo fiore.

Qui se noi meridiana face
   di caritate, e guiso, intra i'mortali,
   se' di speranza fontana vivace.

> Donna, se' tanto grande e tanto vali,
>   che qual vuol grazia ed a te non ricorre,
>   sua disianza vuol volar sanz' ali.
>
> La tura benignita non pur soccorre
>   a chi domanda, ma molte fiate
>   liberamente al dimandar precorre.
>
> In te misericordia, in te pietate,
>   in te magnificenza, in te s'aduna
>   quantunque in creatura e di bontate.

Virgin Mother, daughter of thine own Son, so humble yet more exalted than any creature, fixed goal of the eternal plan, thou art she who did so raise our human nature that its own Creator was not ashamed to take in the timeless peace. In heaven thou art the noonday torch of charity and below on mortal earth thou art the living fountain of hope. Lady, thou art so great and such is thy power that he who seeks grace and does not turn for it to thee leaves his desire trying to fly without wings. Such is thy kindness that it helps not only those who ask but often freely goes before and helps before the asking. In thee mercy, pity, magnificence, and whatever goodness exists in any creature are joined together.

—DANTE
from *The Divine Comedy: Paradiso*

DANTE ALEGHERI (1265–1321)—Born in 1265, Dante is hailed as Italy's greatest poet. His greatest work, *The Divine Comedy,* is divided into three sections: *The Inferno, Purgatorio,* and *Paradiso* and was written between 1306–1321. Dante experienced love at first sight with a young girl named Beatrice. Tragically, she died unexpectedly in 1290 which drove him to both grief and studies in literature and philosophy. While Dante is best known for his writings and poetry, he also held a career as a politician in Florence. Moreover, he served in the Florentine army during the battle of Campaldino against Arezzo and Pisa in 1289. He did marry, in spite of the loss of Beatrice, and he had three children. He died in 1321 upon the completion of quite possibly some of the most notable writing in western civilization.

Putting Christ Back Into Christmas

"Putting Christ back into Christmas" has become a meaningless religious phrase in too many circles. If you want to put Christ back into Christmas, you must start obeying the resurrected Son of God. Obedience is the Christmas spirit. It is the secret of peace and goodwill.

How did Jesus get into the manger? I like to picture it this way: the Father placed His arm around the Crown Prince of Glory, and they walked to the outer limits of space and had a heart-to-heart talk.

The Father said, "Men of earth are dying in Satan's dominion. Death, hell, and the grave hold them in slavery. They live in terror and fear. Son, will You go to earth to be born in a stinking cave with the gut-wrenching odor of cattle, donkeys, and sheep? I want You to live in a carpenter's house and know what it's like to run a small business with a tax-and-spend government in charge. I want You to walk through the stench of a scandalous birth.

> *That's the Christmas spirit—the spirit of absolute obedience.*

"Son, Your best friends will betray You. In Your greatest hour of need they will deny You. The organized church will mock You. The government will look for a way to kill You from day one. They will spit on You, slap You, beat You with a whip until You almost bleed to death, and crown You with thorns. Finally, they will take You outside the walls of Jerusalem and nail Your hands and feet to an old rugged cross and murder You between two thieves.

"Son, that's what I want You to do. Will You do it?"

Time stood still. Every demon in hell waited for the answer. Every angel folded his wings in hushed silence. The souls of humanity hung in the balance.

The Son of God looked at His Father and said, "Father, not My will but Yours, I'll do it!"

That's the Christmas spirit—the spirit of absolute obedience. Do you have it?

How did Jesus get into the manger? A Hebrew girl, sixteen to eighteen years of age, was visited by the angel Gabriel. The angel said, "Hail, Mary, thou art highly favored among women. Behold, thou shalt conceive and bring forth a son, and thou shalt call his name Jesus."

Mary's response was, "How shall this be, seeing I know not a man?" (Luke 1:34 KJV).

The angel said, "The Holy Ghost shall come upon thee, and the power of the Highest shall overshadow thee: therefore also that holy thing which shall be born of thee shall be called the Son of God" (Luke 1:35 KJV).

Mary's response could have been, "Not me. I'm not going to be ridiculed by the women of my church. Those long-tongued hussies will crucify me. I can see them counting on their fingers now. No way, Gabriel. Get someone else!"

Or her response could have been, "Never! As a feminist I'm not going to lose my schoolgirl figure over some baby. I have a career. I'm not having anybody's baby! Marriage is the same as slavery. Being a homemaker is an inferior lifestyle for the thoroughly modern Millie. What do you expect me to do, stay home and bake cookies? Get lost, Gabriel."

A third possible response could have been, "If God does this to me, there is an abortion clinic on the corner. If you think I'm going to live in poverty, have a scandalous pregnancy, ride a donkey to the maternity ward, give birth in a stinking cave, and then let my son be rejected, unwanted, and crucified with criminals, forget it! Abortion is the answer."

But what did Mary say? "Be it unto me according to thy word" (Luke 1:38 KJV). She obeyed with joy, instantly! That's the spirit of Christmas! She said,

My soul doth magnify the Lord,
and my spirit hath rejoiced in God my Savior . . .
For he that is mighty hath done to me great things;
and holy is his name.

—1:46–49 KJV

Please understand this: you obey God only when you do what you don't want to do. If God asks you to do what you want to do, you don't obey, you agree. When He asks you to do what you don't want to do, that's obedience.

—JOHN HAGEE
from *The Spirit of Christmas*

I Sing of a Maiden

I sing of a maiden
  That is makeless;
King of all kings
  To her son she ches;
He came also still
  There his mother was,
As dew in April
  That falleth on the grass.
He came also still
  To his mother's bower,
As dew in April
  That falleth on the
    flower.
He came also still
  There his mother lay,
As dew in April
  That falleth on the
    spray.
Mother and maiden
  Was never none but she;
Well may such a lady
  God's mother be.

—ANONYMOUS, 15th Century

A New Carol of Our Lady

Lords and ladies all by dene
For your goodness and honour,
I will you sing all of a queen;
Of all women she is the flower
    Nowell, Nowell, Nowell, Nowell,
    This said the angel Gabriel.

Of Jesse there sprang a wight,
Isay said by prophecy,
Of whom shall come a man of might,
From death to life he will us buy.
                        Nowell, etc.

There came an angel bright of face,
Flying from heaven with full great light,
And said, Hail! Mary, full of grace,
For thou shalt bear a man of might.
                        Nowell, etc.

Astonied was that lady free,
And had marvell of that greeting;
Angel, she said, how may that be,
For never of man I had knowing?
                        Nowell, etc.

Dread thou nothing, Mary mild,
Thou art fulfilled with great virtue,
Thou shalt conceive and bear a child
That shall be named sweet Jesu.
                        Nowell, etc.

She kneeled down upon her knee;
As thou hast said, so may it be,
With heart, thought and mild cheer,
God's hand-maid I am here.

Nowell, etc.

Then began her womb to spring,
She went with child without man,
He that is lord over all thing,
His flesh and blood of her had than.

Nowell, etc.

The Holy Mother

Anyone who would understand the nature of a tree should examine the earth that encloses its roots, the soil from which its sap climbs into branch, blossom, and fruit. Similarly to understand the person of Jesus Christ, one would do well to look to the soil that brought him forth: Mary, his mother.

We are told that she was of royal descent. Mary's response to the message of the angel was queenly. In that moment she was confronted with something of unprecedented magnitude, something that exacted a trust in God reaching into a darkness far beyond human comprehension. And she gave her answer simply, utterly unconscious of the greatness of her act. A large measure of that greatness was certainly the heritage of her blood.

From that instant until her death, Mary's destiny was shaped by that of her child. This is soon evident in the grief that steps between herself and her betrothed; in the journey to Bethlehem; the birth in danger and poverty; the sudden break from the protection of her home and the flight to a strange country with all the rigors of exile—until at last she is permitted to return to Nazareth.

It is not until much later—when her twelve-year-old son remains behind in the temple, to be found after an agony of seeking—that the divine

"otherness" of that which stands at the center of her existence is revealed (Luke 2:41–50). To the certainly understandable reproach: "Son, why hast thou done so to us? Behold, in sorrow thy father and I have been seeking thee," the boy replies, "How is it that you sought me? Did you not know that I must be about my Father's business?" In that hour Mary must have begun to comprehend Simeon's prophecy: "And thy own soul a sword shall pierce" (Luke 2:35). For what but the sword of God can it mean when a child in such a moment answers his disturbed mother with an amazed: "How is it that you sought me"? We are not surprised to read further down the page: "And they did not understand the word that he spoke to them." Then directly: "And his mother kept all these things carefully in her heart." Not understanding, she buries the words like precious seed within her. The incident is typical: the mother's vision is unequal to that of her son, but her heart, like chosen ground, is deep enough to sustain the highest tree.

> *Her heart, like chosen ground, is deep enough to sustain the highest tree.*

Eighteen years of silence follow. Not a word in the sacred records, save that the boy "went down with them" and "advanced" in wisdom, years, and grace "before God and men." Eighteen years of silence passing through this heart—yet to the attentive ear, the silence of the gospels speaks powerfully. Deep, still eventfulness enveloped in the silent love of this holiest of mothers.

Then Jesus leaves his home to shoulder his mission. Still Mary is near him; at the wedding feast at Cana, for instance, with its last gesture of maternal direction and care (John 2:1–11). Later, disturbed by wild rumors circulating in Nazareth, she leaves everything and goes to him, stands fearfully outside the door (Mark 3:21, 31–35). And at the last she is with him, under the cross to the end (John 19:25).

From the first hour to the last, Jesus' life is enfolded in the nearness of his mother. The strongest part of their relationship is her silence. Nevertheless, if we accept the words Jesus speaks to her simply as they arise from each situation, it seems almost invariably as if a cleft gaped between him and her. Take the incident in the temple of Jerusalem. He was, after all, only a child when he stayed behind without a word,

at a time when the city was overflowing with pilgrims of all nationalities, and when not only accidents but every kind of violence was to be expected. Surely they had a right to ask why he had acted as he did. Yet his reply expresses only amazement. No wonder they failed to understand!

It is the same with the wedding feast at Cana in Galilee. He is seated at the table with the wedding party, apparently poor people, who haven't much to offer. They run out of wine, and everyone feels the growing embarrassment. Pleadingly, Mary turns to her son: "They have no wine."

But he replies only: "What wouldst thou have me do, woman? My hour has not yet come." In other words, I must wait for my hour; from minute to minute I must obey the voice of my Father—no other. Directly he does save the situation, but only because suddenly (the unexpected, often instantaneous manner in which God's commands are made known to the prophets may help us to grasp what happens here) his hour *has* come (John 2:1–11). Another time, Mary comes down from Galilee to see him: "Behold, thy mother and thy brethren are outside, seeking thee." He answers, "Who are my mother and my brethren? Whoever does the will of God, he is my brother and sister and mother" (Mark 3:32–35). And though certainly he goes out to her and receives her with love, the words remain, and we feel the shock of his reply and sense something of the unspeakable remoteness in which he lived.

Deep, still eventfulness enveloped in the silent love of this holiest of mothers.

Even his reply to the words "Blessed is the womb that bore thee," sometimes interpreted as an expression of nearness, could also mean distance: "Rather, blessed are they who hear the word of God and keep it."

Finally on Calvary, his mother under the cross, thirsting for a word, her heart crucified with him, he says with a glance at John: "Woman, behold, thy son." And to John: "Behold, thy mother" (John 19:26–27). Expression, certainly, of a dying son's solicitude for his mother's future, yet her heart must have twinged. Once again she is directed away from him. Christ must face the fullness of his ultimate hour, huge, terrible, all-demanding, alone; must fulfill it from the reaches of extreme isolation, utterly alone with the load of sin that he has shouldered, before the justice of God.

Everything that affected Jesus affected his mother, yet no intimate understanding existed between them. His life was hers, yet constantly escaped her. Scripture puts it clearly: he is "the Holy One" promised by the angel, a title full of the mystery and remoteness of God. Mary gave that holy burden everything: heart, honor, flesh and blood, all the wonderful strength of her love. In the beginning she had contained it, but soon it outgrew her, mounting steadily higher and higher to the world of the divine beyond her reach.

Here he had lived, far removed from her. Certainly, Mary did not comprehend the ultimate. How could she, a mortal, fathom the mystery of the living God! But she was capable of something which on earth is more than understanding, something possible only through that same divine power which, when the hour has come, grants understanding: faith. She believed, and at a time when in the fullest sense of the word probably no one believed. "And blessed is she who has believed . . ." If anything voices Mary's greatness, it is this cry of her cousin Elizabeth.

> *His life was hers, yet constantly escaped her.*

Mary believed blindly. Again and again she had to confirm that belief, and each time with more difficulty. Her faith was greater, more heroic than that of any other human being. Involuntarily we call to mind Abraham and the sudden, terrible sublimity of his faith; but more was demanded of Mary than Abraham. For years she had to combat an only too natural confusion. Who was this "Holy One" whom she, a mere girl, had borne? This "great" one she had suckled and known in all his helplessness? Later she had to struggle against the pain of seeing him steadily outgrow her love, even purposely flee it to that realm of ineffable remoteness which she could not enter. Not only did she have to accept this, but to rejoice in it as in the fulfillment of God's will. Not understanding, never was she to lose heart, never to fall behind. Inwardly she accompanied the incomprehensible figure of her son every step of his journey, however dark. Perseverance in faith, even on Calvary—this was Mary's inimitable greatness.

And literally, every step the Lord took towards fulfillment of his godly destiny Mary followed—in bare faith. Comprehension came only

with Pentecost. Then she understood all that she had so long reverently stored in her heart. It is this heroic faith which places her irrevocably at Christ's side in the work of redemption, not the miracles of Marianic legend. What is demanded of us, as of her, is a constant wrestling *in fide* with the mystery of God and with the evil resistance of the world. Our obligation is not delightful poetry but granite faith.

Mary's vital depths supported the Lord throughout his life and death. Again and again he left her behind to feel the blade of the "sword"—but each time, in a surge of faith, she caught up with him and enfolded him anew, until at last he severed the very bond of sonship, appointing another, the man beside her under the cross, to take his place! On the highest, thinnest pinnacle of creation Jesus stood alone, face to face with the justice of God. From the depths of her co-agony on Golgotha, Mary, with a final bound of faith, accepted this double separation—and once again stood beside him! Indeed, "Blessed is she who has believed!"

—ROMANO GUARDINI
from *The Lord*

Advent

Earth grown old, yet still so green,
    Deep beneath her crust of cold
Nurses fire unfelt, unseen:
    Earth grown old.

    We who live are quickly told:
Millions more lie hid between
    Inner swathings of her fold.

When will fire break up her screen?
    When will life burst thro' her mould?
Earth, earth, earth, thy cold is keen,
    Earth grown old.

—CHRISTINA ROSSETTI

Annunciation

Gabriel paused near the well in the square, letting the moonlight spill over his face and chest. Six months had passed since his last sojourn on earth, and he had nearly forgotten how lovely the night could be. Surely the Almighty smiled down upon this glorious evening—the moment when the Blessed One would learn just how blessed she truly was.

Tonight, under this full smiling moon, he had the joy and privilege of making the greatest announcement in the history of human life. Tonight he would fulfill, for one woman, the dream and hope of every Jewish mother in every age. He would tell the Vessel, Mary, that God had chosen her to bear the Messiah.

He hoped she would take the news with more grace and acceptance than Zechariah had. The old man hadn't believed, and now he would have no voice until the Voice Crying in the Wilderness uttered *his* first cry.

Gabriel wondered again why humans had so much trouble accepting the answers to their prayers. They seemed not only determined to tell the Lord *what* to do, but when and where and how. The old priest should have known better; he had served in the House of God all his life. But then, maybe religious activity didn't necessarily correlate directly to real faith. Gabriel hoped—trusted—that Mary would be different. Gabriel imagined her in his head—a regal, mature woman, a true daughter of Sarah, settled in heart and soul and fully prepared to take on the awesome task of bearing and raising the Messiah.

The archangel found the house, modest by any standards, and went inside. There, on a grass mat with her eyes closed and her hands lifted to heaven, sat a young girl. Praying, Gabriel thought. A devout daughter of Zion. He smiled, then frowned. Surely this girl was not Mary's daughter—the Vessel was supposed to be a virgin.

The word of confirmation resounded in his mind, and he looked closer. *This* was Mary? Why, she was little more than a babe herself! She couldn't be more than thirteen, in the revolutions humans counted as years. Slim and lithe, with long dark hair and a clear, guileless face,

she looked as if she should be out laughing and talking with the other girls. Not preparing herself, soul and body, to bear the Holiest of All.

Gabriel pushed back the questions and doubts that nagged at him. He had a job to do, and he would do it, despite his reservations. He was about to change her life forever, and he could only hope that the change would bring joy rather than sorrow to this lovely woman-child. He took in a breath, infused his human form with angelic brightness, and cleared his throat. "Greetings, favored one," he said. "The Lord is with you. Blessed are you among all women."

The girl's eyes flew open, and she shrank back against the wall. Clearly she was terrified at the apparition before her. Gabriel's heart went out to her, and he reached a hand in her direction. "Do not be afraid, Mary, You have found favor with God. You shall conceive and give birth to a son, and you shall call his name Jesus. He will be great, the Son of the Most High God, and will rule over God's people forever."

Tonight he would fulfill, for one woman, the dream and hope of every Jewish mother in every age.

A strange look crossed Mary's innocent face, an expression of wonder and confusion. "But how is this possible?" she asked. "I have never been with a man."

The archangel suppressed a smile. Leave it to humans to raise the practical dilemmas of life, even in the midst of divine intervention. But he had to give her credit. She didn't argue or protest, the way Moses had when God called him to lead the children of Israel out of bondage. She wasn't trying to figure out a human way to do it, as Abraham did when God told him he was going to be the father of many nations. She didn't doubt, as Zechariah had. She only asked one simple, profound question: "How can this be?"

And he had only one answer: God will do it. "The Holy Spirit will come upon you," he said, "and the child you will bear will be holy, and will be called the Son of God."

She waited, watching him with wide eyes. She did not ask for proof, or for further explanation. She merely accepted.

"Your cousin Elizabeth," he went on, "even now is pregnant with a son. She is very old, and everyone thought she could not have a baby, but she is six months along. With God, you see, nothing is impossible."

Gabriel watched a surge of joy flash in Mary's eyes. She was happy for her cousin's good news—that was a positive sign. The pure of heart can rejoice when others are blessed. But she was young, so very young. How could she bear the weight of such responsibility?

> *Radiant with heaven's light, she looked as if she herself could be an angel.*

The archangel lifted his eyes to heaven and offered a prayer on her behalf, that God would strengthen her and make her equal to the task that lay before her. Then, as if in answer, a shaft of moonlight pierced through the narrow window and illuminated Mary's face. Bathed in the glow, radiant with heaven's light, she looked as if she herself could be an angel, a celestial messenger charged with bringing good news to God's people. The strong planes of her young face and the determined set of her jaw told Gabriel all he needed to know.

Her age was not important. She had been chosen for her character.

She rose from the mat and flipped her dark hair out of her eyes, then faced him with a clear gaze and a slightly stubborn tilt of her head. "I am God's servant," she said deliberately. "Let it be as you have spoken."

The light from the moon increased and filled the humble room. Mary sank back to the floor, trembling a little when the glory cascaded over her. As the Shekinah of the Holy One descended, Gabriel removed himself from the house. She had responded with an obedience unlike anything he had ever witnessed. It was time to give her privacy in God's presence.

Besides, he had other work to do before he could return to his place near the throne. There was a man to deal with, one Joseph the Carpenter, Mary's betrothed. Only God knew what his response would be when he found out his intended was pregnant.

With another glance at the dazzling moonlit sky, Gabriel made his way through the streets of Nazareth. None of the people asleep in these darkened houses had any idea of the miracle that had taken place

this night. But high above them, Gabriel knew, the heavenly chorus was singing hosannas in celebration of the long-awaited Incarnation.

He looked back over his shoulder in the direction of Mary's house. "Blessed are you among women," he whispered into the night air. "I hope Joseph knows what a gift he has been given."

—PENELOPE STOKES
from *The Miracle of the Christmas Child*

From East to West, From Shore to Shore

From east to west, from shore to shore
Let every heart awake and sing
The holy Child Whom Mary bore,
The Christ, the everlasting King.

Behold, the world's Creator wears
The form and fashion of a slave;
Our very flesh our Maker shares,
His fallen creature, man, to save.

For this how wonderously He wrought!
A maiden, in her lowly place,
Became, in ways beyond all thought,
The chosen vessel of His grace.

She bowed her to the angel's word
Declaring what the Father willed,
And suddenly the promised Lord
That pure and hallowed temple filled.

He shrank not from the oxen's stall,
He lay within the manger bed,
And He whose bounty feedeth all
At Mary's breast Himself was fed.

And while the angels in the sky
Sang praise above the silent field,
To shepherds poor the Lord Most High,
The one great Shepherd, was revealed.

All glory for this blessed morn
To God the Father ever be;
All praise to Thee, O virgin born,
All praise, O Holy Ghost, to Thee.

  —CAELIUS SEDULIUS, 5th Century
   Translated from Latin to English
   by John Ellerton

The Annunciation

He tiptoes into the room almost as if he were an intruder. Then kneels, soundlessly. His white robe arranges itself. His breath slows. His muscles relax. The lily in his hand tilts gradually backward and comes to rest against his right shoulder.

She is sitting near the window, doing nothing, unaware of his presence. How beautiful she is. He gazes at her as a man might gaze at his beloved wife sleeping beside him, with all the concerns of the day gone and her face as pure and luminous as a child's and nothing now binding them together but the sound of her breathing.

Ah: wasn't there something he was supposed to say? He feels the whisper far back in his mind, like a mild breeze. Yes, yes, he will remember the message, in a little while. In a few more minutes. But not just now.

  — STEPHEN MITCHELL
   from *Parables and Portraits*

STEPHEN MITCHELL (1943–   )—Born during WWII in Brooklyn, NY, Stephen Mitchell received fine educations at Amherst, the Sorbonne, and Yale. His love for languages has led him in a career in which he has translated many books from Chinese, Hebrew, and German into English. Stephen is also a poet with several writings of his own including *Parables and Portraits*. Currently, he lives in Berkeley, CA.

The Angelic Encounter: Mary and Gabriel

No matter where the angelic ambassador appeared to Mary, he stunned her with his choice of salutations: "Greetings, you who are highly favored! The Lord is with you." Prior to Zechariah's encounter, centuries had passed since God had graced the earth with a heavenly visitation. I doubt the thought occurred to anyone that He would transmit the most glorious news yet heard to a simple Galilean girl.

How I love the way God works! Just when we decide He's too complicated to comprehend, He draws stick pictures.

I'm sure Mary wasn't looking for an angelic encounter that day, but if a town could have eyes to see, Nazareth should have seen. The word *Nazareth* means "watchtower." A watchtower was a human-sized compartment built at a strategic place on the city wall for the designated watchman. He was one of the most important civil servants in any city. From the watchtower, the watchmen stayed on red alert for friend or foe. Two thousand years ago, Nazareth received an unfamiliar friend.

> *Indeed, if towns could see, Nazareth would have been looking.*

Indeed, if towns could see, Nazareth would have been looking. But the recipient of the news was totally unsuspecting. Humble. Meek. Completely caught off guard. Luke 1:29 tells us "Mary was greatly troubled at his words." The phrase actually means "to stir up throughout." You know the feeling: when butterflies don't just flutter in your stomach but land like a bucket at your feet, splashing fear and adrenaline through every appendage. Mary felt the fear through and through, wondering what kind of greeting this might be. How could this young girl comprehend that she was "highly favored" by the Lord God Himself (Luke 1:28)?

The angel's next statement was equally stunning: "The Lord is with you." Although similar words were spoken over lives like Moses, Joshua, and Gideon, I'm not sure they had ever been spoken over a woman.

I'm not suggesting the Lord is not as present in the lives of women as He is in men, but this phrase was suggesting a unique presence and power for the purpose of fulfilling a divine kingdom plan. The sight of the young girl gripped by fear provoked Gabriel to continue with the words, "Do not be afraid, Mary, you have found favor with God" (v. 30). Not until his next words did she have any clue why he had come or for what she had been chosen.

"You will be with child and give birth to a son" (v. 31). Not just any son—"the Son of the Most High" (v. 32). Probably only Mary's youth and inability to absorb the information kept her from fainting in a heap!

My favorite line of all: "And you are to give Him the name Jesus" (v. 31). Do you realize this was the first proclamation of our Savior's personal name since the beginning of time? *Jesus.* The very name at which every knee will one day bow. The very name that every tongue will one day confess. A name that has no parallel in my vocabulary or yours. A name I whispered into the ears of my infant daughters as I rocked them and sang lullabies of His love. A name by which I've made every single prayerful petition of my life. A name that has meant my

> *When the winds of heaven converge with the winds of earth, lightning is bound to strike.*

absolute salvation, not only from eternal destruction, but from myself. A name with power like no other name. Jesus.

What a beautiful name. I love to watch how it falls off the lips of those who love Him. I shudder as it falls off the lips of those who don't. Jesus. It has been the most important and most consistent word in my life. Dearer today than yesterday. Inexpressibly precious to me personally, so I am at a loss to comprehend what the name means universally . . . .

God sent a message through Gabriel that could not have been accurately interpreted as anyone but the long-awaited Messiah.

Whatever the reason, Gabriel met Mary's question with a beautifully expressive response. "The Holy Spirit will come upon you, and the power of the Most High will overshadow you." The Greek word

for *come upon* is *eperchomai,* meaning "to . . . arrive, invade, . . . resting upon and operating in a person." Only one woman in all of humanity would be chosen to bear the Son of God, yet each one of us who are believers have been invaded by Jesus Christ through His Holy Spirit (see Rom. 8:9). He has been invading the closets, the attic, and the basement of my life ever since. How I praise God for the most glorious invasion of privacy that ever graces a human life!

I wonder if Mary knew when He arrived in her life . . . in her womb. Our brothers in the faith might be appalled that we would ask such a question, but we are women! Our female minds were created to think intimate, personal thoughts like these! I have at least a hundred questions to ask Mary in heaven.

Gabriel ultimately wrapped up the story of the divine conception with one profound statement: "So the holy one to be born will be called the Son of God" (v. 35). The term *holy one* has never been more perfectly and profoundly applied than in Gabriel's statement concerning the Son of God. The Greek word is *hagios,* meaning "holy, set apart, sanctified, consecrated . . . sharing in God's purity and abstaining from earth's defilement." . . .

Mary only asked the one question. When all was said and done, her solitary reply was: "I am the Lord's servant. May it be to me as you have said." The Greek word for *servant* is *doule,* which is the feminine equivalent to *doulos,* a male bondservant. In essence, Mary was saying: "Lord, I am your handmaid. Whatever You want, I want." Total submission. No other questions.

We might be tempted to think: *Easy for her to say! Her news was good! Who wouldn't want to be in her shoes? Submitting isn't hard when the news is good!* Oh yes, the news was good. The best. But the news was also hard. When the winds of heaven converge with the winds of earth, lightning is bound to strike. Seems to me that Gabriel left just in time for Mary to tell her mother. I have a feeling Nazareth was about to hear and experience a little thunder.

—BETH MOORE
from *Jesus, the One and Only*

I Know of a Name

I know of a name, a beautiful name,
That angels brought down to earth;
They whispered it low, one night long ago,
To a maiden of lowly birth.

Refrain
That beautiful name, that beautiful name,
From sin has power to free us!
That beautiful name, that wonderful name,
That matchless name is Jesus!

I know of a name, a beautiful name,
That unto a Babe was given.
The stars glittered bright throughout that glad night,
And angels praised God in heav'n.

Refrain

The One of that name, my Savior became,
My Savior of Calvary.
My sins nailed Him there; my burdens he bare.
He suffered all this for me.

Refrain

I love that blest name, that wonderful name,
Made higher than all in heav'n.
'Twas whispered, I know, in my heart long ago
To Jesus my life I've giv'n.

Refrain

—JEAN PERRY

Good Tidings of Great Joy

God never sends a messenger empty-handed. When God sends an angel, he brings a message. The angel said, "Fear not: for, behold, I bring you good tidings of great joy" (Luke 2:10 KJV). The angel was the first to bring the gospel message of good tidings. Jesus is the gospel. Without Jesus there is no gospel. Those of us who are redeemed and washed in the blood of the Lamb can cry out to others, "I bring you good tidings of great joy!"

This season we must no longer preach messages couched in depression. When dysfunctional preachers share their emotional problems in the midst of Christmas, they make us depressed because they're depressed. But this is not a season to be depressed. The drunkard, the sinner, the whoremonger, and the liar are the ones who are depressed. But Christians, in spite of circumstances, should celebrate who Jesus is. We must not get into the pulpit and talk as if we do not have a Savior. Jesus came to rebuke depression and bring good tidings. Your home may be about to break up, but I bring you good tidings. You may not see a way out of your circumstances, but I bring you good tidings: God will make a way!

> *Christians, in spite of circumstances, should celebrate who Jesus is.*

The problem is, we're not ready to receive these good tidings because we are afraid of what's happening to us and what God is doing. We don't understand a lot of things that God does, so we reject them. Don't be afraid of what you see. Don't be afraid of what you're experiencing right now. In the midst of it there are good tidings. This is the season when God brings you something. Look to God. This is the season when God wants to give you good tidings of great joy—good news.

Geographically, Palestine is sandwiched between Egypt and Syria, so the Roman Empire, which conquered all that area, also conquered Palestine. The Jews had no army or political leader of their own. They

were subjected to the Roman Empire, and their only ruling bodies were their Sanhedrin court, their synagogues, and the Mosaic Law. The people were under Roman power. Previously, they were under the power of Greek and Medo-Persian Empires, and before them, the Jews were under Babylonian rule. They had been passed politically from one power to another, but in the midst of that political mess Jesus was coming. He came to the Jews first because the Bible says, "He came to His own, and His own did not receive Him" (John 1:11 NKJV).

> *This is the season when God wants to give you good tidings of great joy— good news.*

Do not be distracted by what you see and hear. When politicians cut the budget and make changes in the federal government, many people are affected. Look at the post office, the immigration office, and any other bureaucracy. Most of the people are shuffling paper and paper clips, with one person licking a stamp, another posting a stamp, and another mailing. We're all caught up in bureaucracy, not a thinking job or one with any identity. Just pushing paper and getting a check. That's the way plantations were run, so when they got ready to close plantations down, there was nowhere for people to go. But God is saying in the midst of all this, "I bring you good tidings of great joy." Not just a little bit of joy. When God does what He wants to do, it's joy unspeakable and full of glory. The half has never been told! For unto you common people, unto you ordinary people, is born in the City of David a Savior, an Emancipator, a Liberator.

God can handle anything. God can turn around anything happening in the White House. God can fix anything going on in your house. We must rebuke the spirit of the world that comes to steal our joy and distract us from the true meaning of Christmas. We must celebrate Christmas within the context of the Word of God. Jesus is Christ the Messiah, Christ the Shining One, the Lord.

—JACKIE MCCULLOUGH
in *The Spirit of Christmas* from
"Celebrate the Gift of Worship"

The Second Nun's Tale

Thou Maid and Mother, Daughter of Thy Son,
Thou well of ruth, of sinful souls the cure,
In Whom, for goodness, God was embryon,
Thou humble One, high over each creature,
Thou did'st ennoble so far our nature
That no disdain God had of humankind
His Son in blood and flesh to clothe and wind.
Within the blessed cloister of Thy sides
Took human shape eternal love and peace
Who all the threefold world as sovereign guides,
Whom earth and sea and heaven, without cease,
Do praise; and Thou, O stainless Maid, increase
Bore of Thy body—and wert kept a maid—
The mighty God Who every creature made.
Assembled is in Thee magnificence,
With mercy, goodness, and with such pity
That Thou, Who art the sun of excellence,
Not only keepest those that pay to Thee,
But oftentimes, of Thy benignity,
Freely, or ever men Thy help beseech,
Thou goest before and art their spirits' leech.

—GEOFFREY CHAUCER
from *The Canterbury Tales*

GEOFFREY CHAUCER (1340–1400)—While there are little known facts about Geoffrey Chaucer, he stands as one of the greatest poets in British literature. He was born in 1340 in London where he served as a page to Prince Lionel. Like Dante, he served in the army for a time and later as a politician that included diplomatic missions to the Continent and Italy. From 1374 on he held a number of official positions, among them comptroller of customs on furs, skins, and hides for the port of London (1374–86) and clerk of the king's works (1389–91). Geoffrey married one of Edward III's queens' ladies in waiting. He died in 1400, and he was buried in Westminster Abbey.

Annunciation

The sun erupts windows frame
a cold blue sea
a breeze feathers her untucked hair as
she leaves her lean to
finish sweeping
under worn mats old painted chairs

in a start she stops
sees her shadow shorten

an angel's face grows
wide in delight
"Rejoice you so highly favored
your womb shall seed promised land and
sky."

With one hand behind her she
backs through her mind

She listens
peace finds peace
"yes." leaves her room and its filling

the grey table sways
her heart follows her down
last leaf to the ground
fall colors every girlish way.

—DAVID CRAIG
from *A Widening Light:*
Poems of the Incarnation

Annunciation to Mary

The angel's entrance (you must realize)
was not what made her frightened. The surprise
he gave her by his coming was no more
than sun- or moon-beam stirring on the floor
would give another,—she had long since grown
used to the form that angels wear, descending;
never imagining this coming-down
was hard for them. (O it's past comprehending,
how pure she was. Did not, one day, a hind
that rested in a wood, watchfully staring,
feel her deep influence, and did it not
conceive the unicorn, then, without pairing,
the pure beast, beast which light begot.—)
No, not to see him enter, but to find
the youthful angel's countenance inclined
so near to her; that when he looked, and she
looked up at him, their looks so merged in one,
the world outside grew vacant suddenly,
and all things being seen, endured and done
were crowded into them: just she and he;
eye and its pasture, vision and its view,
here at this point and at this point alone:—
see, this arouses fear. Such fear both knew.

Then he sang out and made his tidings known.

> —RAINER MARIA RILKE
> Translated by J. B. Leishman
> from *Selected Works of R. M. Rilke:*
> *Poetry, Vol. II*

CHAPTER THREE

Mary's Song

LUKE 1:39–45
³⁹Now Mary arose in those days and went into the hill country with haste, to a city of Judah, ⁴⁰and entered the house of Zacharias and greeted Elizabeth. ⁴¹And it happened, when Elizabeth heard the greeting of Mary, that the babe leaped in her womb; and Elizabeth was filled with the Holy Spirit. ⁴²Then she spoke out with a loud voice and said, "Blessed are you among women, and blessed is the fruit of your womb! ⁴³"But why is this granted to me, that the mother of my Lord should come to me? ⁴⁴"For indeed, as soon as the voice of your greeting sounded in my ears, the babe leaped in my womb for joy. ⁴⁵"Blessed is she who believed, for there will be a fulfillment of those things which were told her from the Lord."

⁴⁶And Mary said:

> "My soul magnifies the Lord,
> ⁴⁷ And my spirit has rejoiced in God my Savior.
> ⁴⁸ For He has regarded the lowly state of His maidservant;
> For behold, henceforth all generations will call me blessed.
> ⁴⁹ For He who is mighty has done great things for me,
> And holy *is* His name.
> ⁵⁰ And His mercy *is* on those who fear Him
> From generation to generation.
> ⁵¹ He has shown strength with His arm;
> He has scattered *the* proud in the imagination of their hearts.
> ⁵² He has put down the mighty from *their* thrones,
> And exalted *the* lowly.
> ⁵³ He has filled *the* hungry with good things,
> And *the* rich He has sent away empty.
> ⁵⁴ He has helped His servant Israel,

In remembrance of *His* mercy,
⁵⁵ As He spoke to our fathers,
To Abraham and to his seed forever."

⁵⁶*And Mary remained with her about three months, and returned to her house.*

Mary's Song

Blue homespun and the bend of my breast
keep warm this small hot naked star
fallen to my arms. (Rest . . .
you who have had so far
to come.) Now nearness satisfies
the body of God sweetly. Quiet he lies
whose vigor hurled
a universe. He sleeps
whose eyelids have not closed before.
His breath (so slight it seems
no breath at all) once ruffled the dark deeps
to sprout a world.
Charmed by doves' voices, the whisper of straw,
he dreams,
hearing no music from his other spheres.
Breath, mouth, ears, eyes
he is curtailed
who overflowed all skies,
all years.
Older than eternity, now he
is new. Now native to earth as I am, nailed
to my poor planet, caught that I might be free,
blind in my womb to know my darkness ended,
brought to this birth
for me to be new-born,

and for him to see me mended
I must see him torn.

—LUCI SHAW
from *A Widening Light:*
Poems of the Incarnation

The Wondrous Soul

She had no thought but this: if any other maiden had got such good things from God, she would be just as glad and would not grudge them to her; indeed, she regarded herself alone as unworthy of such honor and all others as worthy of it. She would have been as well content had God withdrawn these blessings from her and bestowed them upon another before her very eyes. So little did she lay claim to anything, but left all of God's gifts freely in His hands, being herself no more than a cheerful guest chamber and willing hostess to so great a Guest. Therefore she also kept all these things forever. That is to magnify God alone, to count only Him great and lay claim to nothing. We see here how strong an incentive she had to fall into sin, so that it is no less a miracle that she refrained from pride and arrogance than that she received the gifts she did. Tell me, was not hers a wondrous soul? She finds herself the Mother of God, exalted above all mortals, and still remains so simple and so calm that she does not think of any poor serving maid as beneath her. Oh, we poor mortals! If we come into a little wealth or might or honor, or even if we are a little prettier than other men, we cannot abide being made equal to anyone beneath us, but are puffed up beyond all measure. What should we do if we possessed such great and lofty blessings? . . . But Mary's heart remains the same at all times; she lets God have his Will with her and draws from it all only a good comfort, joy, and trust in God. Thus we too should do; that would be to sing a right Magnificat.

> *Was not hers a wondrous soul?*

—MARTIN LUTHER
from *Luther's Works*

The Blessed Virgin Compared to the Air We Breathe

Wild air, world-mothering air,
Nestling me everywhere,
That each eyelash or hair
Girdles; goes home betwixt
The fleeciest, frailest-flixed
Snowflake; that's fairly mixed
With, riddles, and is rife
In every least thing's life;
This needful, never spent,
And nursing element;
My more than meat and drink,
My meal at every wink;
This air, which, by life's law,
My lung must draw and draw
Now but to breathe its praise,
Minds me in many ways
Of her who not only
Gave God's infinity
Dwindled to infancy
Welcome in womb and breast,
Birth, milk, and all the rest
But mothers each new grace
That does now reach our race
Mary Immaculate,
Merely a woman, yet
Whose presence, power is
Great as no goddess's
Was deemed, dreamed; who
This one work has to do
Let all God's glory through,
God's glory which would go
Through her and from her flow
Off, and no way but so.

I say that we are wound
With mercy round and round
As if with air: the same
Is Mary, more by name.
She, wild web, wondrous robe,
Mantles the guilty globe,
Since God has let dispense
Her prayers his providence:
Nay, more than almoner,
The sweet alms' self is her
And men are meant to share
Her life as life does air.

If I have understood,
She holds high motherhood
Towards all our ghostly good
And plays in grace her part
About man's beating heart,
Laying, like air's fine flood,
The deathdance in his blood;
Yet no part but what will
Be Christ our Saviour still.
Of her flesh he took flesh:
He does take fresh and fresh,
Though much the mystery how,
Not flesh but spirit now
And makes, O marvellous!
New Nazareths in us,
Where she shall yet conceive
Him, morning, noon, and eve;
New Bethlems, and he born
There, evening, noon, and morn
Bethlem or Nazareth,
Men here may draw like breath
More Christ and baffle death;
Who, born so, comes to be

New self and nobler me
In each one and each one
More makes, when all is done,
Both God's and Mary's Son.
   Again, look overhead
How air is azured;
O how! nay do but stand
Where you can lift your hand
Skywards: rich, rich it laps
Round the four fingergaps.
Yet such a sapphire-shot,
Charged, steeped sky will not
Stain light. Yea, mark you this:
It does no prejudice
The glass-blue days are those
When every colour glows,
Each shape and shadow shows.
Blue be it: this blue heaven
The seven or seven times seven
Hued sunbeam will transmit
Perfect, not alter it.
Or if there does some soft,
On things aloof, aloft,
Bloom breathe, that one breath more
Earth is the fairer for.
Whereas did air not make
This bath of blue and slake
His fire, the sun would shake,
A blear and blinding ball
With blackness bound, and all
The thick stars round him roll
Flashing like flecks or coal,
Quartz-fret, or sparks of salt,
In grimy vasty vault.
   So God was god of old:
A mother came to mould

Those limbs like ours which are
What must make our daystar
Much dearer to mankind;
Whose glory bare would blind
Or less would win man's mind.
Through her we may see him
Made sweeter, not made dim,
And her hand leaves his light
Sifted to suit our sight.

Be thou then, O thou dear
Mother, my atmosphere;
My happier world, wherein
To wend and meet no sin;
Above me, round me lie
Fronting my forward eye
With sweet and scarless sky;
Stir in my ears, speak there
Of God's love, O live air,
Of patience, penance, prayer:
World-mothering air, air wild,
Wound with thee in thee isled,
Fold home, fast fold thy child.

—GERARD MANLEY HOPKINS

GERARD MANLEY HOPKINS (1844–1889)—Gerard Manley Hopkins was born in 1844 in Essex, England. He attended Balliol College, Oxford, where he read Classics and began his lifelong friendship with Robert Bridges. Deeply affected by the Oxford Movement and the conversions from Anglican to Catholicism, Hopkins entered the Roman Catholic Church and two years later he became a member of the Society of Jesus. In 1877, he was ordained and was priest in a number of parishes, including a slum district in Liverpool. Several years later, he left the ministry to teach at the academy. During this period, he taught at Stonyhurst College, and in 1884, he became Classics Professor at University College, Dublin. In his lifetime Hopkins was hardly known as a poet, except to one or two friends; his poems were not published until after his death in 1918, in a volume edited by Robert Bridges. Hopkins died in Dublin from a contagious fever.

The Angel Assured Mary That Nothing Is *Impossible* With God

For with God nothing shall be impossible.
LUKE 1:37 KJV

I rarely point out passages of Scripture in which there is an omission in the translation. To begin with, there aren't very many places where that happens. Also, sometimes people get too nervous about their translations, and I don't think you need to be. But here there is a word that should have been translated another way. Almost every commentary acknowledges it. The word that's translated "thing" should be translated "word." "Thing" refers to the spoken word of God.

> *God will hasten His word to perform it.*

When God speaks His word, the word *rama* is used. So it's saying here, "For with God, no word shall be without power." Consider how the Amplified Bible translates this: "For with God nothing is ever impossible and no word from God shall be without power or impossible of fulfillment." The Oxford translation is beautiful: "For no word of God is without power." With God, any word is attended with power to see that it's executed. When God speaks His word, He commissions the ministry of the Holy Spirit to perform it. God will hasten His word to perform it.

When the Lord makes a commitment to you or me, we can know that it is not just so many verbs, adjectives, and nouns tumbling out of His lips. He's not saying; "Here's something you can hang on and play with for a while." His word comes with the attendant ministry of the Holy Spirit to make it work.

This miracle of life in the dark womb of this virgin girl is not the first or only time God has moved in the darkness. In creation we see Him doing the same thing: In the midst of chaos and confusion, His word brings life. Into the darkness of slavery in Egypt, God worked out deliverance. In the darkness of this present world, the Son of Righteousness

is going to come and take His church. The Lord will come and meet you in the darkness of your situation, and He will work His glory there.

—JACK HAYFORD
from "I Wish You a 'Mary' Christmas,"
in *The Heart of Christmas*

A Virgin Most Pure

A virgin most pure, as the prophets do tell,
Hath brought forth a Baby, as it hath befell,
To be our Redeemer from death, hell and sin,
Which Adam's transgression has wrapped us in.

Refrain
And therefore be merry, set sorrow aside;
Christ Jesus our Savior was born on this tide.

At Bethlehem city, in Jewry it was
Where Joseph and Mary together did pass,
And there to be taxed, with many one more,
For Caesar commanded the same should be so.

Refrain

But, when they had entered the city so fair
A number of people so mighty was there,
That Joseph and Mary, whose substance was small,
Could get in the city no lodging at all.

Refrain

Then were they constrained in a stable to lie,
Where oxen and asses they used to tie;
Their lodging so simple, they held it no scorn,
But against the next morning our Savior was born.

Refrain

The King of all glory to this world being brought,
Small store of fine linen to wrap Him was sought,
When Mary had swaddled her young Son so sweet,
Within an ox manger she laid Him to sleep.

Refrain

Then God sent an angel from heaven so high,
To certain poor shepherds in fields where they lie,
And bade them no longer in sorrow to stay,
Because that our Savior was born on this day.

Refrain

Then presently after, the shepherds did spy
A number of angels appear in the sky;
Who joyfully talked and sweetly did sing,
To God be all glory, our heavenly King.

Refrain

Three certain wise princes, they thought it most meet
To lay their rich offerings at our Savior's feet;
Then the Shepherds consented, and to Bethlehem did go,
And when they came thither, they found it was so.

Refrain

Mary's Visitation

In those first days she moved lightly still,
though she grew aware from time to time
of her marvellous body on a hill,—
and she rested, breathing, from her climb

to the heights of Juda. But her own,
not the fields', abundance lay around her;
walking on she felt: O a profounder
sense of greatness never has been known.

And it moved her, entering, to laying
her hand on the riper body there.
And the women came together swaying
and they touched each other's robes and hair.

Each, big with the shrine that she was keeping,
soothed her cousin and forgot her fear.
Ah the Saviour was a flower still, sleeping,
but the other felt the Baptist leaping
in her womb, for joy, to have him near.

      —RAINER MARIA RILKE
      Translated by J. B. Leishman
      from _Selected Works of R. M. Rilke: Poetry, Vol. II_

Be Compassionate

Now that Mary knew she was to become a mother, and that her kinswoman Elisabeth would give birth in three months, she wanted to see Elisabeth so they could rejoice together. "Joy" is the major theme of this section as you see three persons rejoicing in the Lord . . . there was the joy of Mary (vv. 46–56), a joy that compelled her to lift her voice in a hymn of praise. The fullness of the Spirit should lead to joyful praise in our lives (Eph. 5:18–20), and so should the fullness of the Word (Col. 3:16–17). Mary's song contains quotations from and references to the Old Testament Scriptures, especially the Psalms and the song of Hannah in 1 Samuel 2:1–10. Mary hid God's Word in her heart and turned it into a song.

This song is called "The Magnificat" because the Latin version of verse 46 is "Magnificat anima mea Dominum." Her great desire was

to magnify the Lord, not herself. She used the phrase *He hath* eight times as she recounted what God had done for three recipients of His blessing . . . Mary saw the Lord turning everything upside down: the weak dethrone the mighty, the humble scatter the proud, the nobodies are exalted, the hungry are filled, and the rich end up poor! The grace of God works contrary to the thoughts and ways of this world system (1 Cor. 1:26–28). The church is something like that band of men that gathered around David (1 Sam. 22:2).

—WARREN WIERSBE
from *Be Compassionate*

WARREN WIERSBE—Warren Wiersbe is both a prolific writer and the former pastor of the Moody Church in Chicago, IL. He has authored over 80 books including his famous "Be" series. He has a unique style of writing and speaking for many audiences. He has a heart for missions and is recognized internationally as a Bible Conference speaker. In this way, he has brought the good news to people all over the world.

A Great and Mighty Wonder

A great and mighty wonder, a full and holy cure:
The virgin bears the Infant with virgin honor pure!
Repeat the hymn again: "To God on high be glory
And peace on earth to men!"

The Word becomes incarnate and yet remains on high,
And cherubim sing anthems to shepherds from the sky.
Repeat the hymn again: "To God on high be glory
And peace on earth to men!"

While thus they sing your Monarch, those bright angelic bands,
Rejoice, ye vales and mountains, ye oceans, clap your hands.
Repeat the hymn again: "To God on high be glory
And peace on earth to men!"

Since all He comes to ransom, by all be He adored,
The Infant born in Bethl'em, the Savior and the Lord.
Repeat the hymn again: "To God on high be glory
And peace on earth to men!"

And idol forms shall perish, and error shall decay,
And Christ shall wield His scepter, our Lord and God for aye.
Repeat the hymn again: "To God on high be glory
And peace on earth to men!"

> —ST. GERMANUS
> Translated from Greek to
> English by John M. Neale

Mother Mary

Who am I, what am I? That He should think of me,
To bring His Son into the World and teach Him at my knee?
As there they sat with hay all strewn about them on the
    ground,
She pondered all that lie ahead when they'd leave fair
    David's town.
By candle light she held her son, and nursed him at her
    breast.
Then lay him on the golden hay so they could get some rest.
With stalwart Joseph at her side and cattle softly lowing,
She welcomed all, shepherd to king, who came by starlight
    glowing.
In harmony, the angels sang reverent hymns of glory.
Mary listened as they told her little one's sacred story.
The bleating of the fleecy lambs was His first lullaby.
A straw filled manger for a crib with animals standing by.
But Mary filled that nursery as only a mother could,
With love and hope and promise, as Father knew she would.

> —SALLY MEYER

Bethlehem

He came all so still
To his mother's bour,
As dew in April
That falleth on the flour.

He came all so still
There his mother lay,
As dew in April
That falleth on the spray.

Mother and maiden
Was never none but she;
Well may such a lady
Goddess mother be.

—A Fifteenth-Century Carol

On the Favored One, the Virgin Mary

There can be no doubt, however, that Mary was a special object of the grace of God. Her choice was an act of election on the part of the Lord. Mary was highly favored because she was the recipient of this divine selection and grace. She was to be the closest to the Son of God during his earthly life and was to share His filial affection during His years in the Nazareth home. Mary's reply to the angel, "Be it unto me according to thy word," reveals that she was a woman of faith. She accepted the announcement of God to her concerning this great wonder of a virgin birth and the coming of the Son of God. Hence, when Elisabeth greeted her, she said, "Blessed is she that believed, for there shall be a performance of those things which were told her from the

Lord." We acknowledge that Mary's faith was a gift from almighty God and there was no merit in it, but from the very beginning, Mary believed.

Many were the women from the beginning of creation, when Eve received the protoevangelium, who had hoped that they might be the mother of the Messiah. This was the hope of Sarah, again of Hannah, again of Elisabeth, and of others throughout the centuries, but God looked down on the human race and chose the one lone, demure Jewish maiden from the town of Nazareth, and we ask why. The answer can only be, if we exclude the sovereign grace of God, that God looks upon the heart. In looking upon the heart of Mary, what did He see? The record concerning her suggests to us that He saw first, *A Pure Heart;* second, He saw *A Pondering, Meditative Heart;* and third, He saw *A Pierced Heart of Sympathetic Suffering . . .*

> *The meaning of the Virgin Birth is that God is with us.*

The meaning of the Virgin Birth is that God is with us, that the Incarnation has taken place, and that once in time the eternal Deity became flesh and dwelt among us, that He suffered as we suffer, that He died and rose again. Quite truly we may see that this Child of Mary was God. The whole composite picture proves this—the picture of His miracles, of His sinlessness, of His teaching, of His death upon the cross, and of His resurrection from the dead . . .

. . . If there is any clue to the reason Mary was chosen by God to become the mother of the Lord, it would be contained in the statement, "She pondered all these things in her heart" (Luke 2:19). Such pondering followed the salutation of the angel, the prophecy of Simeon, and the sayings of the boy Jesus. It reveals a meditative, devout, modest, reticent, worshipful, Jewish maiden, who was the example of all that is best in woman. We hold that Mary symbolizes all that is good and pure and beautiful in motherhood.

Perhaps Mary had more about which to ponder in connection with the birth of her Son than other mothers have in connection with the birth of their children, but there is sufficient of the mysterious, the supernatural, and the wonderful in the life of any child to cause a mother's heart to ponder over whence that life came, where it would

go, and what it would be while it was here upon earth. How often as we look into the life of a little child being presented for Christian baptism, we wonder what will be the future for that life. Will it be hardship and shame or will it be honor and fame?

. . . Mary's was a high state of faith, for she believed, due to her meditations upon the Lord Jesus Christ. She believed what the angel said about Him and thus was convinced that this was to be a Virgin Birth and her Son was to be the Son of God. She did not declare this unto others, but kept it in her own heart, quietly meditating upon its meaning. Moreover, Mary believed from the very beginning in the Messiahship of her Son, with all that the Scriptures promised to be fulfilled through Him. She may have wondered why the kingdom was not established, why all the Old Testament prophecies about that kingdom were not fulfilled if her Son were the King, and yet, in spite of it all, she commanded the servants of the house at Cana of Galilee, saying, "Whatsoever He saith unto you, do it" (John 2:5) . . .

. . . Here, then, we see the noblest woman of all, the woman whose life fulfilled all that God promised to the women of the Old Testament who were good and precious and noble and true. Her Son was her own Saviour and Lord, just as He may be yours and He may be mine.

—Harold John Ockenga
from *Women Who Made Bible History*

Gentle Mary Laid Her Child

Gentle Mary laid her Child lowly in a manger;
There He lay, the undefiled, to the world a Stranger:
Such a Babe in such a place, can He be the Savior?
Ask the saved of all the race who have found His favor.

Angels sang about His birth; wise men sought and found Him;
Heaven's star shone brightly forth, glory all around Him:

Shepherds saw the wondrous sight, heard the angels singing;
All the plains were lit that night, all the hills were ringing.

Gentle Mary laid her Child lowly in a manger;
He is still the undefiled, but no more a stranger:
Son of God, of humble birth, beautiful the story;
Praise His Name in all the earth, hail the King of glory!

—JOSEPH SIMPSON COOK

The Virgin Mary

For that fair blessed mother-maid,
Whose flesh redeem'd us, that she-cherubin,
   Which unlock'd paradise, and made
One claim for innocence, and disseized sin,
     Whose womb was a strange heaven, for there
     God clothed Himself, and grew,
Our zealous thanks we pour. As her deeds were
Our helps, so are her prayers; nor can she sue
In vain, who hath such titles unto you.

—JOHN DONNE

The Mary Model

Now let's look at the Mary Model and determine why God has given it to us and what we can learn from it. A pattern in the Mary Model can be applied to our lives:

And in the sixth month, the angel Gabriel was sent from God unto a city of Galilee, named Nazareth, to a virgin espoused to a man whose name was Joseph, of the house of David; and the virgin's name was Mary. And the angel came in unto her, and said, Hail, thou that art highly favored, the Lord is with thee: blessed art thou among women. (Luke 1:26–28 KJV)

When the Lord is with you, you are blessed and highly favored.

And when she saw him, she was troubled at his saying, and cast in her mind what manner of salutation this should be. (Luke 1:29 KJV)

When the Lord speaks to you, sometimes it is troubling. When I was first born-again and found out that God required me to give 10 percent of my increase, that troubled me. Mary heard a word from the angel, and it troubled her:

And the angel said unto her, Fear not, Mary: for thou hast found favor with God. And behold, thou shalt conceive in thy womb, and bring forth a son, and shalt call his name JESUS. (Luke 1:30–31 KJV)

The first thing Mary had to do was to get rid of fear. If you walk in fear, you will not be able to follow the Mary Model. The greatest fear Satan tries to put in your life is that the Word of God won't come to pass. He wants you to fear that the Word will not be conceived within you, that you are barren, and that you will never be able to bear fruit.

> *If you walk in fear, you will not be able to follow the Mary Model.*

The angel told Mary that she would conceive and bring forth a son supernaturally. This principle can also be applied to us spiritually. For you, it might be next week's rent, a raise, or a promotion. It might be a family member coming to the Lord. God's Word to you is, "You shall conceive and bring forth!" You can't conceive without bringing forth. Whatever is supernaturally conceived in your heart by the Spirit is going to come forth. If the Word of God is conceived within, it will come forth.

Now ask yourself a question: What have I been trying to bring forth? Perhaps you need peace, healing, or restoration of a broken marriage. The Mary Model shows you how to bring it forth. The Christmas season is a time of spiritual conception—a time when the Word of God enters your spirit, grows within you, and ultimately comes forth through your life.

The angel told Mary, "Call his name JESUS" (Luke 1:31 KJV). He

was named before conception. It is time for you to open your mouth and start calling those things that are not as though they already exist (Rom. 4:17). It's time to call your deliverance forth! It's time to call your healing forth! It's time to call your prosperity forth! It's time to call your favor forth!

Whatever you're believing God for, you must open your mouth and call it forth. God shut Zechariah's mouth because He didn't want Zechariah to speak until he was ready to agree with God. Finally, he wrote, "His name is John" (Luke 1:20, 63 KJV). Then God opened Zechariah's mouth.

> *If the Word of God is conceived within, it will come forth.*

Don't say, "I am no good." Don't call yourself a failure. Call yourself what God Almighty called you before you were conceived. He called you blessed! He called you healed! He called you prosperous! The angel explained to Mary who Jesus was and what He would do:

> *He shall be great, and shall be called the Son of the Highest: and the Lord God shall give unto him the throne of his father David: and he shall reign over the house of Jacob for ever; and of his kingdom, there shall be no end. Then said Mary unto the angel, How shall this be, seeing I know not a man?* (Luke 1:32–34 KJV)

Mary asked, "How shall this be?" How many times have you asked that question? In her case it was, "How shall this be, seeing that I've not been intimate with a man?" In your case it may be, "How shall this be, seeing that my job pays me only $5.15 an hour?" or "How shall this be, seeing that the doctors haven't come up with the cure for this disease?" There is a time factor involved in the anointing:

> *The angel answered and said unto her, The Holy Ghost shall come upon thee, and the power of the Highest shall overshadow thee: therefore also that holy thing which shall be born of thee shall be called the Son of God.* (Luke 1:35 KJV)

The Holy Spirit is your Helper. He won't do what you can do, but He will do what you can't do. The angel told Mary, "For with God nothing shall be impossible" (Luke 1:37 KJV). And Mary said,

Behold the handmaid of the Lord; be it unto me according to thy word. And the angel departed from her. (Luke 1:38 KJV)

Here are the keys to the Mary Model: "For with God nothing shall be impossible" and "Be it unto me according to thy word."

—CREFLO A. DOLLAR
from *The Spirit of Christmas*

Vermeer

Quia respexit humilitatem
    ancillae suae.—LUKE 1:48

She stands by the table, poised
at the center of your vision,
with her left hand
just barely on
the pitcher's handle, and her right
lightly touching the windowframe.
Serene as a clear sky, luminous
in her blue dress and many-toned
white cotton wimple, she is looking
nowhere. Upon her lips
is the subtlest and most lovely
of smiles, caught
for an instant
like a snowflake in a warm hand.
How weightless her body feels
as she stands, absorbed, within this
fulfillment that has brought more
than any harbinger could.
She looks down with an infinite
tenderness in her eyes,

as though the light at the window
were a newborn child
and her arms open enough
to hold it on her breast, forever.

—STEPHEN MITCHELL
from *Parables and Portraits*

Sleep, My Little Jesus

Sleep, my little Jesus,
On Thy bed of hay,
While the shepherds homeward
Journey on their way.
Mother is Thy shepherd
And will her vigil keep:
Did the voices wake Thee?
O sleep, my Jesus, sleep!

Refrain
Softly sleep, sweetly sleep,
My Jesus, sleep!

Sleep, my little Jesus,
While Thou art my own!
Ox and ass Thy neighbors,
Shalt Thou have a throne?
Will they call me blessèd?
Shall I stand and weep?
Be it far, Jehovah!
O sleep, my Jesus, sleep!

Refrain

Sleep, my little Jesus,
Wonder-baby mine!
Well the singing angels
Greet Thee as divine.
Through my heart, as heaven
Low the echoes sweep
Of glory to Jehovah!
O sleep, my Jesus, sleep!

Refrain

—WILLIAM C. GANNETT

On the Purity of Conception

It was not enough that the conception of Jesus takes place without a male role, for if a woman who had previously known a man had conceived him even through the Holy Spirit, 'who would ever have believed that the child that was born was of the Holy Spirit? For nature knows no birth that is not besmirched with stain.' For the same reason she had to be ever a virgin, she who bore the one in whom there could not be even the least suspicion of blemish. For the birth of Jesus to be absolutely pure of every stain, Mary herself had to be free of any pollution of normal child-bearing.

—ULRICH ZWINGLI

ULRICH ZWINGLI (1484–1531)—Ulrich Zwingli was the leader of the fledgling reformation in Zurich. In 1519 he became the people's priest at the Great Minster Church in Zurich. He launched the Reformation by preaching Biblical sermons from the pulpit. While Luther allowed what the Bible did not prohibit, Zwingli prohibited what the Bible did not specifically prescribe. He stressed the ability of common people to interpret the Bible for themselves, taught the memorial view of the Lord's Supper, and called for a return to the Apostolic Church described in the New Testament. However, Zwingli did not only serve as a reformer, for he was a musician, a soldier, and a political figure in the community.

The Love That I Bear

I sing of the life that I bear
I sing to the one who's inside of me
Whose face is familiar
Though I've never seen
Whose life lies ahead
Like a wonderful dream

Chorus:
I sing of the love that I bear
I sing to the Spirit indwelling me
Alive deep inside me
As surely, I know
As my baby is living and grows

Passion and pain
Come together the same
As the flesh and the blood
Come by the way of one love
Sing then to life
And of love come alive
So all that is darkness will die

(Repeat chorus)

Alive deep inside me
As surely, I know
As my baby
Is living and grows

—SCOTT BRASHER and
MICHAEL CARD

The Mother of God

The three-fold terror of love; a fallen flare
Through the hollow of an ear;
Wings beating about the room;
The terror of all terrors that I bore
The Heavens in my womb

Had I not found content among the shows
Every common woman knows,
Chimney corner, garden walk,
Or rocky cistern where we tread the clothes
And gather all the talk?

What is this flesh I purchased with my pains,
This fallen star my milk sustains,
This love that makes my heart's blood stop
Or strikes a sudden chill into my bones
And bids my hair stand up?

—WILLIAM BUTLER YEATS

W. B. YEATS (1865–1939)—Born in Dublin to an Irish painter as a father and a mother interested in the occult, folklore, and mythology, Yeats was immersed in the arts and mysticism. Yeats was educated in fine British schools, and when he graduated he wrote and dabbled in politics. Infatuated with Maud Gonne, he asked her several times to marry him to no avail. Their friendship lasted for many years, and she was the subject of much of his poetry. Elected a senator of the Irish Free Republic in 1922, he is remembered as an important cultural leader, as a major playwright (he was one of the founders of the famous Abbey Theatre in Dublin), and as one of the very greatest poets—in any language—of the century. W. B. Yeats was awarded the Nobel Prize in 1923 and died in 1939 at the age of 73.

Virgin Birth

The earliest of the four Gospels makes no reference to it, and neither does Paul, who wrote earlier still. On later evidence, however, many Christians have made it an article of faith that it was the Holy Spirit rather than Joseph who got Mary pregnant. If you believe God was somehow in Christ, it shouldn't make much difference to you how he got there. If you don't believe, it should make less difference still. In either case, life is complicated enough without confusing theology and gynecology.

In one sense anyway, the doctrine of the Virgin Birth is demonstrably true. Whereas the villains of history can always be seen as the products of heredity and environment, the saints always seem to arrive under their own steam. Evil evolves. Holiness happens.

—FREDERICK BUECHNER
from *Wishful Thinking*

On the Mystery of God's Ways

She experiences in her own body that God's ways with humans are wonderful, that He isn't bound by human standards, that He doesn't follow the path that humans like to lay out for Him—that His way is beyond all understanding, beyond all proof, free, and with a mind of its own.

—DIETRICH BONHOEFFER
from *The Mystery of Holy Night*

CHAPTER FOUR

Room at the Inn

2:1–7

¹*And it came to pass in those days that a decree went out from Caesar Augustus that all the world should be registered. ²This census first took place while Quirinius was governing Syria. ³So all went to be registered, everyone to his own city. ⁴Joseph also went up from Galilee, out of the city of Nazareth, into Judea, to the city of David, which is called Bethlehem, because he was of the house and lineage of David, ⁵to be registered with Mary, his betrothed wife, who was with child. ⁶So it was, that while they were there, the days were completed for her to be delivered. ⁷And she brought forth her firstborn Son, and wrapped Him in swaddling cloths, and laid Him in a manger, because there was no room for them in the inn.*

Room for Jesus

She brought forth her firstborn Son, . . .
and laid Him in a manger,
because there was no room for them in the inn.
— LUKE 2:7

No room for Jesus? No room for the King of kings? No, but room for others and for other things. There was no room for Jesus in the world that He had made—imagine!

Things have not really changed since that Bethlehem night over two thousand years ago. God is still on the fringes of most of our lives. We fit Him in when it is convenient for us, but we become irritated when He makes demands on us. If God would only stay in His little box and come out when we pull the string!

Our lives are so full. There is so much to be done. But in all our busy activities are we in danger of excluding from our hearts and lives the One who made us?

"Oh, come to my heart, Lord Jesus; there is room in my heart for you."

—BILLY GRAHAM
from *Hope for Each Day*

BILLY GRAHAM (1918–   )—Known as one of the leading evangelists for Christianity in the 20th century, Billy Graham is a symbol of pastoral care, leadership, and hope for America and the world. He has spoken to countless millions over his fifty-year preaching career that began in a small Southern Baptist church. Billy Graham has been awarded numerous honors for his missions and work, and he has been an advisor to Presidents and pastors for decades. After his studies at Wheaton College, Graham married Ruth Bell. They have five children and nineteen grandchildren, and they currently live in the mountains of North Carolina.

The Nativity

Among the oxen (like an ox I'm slow)
I see a glory in the stable grow
Which, with the ox's dullness might at length
   Give me an ox's strength.

Among the asses (stubborn I as they)
I see my Saviour where I looked for hay;
So may my beastlike folly learn at least
   The patience of a beast.

Among the sheep (I like a sheep have strayed)
I watch the manger where my Lord is laid;
Oh that my baa-ing nature would win thence
   Some wooly innocence!

—C. S. LEWIS
from *Poems*

New Prince, New Pomp

Behold, a seely tender babe
  In freezing winter night
In homely manger trembling lies—
  Alas, a piteous sight!

The inns are full, no man will yield
  This little pilgrim bed,
But forced he is with seely beasts
  In crib to shroud his head.

Despise him not for lying there;
  First, what he is enquire.
An orient pearl is often found
  In depth of dirty mire.

Weigh not his crib, his wooden dish,
  Nor beasts that by him feed;
Weigh not his mother's poor attire
  Nor Joseph's simple weed.

This stable is a prince's court,
  This crib his chair of state,
The beasts are parcel of his pomp,
  The wooden dish his plate.

The persons in that poor attire
  His royal liveries wear;
The prince himself is come from heaven—
  This pomp is prizèd there.

With joy approach, O Christian wight;
  Do homage to thy king;
And highly prize his humble pomp
  Which he from heaven doth bring.

    —Robert Southwell

Open My Heart

Dearest God,
please never let me
crowd my life
full to the brim
so that, like the keeper
of Bethlehem's inn,
I find I have no room
for Him.
Instead, let my heart's door
be ever open,
ready to welcome
the newborn King.
Let me offer the best that I have
to Him who gives me
everything.

—ROSALYN HART FINCH

The Maid-Servant at the Inn

"It's queer," she said; "I see the light
   As plain as I beheld it then,
All silver-like and calm and bright—
   We've not had stars like that again!

"And she was such a gentle thing
   To birth a baby in the cold.
The barn was dark and frightening—
   This new one's better than the old.

"I mind my eyes were full of tears,
   For I was young, and quick distressed,

But she was less than me in years
    That held a son against her breast.

"I never saw a sweeter child—
    The little one, the darling one!—
I mind I told her, when he smiled
    You'd know he was his mother's son.

"It's queer that I should see them so—
    The time they came to Bethlehem
Was more than thirty years ago;
    I've prayed that all is well with them."

          —DOROTHY PARKER
        from *The Portable Dorothy Parker*

DOROTHY PARKER (1893–1967)—Upon surviving a tragic childhood fraught with the deaths of her parents and brother, Dorothy attended private schools. Her first jobs were writing reviews and poems for *Vanity Fair* and *Vogue*. While working for *Vanity Fair* and *Vogue*, Parker became a founding member of the Algonquin Round Table, an informal gathering of writers who lunched at the Algonquin Hotel. During this time Parker traveled to Europe, where she befriended Ernest Hemingway and contributed articles to the *New Yorker* and *Life*. While her work was successful and she was well regarded as a brilliant, albeit pessimistic wit and conversationalist, she suffered from depression and alcoholism and attempted suicide three times. Parker went on to aid in the writing of the screenplay *A Star Is Born* with Alan Campbell, her second husband. Parker was blacklisted during the 1940s for her support of radical causes and called before the House on Un-American Activities in the 1950s. She continued to write stories and poetry and later became a book reviewer for *Esquire*. She was inducted into the American Academy of Arts and Letters in 1959 and was a visiting professor at California State College in Los Angeles. On June 6, 1967, Parker was found dead of a heart attack in a New York City hotel.

No Room at the Inn

"But don't you have just one room?" Joseph pleaded.

"To be honest, I did. But only moments ago a large delegation arrived and took every last bed. I don't have a place for you and your wife."

Joseph tried to be patient, but his jaw was tightening. He leaned forward so his face was inches from the innkeeper's. "See that lady in the cart?" he asked through his teeth. "She is my wife. She could deliver any minute. She nearly had the baby this afternoon in a wagon. She is in pain right now. Do you want the baby to be born here in your doorway?"

"No, of course not, but I can't help you. Please understand. I have no more rooms."

"I heard you, but it is midnight and cold. Don't you have any place for us to keep warm?"

The man sighed, looked at Mary and then at Joseph. He walked into his house and returned with a lamp. "Behind the inn is a trail which will lead you down a hill. Follow it until you come to a stable. It's clean, at least as clean as stables usually are." With a shrug he added, "You'll be warm there."

Joseph couldn't believe what he was hearing. "You expect us to stay in the stable?"

"Joseph." It was Mary speaking. She'd heard every word. He turned; she was smiling. He knew exactly what the smile meant. Enough arguing.

His sigh puffed his cheeks. "That will be fine," Joseph consented and took the lamp.

"Strange," the clerk muttered to himself as the couple left. Turning to his wife he asked, "Who was the man who took all the rooms?"

Opening the register, the woman read the name aloud. "Different name. Sophio. Must be Greek."

—MAX LUCADO
from *Cosmic Christmas*

Room in the Inn

How much different would things have been,
If maybe there had been room at the inn?
No hay, no manger, no beasts, no stall.
Rather, plenty of beds and blankets for all.

Not a proprietor in his right mind
Would allow all those shepherds, the filthiest kind,
To enter the doors of his establishment,
Not even the ones, who by angels were sent!

And the star overhead, no matter the beam,
Through walls made of mud, would not have been seen.
No bleating of lamb, no cooing of bird.
Would songs of the angels have even been heard?

Maybe the kings would have been turned away.
Foreigners weren't welcome in that place or that day.
Don't blame the innkeepers doing their jobs.
How could they know it was the Son of God?

Like the rest of his life, it was part of the plan.
A humble birth, a humble man.
Yes, it happened as it should have been,
No place to stay. No room in the inn.

—SALLY MEYER

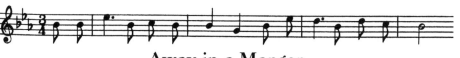

Away in a Manger

Away in a manger, no crib for a bed,
The little Lord Jesus laid down His sweet head.
The stars in the sky looked down where He lay,
The little Lord Jesus, asleep on the hay.

The cattle are lowing, the Baby awakes,
But little Lord Jesus, no crying He makes;
I love Thee, Lord Jesus, look down from the sky
And stay by my cradle til morning is nigh.

Be near me, Lord Jesus, I ask Thee to stay
Close by me forever, and love me, I pray;
Bless all the dear children in Thy tender care,
And fit us for heaven to live with Thee there.

The Nativity

The thatch on the roof was as golden,
   Though dusty the straw was and old,
The wind had a peal as of trumpets,
   Though blowing and barren and cold,
The mother's hair was a glory
   Though loosened and torn,
For under the eaves in the gloaming
   A child was born.

Have a myriad children been quickened,
   Have a myriad children grown old,
Grown gross and unloved and embittered,
   Grown cunning and savage and cold?
God abides in a terrible patience,
   Unangered, unworn,
And again for the child that was squandered
   A child is born.

What know we of aeons behind us,
   Dim dynasties lost long ago.
Huge empires, like dreams unremembered,
   Huge cities for ages laid low?
This at least—that with blight and with blessing,
   With flower and with thorn,
Love was there, and his cry was among them,
   'A child is born.'

Though the darkness be noisy with systems,
    Dark fancies that fret and disprove,
Still the plumes stir around us, above us
    The wings of the shadow of love:
Oh! princes and priests, have ye seen it
    Grow pale through your scorn;
Huge dawns sleep before us, deep changes,
    A child is born.

And the rafters of toil still are gilded
    With the dawn of the stars of the heart,
And the wise men draw near in the twilight,
    Who are weary of learning and art,
And the face of the tyrant is darkened,
    His spirit is torn,
For a new king is enthroned; yea, the sternest,
    A child is born.

And the mother still joys for the whispered
    First stir of unspeakable things,
Still feels that high moment unfurling
    Red glory of Gabriel's wings.
Still the babe of an hour is a master
    Whom angels adorn,
Emmanuel, prophet, anointed,
    A child is born.

And thou, that art still in thy cradle,
    The sun being crown for thy brow,
Make answer, our flesh, make an answer,
    Say, whence art thou come—who art thou?
Art thou come back on earth for our teaching
    To train or to warn—?
Hush—how may we know?—knowing only
    A child is born.

—G. K. CHESTERTON

No Room in the Inn

No beautiful chamber, no soft cradle bed,
No place but a manger, nowhere for His head;
No praises of gladness, no thought of their sin,
No glory but sadness, no room in the inn.

Refrain
No room, no room, for Jesus,
O give Him welcome free,
Lest you should hear at Heaven's gate,
"There is no room for thee."

No sweet consecration, no seeking His part,
No humiliation, no place in the heart;
No thought of the Savior, no sorrow for sin,
No prayer for His favor, no room in the inn.

Refrain

No one to receive Him, no welcome while here,
No balm to relieve Him, no staff but a spear;
No seeking His treasure, no weeping for sin,
No doing His pleasure, no room in the inn.

Refrain

—A. L. SKILTON

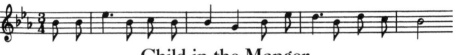

Child in the Manger

Child in the manger, Infant of Mary,
Outcast and Stranger, Lord of all,

Child Who inherits all our transgressions,
All our demerits on Him fall.

Once the most holy Child of salvation
Gently and lowly lived below.
Now as our glorious mighty Redeemer,
See Him victorious o'er each foe.

Prophets foretold Him, Infant of wonder;
Angels behold Him on His throne.
Worthy our Savoir of all of our praises;
Happy forever are His own.

—Mary M. Macdonald
Translated from Gaelic to
English by Lachlan Macbean

Nativity

Immensity cloistered in thy dear womb,
Now leaves his well-beloved imprisonment,
There he hath made himself to his intent
Weak enough, now into our world to come;
But Oh, for thee, for him, hath th' Inn no room?
Yet lay him in this stall, and from the Orient,
Stars, and wisemen will travel to prevent
Th' effect of Herod's jealous general doom.
Seest thou, my Soul, with thy faith's eyes, how he
Which fills all place, yet none holds him, doth lie?
Was not his pity towards thee wondrous high,

That would have need to be pitied by thee?
Kiss him, and with him into Egypt go,
With his kind mother, who partakes thy woe.

—JOHN DONNE

JOHN DONNE (1572–1631)—After attending the prestigious universities of Oxford and Cambridge, John Donne refused degrees from both places on religious grounds. He had been raised Catholic. He went on to study law and receive a position as a secretary for a statesman. While undergoing this job, he was imprisoned for marrying the young Anne More without her parents' consent. After being released, they lived in poverty due to his inability to obtain another job. While writing poetry, he succumbed to his peers and became an ordained minister of the Church of England, renouncing his ties to Catholicism. A mere two years later, his beloved Anne died. Obsessed with death, John began to write his best metaphysical poetry and continued writing until his death.

Prayer at the Manger

O God, whose mighty Son
was born in Bethlehem
those days long ago,
lead us to that same poor place,
where Mary laid her tiny Child.
And as we look on in wonder and praise,
make us welcome him in all new life,
see him in the poor,
and care for his handiwork:
the earth, the sky, and the sea.
O God, bless us again in your great love.
We pray for this through Christ our Lord.
Amen.

—ANONYMOUS

The Oxen

Christmas Eve, and twelve of the clock.
  "Now they are all on their knees,"
An elder said as we sat in a flock
  By the embers in the hearthside ease.

We pictured the meek mild creatures where
  They dwelt in their strawy pen,
Nor did it occur to one of us there
  To doubt they were kneeling then.

So fair a fancy few would weave
  In these years! Yet, I feel,
If someone said on Christmas Eve,
  "Come; see the oxen kneel

"In the lonely barton by yonder coomb
  Our childhood used to know,
I should go with him in the gloom,
  Hoping it might be so."

—THOMAS HARDY

THOMAS HARDY (1840–1928)—Trained as an architect in England, Hardy spent ten years working in this business. Though Hardy began as a novelist, he received critical reviews of his *Jude the Obscure* and *Tess of the D'Urbervilles* and he moved into writing poetry. Against the barren background of his home in Dorset, Hardy writes about the fatalistic outcomes of life and the bleakness of the human condition. Thomas married Emma Gifford who became the subject of many poems. Though his novels were more popular, Thomas was still hailed as one of the greatest poets of England. In fact, he was designated to be buried in Poets' Corner in Westminster Abbey. As a compromise, however, his heart was removed and buried with his family in Dorchester.

Visiting Bethlehem

One of the queerest spots on earth—I hope—is in Bethlehem. This is the patch of planet where, according to tradition, a cave once stabled animals, and where Mary gave birth to a son whose later preaching—scholars of every stripe agree, with varying enthusiasm—caused the occupying Romans to crucify him. Generations of Christians have churched over the traditional Bethlehem spot to the highest degree. Centuries of additions have made the architecture peculiar, but no one can see the church anyway, because many monasteries clamp onto it in clusters like barnacles. The Greek Orthodox Church owns the grotto site now, in the form of the Church of the Nativity.

There, in the Church of the Nativity, I took worn stone stairways to descend to levels of dark rooms, chapels, and dungeonlike corridors where hushed people passed. The floors were black stone or cracked marble. Dense brocades hung down old stone walls. Oil lamps hung in layers. Each polished silver or brass lamp seemed to absorb more light than its orange flame emitted, so the more lamps shone, the darker the space.

Packed into a tiny, domed upper chamber, Norwegians sang, as every other group did in turn, a Christmas carol. The stone dome bounced the sound around. The people sounded like seraphs singing inside a bell, sore amazed.

Descending once more, I passed several monks, narrow men, fine-faced and black, who wore tall black hats and long black robes. Ethiopians, they use the oldest Christian rite. At a lower level, in a small room, I peered over half a stone wall and saw Europeans below; they whispered in a language I could not identify.

Distant music sounded deep, as if from within my ribs. The music was, in fact, people from all over the world in the upper chamber, singing harmonies in their various tongues. The music threaded the vaults.

Now I climbed down innumerable dark stone stairs to the main part, the deepest basement: the Grotto of the Nativity. The grotto was

down yet another smoky stairway, at the back of a stone cave far beneath street level. This was the place. It smelled of wet sand. It was a narrow cave about ten feet wide; cracked marble paved it. Bunched tapers, bending grotesque in the heat, lighted a corner of floor. People had to kneel, one by one, under arches of brocade hangings, and stretch into a crouch down among dozens of gaudy hanging lamps, to see it.

I took worn stone stairways to descend to the levels where hushed people passed.

A fourteen-pointed silver star, two feet in diameter, covered a raised bit of marble floor at the cave wall. This silver star was the X that marked the spot: Here, just here, the infant got born. Two thousand years of Christianity began here, where God emptied himself into man. Actually, many Christian scholars think "Jesus of Nazareth" was likely born in Nazareth. Early writers hooked his birth to Bethlehem to fit a prophecy. Here, now, the burning oils smelled heavy. It must have struck many people that we were competing with these lamps for oxygen.

In the center of the silver star was a circular hole. That was the bull's-eye, God's quondam target.

Crouching people leaned forward to wipe their fingers across the hole's flat bottom. When it was my turn, I knelt, bent under a fringed satin drape, reached across half the silver star, and touched its hole. I could feel some sort of soft wax in it. The hole was a quarter inch deep and six inches across, like a wide petri dish. I have never read any theologian who claims that God is particularly interested in religion, anyway.

Any patch of ground anywhere smacks more of God's presence on earth, to me, than did this marble grotto. The ugliness of the blunt and bumpy silver star impressed me. The bathetic pomp of the heavy, tasseled brocades, the marble, the censers hanging from chains, the embroidered antependium, the aspergillum, the crosiers, the ornate lamps—some humans' idea of elegance—bespoke grand comedy, too, that God put up with it. And why should he not? Things here on earth get a whole lot worse than bad taste.

"Every day," said Rabbi Nachman of Bratslav, "the glory is ready to emerge from its debasement."

The lamps' dozen flames heated my face. Under the altar cloths, in

the corner where the stone wall met the marble floor, there was nothing to breathe but the lamps' oily fumes and people's exhalations. High above my back, layer after layer of stone away, people were singing. After the singing dwindled, the old walls still rang, and soon another group took up the general song in a melody faint and pure.

> *Two thousand years of Christianity began here, where God emptied himself into man.*

In the fourth century, those Jewish mystics devoted to Ezekiel's vision of the chariot wrote a text in which Rabbi Isaac said: "It is a five-hundred-year journey from the earth to the firmament. . . .The thickness of the firmament is a five-hundred-year journey. The firmament contains only the sun, moon and stars . . . The waters above the firmament are a five-hundred-year journey. From the sea to the Heaven of Heavens is a five-hundred-year journey. There are to be found the angels who say the *Kedushah*."

The text goes on to describe more five-hundred-year journeys upward to levels each of a thickness of a five-hundred-year journey: to the level of myriads and myriads ministering to the Prince above the firmament, to the level of the Canopy of the Torah, to the rebuilt Temple, to "the storehouses of snow and the storehouses of hail," and above them to the treasure-houses of blessing and the storehouses of peace. Above all that lies a thick layer of wings and hooves, and "the chariot to come." Above these seven heavens and the seven thicknesses between them is a layer of wings as thick as all the seven heavens and the distances between them together, and "above them is the Holy One, blessed be He."

Standing again, rubbing my fingers together, I found more stone stairways, more levels, and the street, the sunlight, the world. I found a van in the parking lot of what used to be, I try to tell myself, a stable—but this story was worn out for now, the paradox and scandal of any incarnation's occurring in a stable. More powerful at the moment was the sight of people converging from all over the world, people of every color in every costume, to rub their fingers across a flat hole in a bossy silver star on the cracked marble floor of a cave.

Rabbi Menahem Mendel brought Hasidic teaching to Palestine in the eighteenth century. He said, "This is what I attained in the Land of Israel. When I see a bundle of straw lying in the street, it seems to me a sign of the presence of God, that it lies there lengthwise, and not crosswise."

I could not keep away from it. I saw I had a minute or two to rush back from the van into the church and down the grotto stairs to kneel again at the silver star behind the brocade, to prostrate myself under the lamps, and to rub my fingers in the greasy wax.

Was it maybe tallow? I felt like Harry Reasoner at the Great Wall of China in 1972, who, pressed on live coverage for a response, came up with, "It's . . . uh . . . it's one of the two or three darnedest things I ever saw."

—LUCI SHEN

—ANNIE DILLARD

from *For the Time Being*

ANNIE DILLARD (1945–)—Raised in an affluent home and afforded the luxuries of literature and art, Annie developed a love for reading at an early age. By high school, her annual read would be *The Field Book of Ponds & Streams.* Annie attended Hollins College where she studied English, creative writing, and theology. While there, she married her writing teacher, Richard Dillard. She continued to pursue a Master in English where she focused on Emerson and Thoreau. Though she was raised Presbyterian, she wandered from Christianity for a time on a spiritual journey through several different religions. However, she was recently converted to Catholicism. Her *Pilgrim at Tinker Creek* won the Pulitzer prize for general non-fiction. After this success, she has continued to write and teach as an adjunct professor at Wesleyan University.

Now Yield We Thanks and Praise

Now yield we thanks and praise to Christ enthroned in glory,
And on this day of days tell out redemption's story,
Who truly have believed that on this blessed morn,
In holiness conceived, the Son of God was born.

What tribute shall we pay to Him who came in weakness,
And in a manger lay to teach His people meekness?
Let every house be bright; let praises never cease;
With mercies infinite our Christ hath brought us peace.

—HOWARD C. ROBBINS

The Nativity
Written in the year 1656

Peace? and to all the world? sure, one
And he the prince of peace, hath none.
He travels to be born, and then
Is born to travel more agen.
Poor *Galile!* thou can'st not be
The place for his Nativity.
His restless mother's call'd away,
And not deliver'd till she pay.
  A *Tax?* 'tis so still! we can see
The Church thrive in her misery;
And like her head at *Bethlem,* rise
When she opprest with troubles, lyes.
Rise? should all fall, we cannot be
In more extremities than he.
Great *Type* of passions! come what will,
Thy grief exceeds all *copies* still.
Thou cam'st from heav'n to earth, that we
Might go from Earth to Heav'n with thee.
And though thou found'st no welcom here,
Thou did'st provide us *mansions* there.
A *stable* was thy *Court,* and when
Men turn'd to *beasts;* Beasts would be *Men.*
They were thy *Courtiers,* others none;
And their poor *Manger* was thy *Throne.*

No swadling *silks* thy Limbs did fold,
Though thou could'st turn thy Rays to gold.
No *Rockers* waited on thy birth,
No *Cradles* stirr'd: nor songs of mirth;
But her chast *Lap* and sacred *Brest*
Which lodg'd thee first, did give thee *rest*.
    But stay: what light is that doth stream,
And drop here in a gilded beam?
It is thy Star runs *page*, and brings
Thy tributary *Eastern* Kings.
Lord! grant some *Light* to us, that we
May with them find the way to thee.
Behold what mists eclipse the day:
How dark it is! shed down one *Ray*
To guide us out of this sad night,
And say once more, *Let there be Light*.

—HENRY VAUGHAN

The Friendly Beasts

Jesus, our Brother, strong and good,
Was humbly born in a stable rude,
And the friendly beasts around Him stood,
Jesus, our Brother, strong and good.

"I," said the donkey, shaggy and brown,
"I carried His mother uphill and down,
 I carried His mother to Bethlehem town;
 I," said the donkey, shaggy and brown.

"I," said the cow, all white and red,
"I gave Him my manger for His bed,

I gave Him hay to pillow His head;
I," said the cow, all white and red.

"I," said the sheep with curly horn,
"I gave Him my wool for His blanket warm,
He wore my coat on Christmas morn;
I," said the sheep with curly horn.

"I," said the dove, from rafters high,
"I cooed Him to sleep that He should not cry,
We cooed Him to sleep, my mate and I;
I," said the dove, from the rafters high.

Thus all the beasts, by some good spell,
In the stable dark were glad tell
Of the gifts they gave Emmanuel,
The gifts they gave Emmanuel.

—ANONYMOUS

Upon Christ His Birth

Strange news! a city full? will none give way
To lodge a guest that comes not every day?
No inn, nor tavern void? yet I descry
One empty place alone, where we may lie:
In too much fullness is some want: but where?
Men's empty hearts: let's ask for lodging there.
But if they not admit us, then we'll say
Their hearts, as well as inns, are made of clay.

—SIR JOHN SUCKLING

SIR JOHN SUCKLING (1609–1642)—Born in Whitton, England into a family that had descended from a prominent Norfolk line, Suckling was graced with a fine education at Cambridge but left without taking a degree. His father died shortly thereafter, and Suckling inherited extensive estates. However, Suckling chose to pursue a military and ambassadorial career to serve in the British army. He was knighted in 1630. Welcomed back to the English court, he became quite popular as a gamester, writer, and political figure. Furtively taking an active role in a royalist plot to rescue Strafford from the tower of London, Suckling was found out and he fled to Paris. Shortly thereafter, he died by suicide, poison, or as tradition has it, by a servant who placed a razor in his boot. His works of poetry, prose, and plays are witty, fun pieces that are still read today.

Christmas Day Prayer

O God, my Father,
looking up at the shining stars
of the cold December sky
I remember the patient mother
and the rock-hewn manger
in lowly Bethlehem where lay cradled
Thy Love for the world.
In the shadows of the silent stall
I stand beside the Christ.
Speak to my soul as I wait, I pray Thee.
Let the trusting, loving spirit of the Child
steal into my life until it calms
my fears and soothes my pain.
In willing surrender and passionate longing
let me take the Christ child to my heart,
that henceforth I may live as He lived,
love as He loved, and, following His footsteps,
bring help to the needy, courage to the weak,
comfort to the sorrowing, and hope to the lost.
Amen.

—ANONYMOUS

Once in Royal David's City

Once in royal David's city
Stood a lowly cattle shed,
Where a mother laid her Baby
In a manger for His bed:
Mary was that mother mild,
Jesus Christ her little Child.

He came down to earth from heaven,
Who is God and Lord of all,
And His shelter was a stable,
And His cradle was a stall;
With the poor, and mean, and lowly,
Lived on earth our Savior holy.

And through all His wondrous childhood
He would honor and obey,
Love and watch the lowly maiden,
In whose gentle arms He lay:
Christian children all must be
Mild, obedient, good as He.

Jesus is our childhood's pattern;
Day by day, like us He grew;
He was little, weak and helpless,
Tears and smiles like us He knew;
And He feeleth for our sadness,
And he shareth in our gladness.

And our eyes at last shall see Him,
Through His own redeeming love;
For that Child so dear and gentle
Is our Lord in heaven above,

And He leads His children on
To the place where He is gone.

Not in that poor lowly stable,
With the oxen standing by,
We shall see Him, but in heaven,
Set at God's right hand on high;
Where like stars His children crowned
All in white shall wait around.

—Cecil F. Alexander

On the Morning of Christ's Nativity

This is the Month, and this is the happy morn
Wherin the Son of Heav'ns eternal King,
Of wedded Maid, and Virgin Mother born,
Our great redemption from above did bring;
For so the holy sages once did sing,
   That he our deadly forfeit should release,
And with his Father work is a perpetual peace.

That glorious Form, that Light unsufferable,
And that far-beaming blaze of Majesty,
Wherwith he wont at Heav'ns high Councel-Table,
To sit the midst of Trinal Unity,
He laid aside; and here with us to be,
   Forsook the Courts of everlasting Day,
And chose with us a darksom House of mortal Clay.

Say Heav'nly Muse, shall not thy sacred vein
Afford a present to the Infant God?
Hast thou no verse, no hymn, or solemn strein,
To welcom him to this his new abode,

Now while the Heav'n by the Suns team untrod,
   Hath took no print of the approaching light,
And all the spangled host keep watch in squadrons bright?

See how from far upon the Eastern rode
The Star-led Wisards haste with odours sweet,
O run, prevent them with thy humble ode,
And lay it lowly at his blessed feet;
Have thou the honour first, thy Lord to greet,
   And joyn thy voice unto the Angel Quire,
From out his secret Altar toucht with hallow'd fire.

The Hymn

It was the Winter wilde,
While the Heav'n-born-childe,
   All meanly wrapt in the rude manger lies;
Nature in aw to him
Had doff't her gawdy trim,
   With her great Master so to sympathize:
It was no season then for her
To wanton with the Sun her lusty Paramour.

Only with speeches fair
She woo's the gentle Air
   To hide her guilty front with innocent Snow,
And on her naked shame,
Pollute with sinfull blame,
   The Saintly Vail of Maiden white to throw,
Confounded, that her Maker's eyes
Should look so ne'er upon her foul deformities.

But he her fears to cease,
Sent down the meek-eyd Peace,
   She crown'd with Olive green, came softly sliding
Down through the turning sphear

His ready Harbinger,
    With Turtle wing the amorous clouds dividing,
and waving wide her mirtle wand,
She strikes a universall Peace through Sea and Land.

No War, or Battails sound
Was heard the World around,
    The idle spear and shield were high up hung;
The hooked Chariot stood
Unstain'd with hostile blood,
    The Trumpet spake not to the armed throng,
And Kings sate still with awfull eye,
As if they surely knew their sovran Lord was by.

But peacefull was the night
Wherin the Prince of light
    His raign of piece upon the earth began:
The Windes with wonder whist,
Smoothly the waters kist,
    Whispering new joyes to the milde Ocean,
Who now hath quite forgot to rave,
While Birds of Calm sit brooding on the charmed wave.

The Stars with deep amaze
Stand fixt in stedfast gaze,
    Bending one way their pretious influence,
And will not take their flight,
For all the morning light,
    Or *Lucifer* that often warn'd them thence,
But in their glimmering Orbs did glow,
Untill their Lord himself bespake, and bid them go.

And though the shady gloom
Had given day her room,
    The Sun himself with-held his wonted speed,
And hid his head for shame,

As his inferiour flame,
   The new enlightn'd world no more should need;
He saw a greater Sun appear
Than his bright Throne, or burning Axletree could bear.

The Shepherds on the Lawn,
Or ere the point of dawn,
   Sate simply chattering in a rustick row;
Full little thought they than,
That the mighty *Pan*
   Was kindly com to live with them below;
Perhaps their loves, or els their sheep,
Was all that did their silly thoughts so busie keep.

When such musick sweet
Their hearts and ears did greet,
   As never was by mortall finger strook,
Divinely-warbled voice
Answering the stringed noise,
   As all their souls in blisfull rapture took:
The Air such pleasure loth to lose,
With thousand echo's still prolongs each heav'nly close.

Nature that heard such sound
Beneath the hollow round
   Of *Cynthia's* seat, the Airy region thrilling,
Now was almost won
To think her part was don,
   And that her raign had here its last fulfilling;
She knew such harmony alone
Could hold all Heav'n and Earth in happier union.

At last surrounds their sight
A Globe of circular light,
   That with long beams the shame-fac't night array'd,

The helmed Cherubim
And sworded Seraphim,
   Are seen in glittering ranks with wings displaid,
Harping in loud and solemn quire,
With unexpressive notes to Heav'ns new-born Heir.

Such Musick (as 'tis said)
Before was never made,
   But when of old the sons of morning sung,
While the Creator Great
His constellations set,
   And the well-ballanc't world on hinges hung,
And cast the dark foundations deep,
And bid the weltring waves their oozy channel keep.

Ring out ye Crystall sphears,
Once bless our human ears,
   (If ye have power to touch our senses so)
And let your silver chime
Move in melodious time;
   And let the Base of Heav'ns deep Organ blow,
And with your ninefold harmony
Make up full consort to th' Angelike symphony.

For if such holy Song
Enwrap our fancy long,
   Time will run back, and fetch the age of gold,
And speckl'd vanity
Will sicken soon and die,
   And leprous sin will melt from earthly mould,
And Hell it self will pass away,
And leave her dolorous mansions to the peering day.

Yea Truth, and Justice then
Will down return to men,
   Th' enameled *Arras* of the Rain-bow wearing,

And Mercy set between,
Thron'd in Celestiall sheen,
   With radiant feet the tissued clouds down stearing,
And Heav'n as at som festivall,
Will open wide the Gates of her high Palace Hall.

But wisest Fate sayes no,
This must not yet be so,
   The Babe lies yet in smiling Infancy,
That on the bitter cross
Must redeem our loss;
   So both himself and us to glorifie:
Yet first to those ychain'd in sleep,
The wakefull trump of doom must thunder through
   the deep,

With such a horrid clang
As on mount *Sinai* rang
   While the red fire, and smouldring clouds out brake:
The aged Earth agast
With terrour of that blast,
   Shall from the surface to the center shake;
When at the worlds last session,
The dreadfull Judge in middle Air shall spread his throne.

And then at last our bliss
Full and perfect is,
   But now begins; for from this happy day
Th' old Dragon under ground
In straiter limits bound
   Not half so far casts his usurped sway,
And wrath to see his Kingdom fail,
Swindges the scaly Horrour of his foulded tail.

The Oracles are dumm,
No voice or hideous humm
   Runs through the arched roof in words deceiving.
Apollo from his shrine
Can no more divine,
   With hollow shreik the steep of *Delphos* leaving.
No nightly trance, or breathed spell,
Inspire's the pale-ey'd Priest from the prophetic cell.

The lonely mountains o're,
And the resounding shore,
   A voice of weeping heard, and loud lament;
From haunted spring, and dale
Edg'd with poplar pale,
   The parting Genius is with sighing sent,
With flowre-inwov'n tresses torn
The Nimphs in twilight shade of tangled thickets
     mourn.

In consecrated Earth,
And on the holy Hearth,
   The *Lars*, and *Lemures* moan with midnight plaint,
In Urns, and Altars round,
A drear, and dying sound
   Affrights the *Flamins* at their service quaint;
And the chill Marble seems to sweat,
While each peculiar power forgoes his wonted seat.

Peor, and *Baalim*,
Forsake their Temples dim,
   With that twice-batter'd god of *Palestine*,
And mooned *Ashtaroth*,
Heav'ns Queen and Mother both,
   Now sits not girt with Tapers holy shine,

The Libyc *Hammon* shrinks his horn,
In vain the *Tyrian* Maids their wounded *Thamuz* mourn.

And sullen *Moloch* fled,
Hath left in shadows dred,
   His burning Idol all of blackest hue,
In vain with Cymbals ring,
They call the grisly king,
   In dismall dance about the furnace blue;
The brutish gods of *Nile* as fast,
Iris and *Orus*, and the Dog *Anubis* hast.

Nor is *Osiris* seen
In *Memphian* Grove, or Green,
   Trampling the unshowr'd Grasse with lowings loud:
Nor can he be at rest
Within his sacred chest,
   Naught but profoundest Hell can be his shroud,
In vain with Timbrel'd Anthems dark
The sable-stoled Sorcerers bear his worshipt Ark.

He feels from *Juda's* Land
The dredded Infants hand,
   The rayes of *Bethlehem* blind his dusky eyn;
Nor all the gods beside,
Longer dare abide,
   Not *Typhon* huge ending in snaky twine:
Our Babe to shew his Godhead true,
Can in his swadling bands controul the damned crew.

So when the Sun in bed,
Curtain'd with cloudy red,
   Pillows his chin upon an Orient wave,
The flocking shadows pale,

Troop to th' infernall jail,
   Each fetter'd Ghost slips to his severall grave,
And the yellow-skirted *Fayes*,
Fly after the Night-steeds, leaving their Moon-lov'd maze.

But see the Virgin blest,
Hath laid her Babe to rest.
   Time is our tedious Song should here have ending,
Heav'ns youngest teemed Star,
Hath fixt her polisht Car,
   Her sleeping Lord with Handmaid Lamp attending:
And all about that Courtly Stable,
Bright-harnest Angels sit in order serviceable.

—JOHN MILTON

Cradled in a Manger, Meanly

Cradled in a manger, meanly,
Laid the Son of Man His head;
Sleeping His first earthly slumber
Where the oxen had been fed.
Happy were those shepherds listening
To the holy angel's word;
Happy they within that stable
Worshipping their infant Lord.

Happy all who hear the message
Of His coming from above;
Happier still who hail His coming,
And with praises greet His love.
Blessed Savior, Christ most holy,
In a manger Thou didst rest;

Canst Thou stoop again, yet lower,
And abide within my breast?

Evil things are there before Thee;
In the heart, where they have fed,
Wilt Thou pitifully enter,
Son of Man, and lay Thy head?
Enter, then, O Christ most holy;
Make a Christmas in my heart;
Make a heaven of my manger:
It is heaven where Thou art.

And to those who never listened
To the message of Thy birth,
Who have winter, but no Christmas
Bringing them Thy peace on earth,
Send to these the joyful tidings;
By all people, in each home,
Be there heard the Christmas
   anthem;
Praise to God, the Christ has come!

—GEORGE STRINGER ROWE

There Came a Little Child to Earth

There came a little Child to earth
Long ago;
And the angels of God proclaimed His birth,
High and low.

Out on the night, so calm and still,
Their song was heard;

For they knew that the Child on Bethlehem's hill
Was Christ the Lord.

—Emily E. Elliott

Infant Holy, Infant Lowly

Infant holy, Infant lowly, for His bed a cattle stall;
Oxen lowing, little knowing, Christ the Babe is Lord of all.
Swift are winging angels singing, noels ringing, tidings bringing:
Christ the Babe is Lord of all.

Flocks were sleeping, shepherds keeping vigil till the morning new
Saw the glory, heard the story, tidings of a Gospel true.
Thus rejoicing, free from sorrow, praises voicing, greet the morrow:
Christ the Babe was born for you.

—Traditional Carol
Translated from Polish to
English by Edith M. Reed

A Christmas Carol

Before the paling of the stars,
Before the winter morn,
Before the earliest cock-crow
Jesus Christ was born:
Born in a stable,
Cradled in a manger,
In the world His hands had made
Born a stranger.

Priest and king lay fast asleep
In Jerusalem,

Young and old lay fast asleep
    In crowded Bethlehem:
Saint and angel, ox and ass,
    Kept a watch together,
Before the Christmas daybreak
    In the winter weather.

Jesus on His mother's breast
    In the stable cold,
Spotless Lamb of God was He,
    Shepherd of the fold:
Let us kneel with Mary maid,
    With Joseph bent and hoary,
With saint and angel, ox and ass,
    To hail the King of Glory.

—Christina Rossetti

O Jesus Christ, Thy Manger Is

O Jesus Christ, Thy manger is
My paradise at which my soul reclineth.
For there, O Lord, doth lie the Word
Made flesh for us; herein Thy grace forthshineth.

He Whom the sea and wind obey
Doth come to serve the sinner in great meekness.
Thou, God's own Son, with us art one,
Dost join is and our children in our weakness.

Thy light and grace our guilt efface,
Thy heavenly riches all our loss retrieving.

Immanuel, Thy birth doth quell
The power of hell and Satan's bold deceiving.

Thou Christian heart, whoe'er thou art,
Be of good cheer and let no sorrow move thee!
For God's own Child, in mercy mild,
Joins thee to Him—how greatly God must love thee!

Remember thou what glory now
The Lord prepared thee for all earthly sadness.
The angel host can never boast
Of greater glory, greater bliss or gladness.

The world may hold her wealth and gold;
But thou, my heart, keep Christ as thy true Treasure.
To Him hold fast until at last
A crown be thine and honor in full measure.

—Paul Gerhardt

Christmas I

All after pleasures as I rid one day,
    My horse and I, both tired, body and mind,
    With full cry of affections, quite astray;
I took up in the next inn I could find.
There when I came, whom found I but my dear,
    My dearest Lord, expecting till the grief
    Of pleasures brought me to him, ready there
To be all passengers, most sweet relief?
O Thou, whose glorious, yet contracted light,
    Wrapped in night's mantle, stole into a manger,
    Since my dark soul and brutish is thy right,

To Man of all beasts be not thou a stranger:
    Furnish and deck my soul, that thou mayst have
    A better lodging, than a rack, or grave.

The shepherds sing; and shall I silent be?
    My God, no hymn for thee?
My soul's a shepherd too; a flock it feeds
    Of thoughts, and words, and deeds.
The pasture is thy word: the streams, thy grace
    Enriching all the place.
Shepherd and flock shall sing, and all my powers
    Out-sing the day-light hours.
Then we will chide the sun for letting night
    Take up his place and right:
We sing one common Lord; wherefore he should
    Himself the candle hold.
I will go searching, till I find a sun
    Shall stay, till we have done;
A willing shiner, that shall shine as gladly,
    As frost-nipped suns look sadly.
Then we will sing, and shine all our own day,
    And one another pay:
His beams shall cheer my breast, and both so twine,
Till ev'n his beams sing, and my music shine.

—GEORGE HERBERT

GEORGE HERBERT (1593–1633)—As the fifth son to a wealthy Welsh family, Herbert was truly the middle child in a family of ten. His father died when he was four leaving these children to his mother's care. George received a good education at Westminster and later Trinity College, Cambridge. After his schooling, he was elected a public orator and then a representative in the Parliament. Only after a few years, he resigned from his political career to be ordained as a rector and to marry Jane Danvers. In a small town near Salisbury, George preached and wrote poetry. His metaphysical poetry, characterized by a deep religious devotion, linguistic precision, metrical agility, and ingenious use of conceit, has been paralleled to that of John Donne's. He died at the age of forty from consumption, and *The Temple* was published the same year.

A Small Cathedral

A small cathedral outside Bethlehem marks the supposed birthplace of Jesus. Behind a high altar in the church is a cave, a little cavern lit by silver lamps.

You can enter the main edifice and admire the ancient church. You can also enter the quiet cave where a star embedded in the floor recognizes the birth of the King. There is one stipulation, however. You have to stoop. The door is so low you can't go in standing up.

The same is true of the Christ. You can see the world standing tall, but to witness the Savior, you have to get on your knees.

So . . .

while the theologians were sleeping
    and the elite were dreaming
        and the successful were snoring,
            the meek were kneeling.

They were kneeling before the One only the meek will see. They were kneeling in front of Jesus.

—MAX LUCADO
from *The Applause of Heaven*

CHAPTER FIVE

The Incarnation

JOHN 1:14–18

¹⁴And the Word became flesh and dwelt among us, and we beheld His glory, the glory as of the only begotten of the Father, full of grace and truth. ¹⁵John bore witness of Him and cried out, saying, "This was He of whom I said, 'He who comes after me is preferred before me, for He was before me.'" ¹⁶And of His fullness we have all received, and grace for grace. ¹⁷For the law was given through Moses, but *grace and truth came through Jesus Christ. ¹⁸No one has seen God at any time. The only begotten Son, who is in the bosom of the Father, He has declared Him.*

A Hymn on the Nativity of My Saviour

I sing the birth was born to-night,
The author both of life and light;
    The angels so did sound it.
And like the ravished shepherds said,
Who saw the light, and were afraid,
    Yet searched, and true they found it.

The Son of God, th' eternal king,
That did us all salvation bring,
    And freed the soul from danger;
He whom the whole world could not take,
The Word, which heaven and earth did make,
    Was now laid in a manger.

The Father's wisdom willed it so,
The Son's obedience knew no No,
 Both wills were in one stature;
And as that wisdom had decreed,
The Word was now made flesh indeed,
 And took on him our nature.

What comfort by him do we win,
Who made himself the price of sin,
 To make us heirs of glory!
To see this babe all innocence;
A martyr born in our defence:
 Can man forget the story?

—BEN JONSON

On the Incarnation of the Word

"The Word disguised Himself by appearing in a body, that He might, as Man, transfer men to Himself, and center their senses on Himself."

—ATHANASIUS

from *The Nicene and Post-Nicene Fathers*

ATHANASIUS (295?–373)—Living at the beginning of the fourth century, Athanasius was a Church Father who struggled against heretical ideologies that were circulating at the time. After becoming the bishop of Alexandria, Athanasius' principle fight was to combat Arianism. Thus, Athanasius stood for the deity of Christ in the incarnation and the crucifixion as the foundation to the Christian faith. Most of his works surround this issue, yet he wrote several apologetic works as well. He was intimately involved in both the Council of Nicea and the Council of Alexandria. Against Arianism, Athanasius argued from Scripture, appealed to a Christian worship of Jesus Christ, and was the first to devote serious attention to the status of the Holy Spirit.

A Word

A word came forth in Galilee, a word like to a star;
It climbed and rang and blessed and burnt wherever brave
   hearts are;
A word of sudden secret hope, of trial and increase
Of wrath and pity fused in fire, and passion kissing peace.
A star that o'er the citied world beckoned, a sword of flame;
A star with myriad thunders tongued; a mighty word there
   came.

The wedge's dart passed into it, the groan of timber wains,
The ringing of the rivet nails, the shrieking of the planes;
The hammering on the roofs at morn, the busy workshop roar;
The hiss of shavings drifted deep along the windy floor;
The heat-browned toiler's crooning song, the hum of human
   worth
Mingled of all the noise of crafts, the ringing word went forth.

The splash of nets passed into it, the grind of sand and shell,
The boat-hook's clash, the boat-oars' jar, the cries to buy and
   sell,
The flapping of the landed shoals, the canvas crackling free,
And through all varied notes and cries, the roaring of the sea,
The noise of little lives and brave, of needy lives and high;
In gathering all the throes of earth, the living word went by.

Earth's giant sins bowed down to it, in Empire's huge eclipse,
When darkness sat above the thrones, seven thunders on her
   lips,
The woes of cities entered it, the clang of idols' falls,
The scream of filthy Caesars stabbed high in their brazen
   halls,

The dim hoarse floods of naked men, the world-realms'
   snapping girth,
The trumpet of Apocalypse, the darkness of the earth:

The wrath that brake the eternal lamp and hid the eternal
   hill,
A world's destruction loading, the word went onward still—
The blaze of creeds passed into it, the hiss of horrid fires,
The headlong spear, the scarlet cross, the hair-shirt and the
   briars,
The cloistered brethren's thunderous chaunt, the errant
   champion's song,
The shifting of the crowns and thrones, the tangle of the
   strong.

The shattering fall of crest and crown and shield and cross
   and cope,
The tearing of the gauds of time, the blight of prince and
   pope,
The reign of ragged millions leagued to wrench a loaded debt,
Loud with the many throated roar, the word went forward
   yet.
The song of wheels passed into it, the roaring and the smoke
The riddle of the want and wage, the fogs that burn and
   choke.

The breaking of the girths of gold, the needs that creep and
   swell,
The strengthening hope, the dazing light, the deafening
   evangel,
Through kingdoms dead and empires damned, through
   changes without cease,
With earthquake, chaos, born and fed, rose,—and the word
   was 'Peace.'

—G. K. CHESTERTON

When Came in Flesh the Incarnate Word

When came in flesh the incarnate Word,
The heedless world slept on,
And only simple shepherds heard
That God had sent His Son.

When comes the Savior at the last,
From east to west shall shine
The awful pomp, and earth aghast
Shall tremble at the sign.

Then shall the pure of heart be blest;
As mild He comes to them,
As when upon the virgin's breast
He lay at Bethlehem.

As mild to meek eyed love and faith,
Only more strong to save;
Strengthened by having bowed to death,
By having burst the grave.

Lord, who could dare see Thee descend
In state, unless he knew
Thou art the sorrowing sinner's Friend,
The gracious and the true?

Dwell in our hearts, O Savior blest;
So shall Thine advent's dawn
'Twixt us and Thee, our bosom Guest,
Be but the veil withdrawn.

—JOSEPH ANSTICE

Where God Enters

Here in time we make holiday because the eternal birth which God the father bore and bears unceasingly in eternity is now born in time, in human nature. Saint Augustine says this birth is always happening. But if it does not happen in me, what does it profit me? What matters is that it shall happen in me.

We intend therefore to speak of this birth as taking place in us, as being consummated in the virtuous soul, for it is in the perfect soul that God speaks his word. What I shall say is true only of the devout man, of him who has walked and is still walking in the way of God, not of the natural undisciplined man who is entirely remote from and unconscious of this birth.

There is a saying of the wise man, "When all things lay in the midst of silence, then leapt there down into me from on high, from the royal throne, a secret word." This sermon is about this word.

Concerning it three things are to be noted. The first is where in the soul God the father speaks his Word, where she is receptive of this act, where this birth occurs. The second, has to do with man's conduct in relation to this act, this interior speaking, this birth. The third point will deal with the profit, and how great it is, that accrues from this birth.

> *Whatever the soul effects, she effects with her powers.*

Note in the first place that in what I am about to say I intend to use natural proofs that you yourselves can grasp, for though I put more faith in the scriptures than myself, nevertheless it is easier and better for you to learn by arguments that can be verified.

First we will take the words, "In the midst of the silence there was spoken in me a secret word." But, sir, where is the silence and where the place in which the word is spoken?

To begin with, it is spoken in the purest, noblest ground, yes, in the very center of the soul. That is mid-silence, for no creature ever entered there, nor any image, nor has the soul there either activity or

understanding, therefore she is not aware of any image either of herself or any creature. Whatever the soul effects, she effects with her powers. When she understands, she understands with her intellect. When she remembers, she does so with her memory. When she loves, she does so with her will. She works then with her powers and not with her essence.

Now every exterior act is linked with some means. The power of seeing is brought into play only through the eyes; elsewhere she can neither do nor bestow such a thing as seeing. And so with all the other senses; their operations are always effected through some means or other. But there is no activity in the essence of the soul; the faculties she works with emanate from the ground of the essence, but in her actual ground there is a mid-silence; here alone is a rest and habitation for this birth, this act, wherein God the father speaks his word, for she is intrinsically receptive of nothing but the divine essence, without means. Here God enters the soul with his all, not merely with a part. God enters the ground of the soul.

> *God enters the ground of the soul.*

None can touch the ground of the soul but God. No creature is admitted into her ground, it must stop outside in her powers. There it sees the image whereby it has been drawn in and found shelter. For when the soul's powers contact a creature, they set out to make of the creature an image and likeness which they absorb. By it they know the creature. Creatures cannot enter the soul, nor can the soul know anything about a creature whose image she has not willingly taken into herself. She approaches creatures through their present images, an image being a thing that the soul creates with her powers. Be it a stone, a rose, a person, or anything else she wants to know about, she gets out the image of it which she has already taken in and thus is able to unite herself with it. But an image received in this way must of necessity enter from without through the senses. Consequently, there is nothing so unknown to the soul as herself. The soul, says the philosopher, can neither create nor absorb an image of herself. So she has nothing to know herself by. Images all enter through the senses, hence she can have no image of herself. She knows other things but not

herself. Of nothing does she know so little as herself, owing to this arrangement.

Now you must know that inwardly the soul is free from means and images; that is why God can freely unite with her without form or image. You cannot but attribute to God without measure whatever power you attribute to a master. The wiser and more powerful the master, the more immediately is his work effected and the simpler it is. Man requires many instruments for his external works; much preparation is needed before he can bring them forth as he has imagined them. The sun and moon, whose work is to give light, in their master-ship perform this very swiftly: the instant their radiance is poured forth, all the ends of the earth are filled with light. More exalted are the angels, who need fewer means for their works and have fewer images. The highest Seraph has but a single image. He seizes as a unity all that his inferiors regard as manifold. Now God needs no image and has no image: without image, likeness, or means does God work in the soul, in her ground wherein no image ever entered other than himself with his own essence. This no creature can do.

How does God the father give birth to his son in the soul? Like creatures, in image and likeness? No, by my faith, but just as he gives him birth in eternity and not otherwise.

Well, but how does he give him birth there?

See, God the father has perfect insight into himself, profound and thorough knowledge of himself by means of himself, not by means of any image. And thus God the father gives birth to his son in the very oneness of the divine nature. Thus it is, and in no other way, that God the father gives birth to his son in the ground and essence of the soul, and this he unites himself with her. Were any image present, there would be no real union, and in real union lies true bliss.

> *There is nothing so unknown to the soul as herself.*

Now you may say: "But there is nothing innate in the soul but images." No, not so! If that were true, the soul would never be happy, but God made every creature to enjoy perfect happiness, otherwise God would not be the highest happiness and final goal, whereas it is his will and nature to be the alpha and omega of all.

No creature can be happiness. And here indeed can just as little be perfection, for perfection (perfect virtue, that is to say) results from perfection of life. Therefore you truly must sojourn and dwell in your essence, in your ground, and there God shall mix you with his essence without the medium of any image. No image represents and signifies itself: it stands for that of which it is the image. Now seeing that you have no image other than what is outside you, therefore it is impossible for you to be beatified by any image whatsoever.

The second point is, what must a person do to deserve and procure this birth that it may come to pass and be consummated in him? It is better for him to do his part toward it, to imagine and think about God, or should he keep still in peace and quiet so that God can act in him while he merely waits on God's operation? Of course, I am referring to those whose act is only for the good and perfect, those who have so absorbed and assimilated the essence of virtue that it emanates from them naturally, without their seeking. They live a worthy life and have within them the lofty teaching of our Lord Jesus Christ. Such are permitted to know that the very best and utmost of attainment in this life is to remain still and let God act and speak in you. When the powers have all been withdrawn from their bodily forms and functions, then this word is spoken. Thus he says: "In the midst of the silence the secret word was spoken to me."

The more completely you are able to draw in your faculties and forget those things and their images which you have taken in—the more, that is to say, you forget the creature—the nearer you are to this and the more susceptible you are to it. If only you could suddenly be altogether unaware of things, could you but pass into oblivion of your own existence as Saint Paul did when he said: "Whether in the body I know not, or out of the body I know not, God knows!" Here the Spirit had so entirely absorbed the faculties that it had forgotten the body: memory no longer functioned, nor understanding, nor the senses, nor even those powers whose duty it is to govern and grace the body; vital warmth and energy were arrested so that the body remained intact throughout the three days during which he neither ate nor drank. It was the same with Moses when he fasted forty days on the mount and was none the worse for it: on the last day he was as strong as on the first.

Thus a person must abscond from his senses, invert his faculties, and lapse into oblivion of things and of himself. About which the philosopher addressed the soul: "Withdraw from the restlessness of external activities!" And again: "Flee away and hide from the turmoil of outward occupations and inward thoughts, for they create nothing but discord!" If God is to speak his word in the soul, she must be at rest and at peace; then he speaks in his soul his word and *himself:* not an image but himself. Dionysius says: "God has no image or likeness of himself, seeing that he is intrinsically all good, truth and being." God performs all his works in himself and outside himself simultaneously. Do not fondly imagine that God, when he created the heavens and the earth and all creatures, made one thing one day and another the next.

> *If God is to speak his word in the soul, she must be at rest and at peace.*

All God did was: he willed and they were. God works without instrument and without image. And the freer you are from images, the more receptive you are to his interior operation, and the more introverted and oblivious you are, the closer you are to it. All things must be forsaken. God scorns to work among images.

Now you may say, "What is it that God does without images in the ground and essence?" That I am incapable of knowing, for my soul powers can receive only in images; they have to recognize and lay hold of each thing in its appropriate image: they cannot recognize a bird in the image of a man. Now since images all enter from without, this is concealed from my soul, which is most salutary for her. Not knowing makes her wonder and leads her to eager pursuit, for she knows clearly *that* it is but knows not *how* nor *what* it is. No sooner does one know the reason of a thing than he tires of it and goes casting about for something new. Always clamoring to know, we are ever inconstant. The soul is constant only to this unknowing which keeps her pursuing.

The wise man said concerning this: "In the middle of the night when all things were in quiet silence, there was spoken to me a hidden word." It came like a thief, by stealth. What does he mean by a word that was hidden? The nature of a word is to reveal what is hidden. It appeared before me, shining out with intent to reveal and giving me

knowledge of God. Hence it is called a word. But what it was remained hidden from me. That was its stealthy coming "in a whispering stillness to reveal itself." It is just because it is hidden that one is always and must be always after it. It appears and disappears; we are meant to yearn and sigh for it.

Saint Paul says we ought to pursue this until we spy it and not stop until we grasp it. When he returned after being caught up into the third heaven, where God was made known to him and where he beheld all things, he had forgotten nothing, but it was so deep down in his ground that his intellect could not reach it; it was veiled from him. He was therefore obliged to pursue it and search for it in himself, not outside himself. It is not outside, it is inside: wholly within. And being convinced of this, he said: "I am sure that neither death nor any affliction can separate me from what I find within me."

There is a fine saying of one philosopher to another about this. He says: "I am aware of something in me which sparkles in my intelligence;

> *Into this retirement steals the word in the darkness of the night.*

I clearly perceive *that* it is something, but *what* I cannot grasp. Yet it seems if I could only seize it I should know its truth." To which the other philosopher replied, "Follow it boldly! For if you can seize it, you will possess the sum total of all good and have eternal life!" It hides yet it shows. It comes, but after the manner of a thief, with intent to take and to steal all things from the soul. By emerging and showing itself somewhat, it purposes to decoy the soul and to draw it to itself, to rob it and take itself from it. As the prophet said: "Lord, take from them their spirit and give them instead thy spirit." This too the loving soul meant when she said, "My soul dissolved and melted away when Love spoke his word; when he entered I could not but fail." And Christ signified it by his words: "Whosoever shall leave anything for my sake shall be paid an hundredfold, and whosoever will possess me must deny himself and all things, and whosoever will serve me must follow me nor go anymore after his own."

Those who have written of the soul's nobility have gone no further than their natural intelligence could carry them: they never entered

her ground, so that much remained obscure and unknown to them. "I will sit in silence and hearken to what God speaks within me," said the prophet. Into this retirement steals the word in the darkness of the night. Saint John says, "The light shines in the darkness; it came unto its own and as many as received it became in authority sons of God: to them was given power to become God's sons."

Notice the fruit and use of this mysterious word and of this darkness. In this gloom which is his own, the heavenly father's son is not born alone: you too are born there a child of the same heavenly father and no other, and to you also he gives power. Call this if you will an ignorance, an unknowing, yet there is in it more than all knowing and understanding without it, for this outward ignorance lures and attracts you from all understood things and from yourself. This is what Christ meant when he said, "Whosoever denies not himself and leaves not father and mother and is not estranged from all these, he is not worthy of me." As though to say: he who abandons not creaturely externals can neither be conceived nor born in this divine birth. But divesting yourself of yourself and of everything external does indeed give it to you.

May the God who has been born again as man assist us in this birth, continually helping us, weak men, to be born again in him as God. Amen.

—MEISTER ECKHART
from *Whom God Hid Nothing*

Satan Legend

According to a legend Satan and his demons were having a Christmas party. As the demonic guests were departing, one grinned and said to Satan, "Merry Christmas, your majesty." At that, Satan replied with a growl, "Yes, keep it merry. If they ever get serious about it, we'll all be in trouble." Well, get serious about it. It is the birth of the Baby. It is the coming of God. It is the intervention of God's presence among men.

—CHUCK SWINDOLL
from *The Tale of the Tardy Oxcart*

On the Incarnation

"The One person, whom we really know as a human person, is the person of Jesus Christ, and even this is in fact the person of God the Son, in which humanity, without being or having itself a person, is caught up into fellowship with the personality of God."

—KARL BARTH

from *Church Dogmatics*, II/1

KARL BARTH (1886–1968)—Proclaimed one of the greatest theologians of the 20th century and possibly since the Reformation, Karl Barth, between 1920 and 1950, ushered in a new era of theology: Neo-Orthodoxy. In the aftermath of WWI, Barth critiqued the liberal theology of the social order in America due to its accommodation of culture. Born to a New Testament scholar, Barth began his studies early in life and attended the best schools in Germany. His *Epistle to the Romans* and *Church Dogmatics* are his most notable works that emphasize the transcendence of God, the sinfulness of humanity, and the gift of revelation in Jesus Christ.

The Birth of Christ

The time draws near the birth of Christ;
　　The moon is hid—the night is still;
　　The Christmas bells from hill to hill
Answer each other in the mist.

Four voices of four hamlets round,
　　From far and near, on mead and moor,
　　Swell out and fail, as if a door
Were shut between me and the sound.

Each voice four changes on the wind,
　　That now dilate and now decrease,
　　Peace and good-will, good-will and peace,
Peace and good-will to all mankind.

Rise, happy morn! rise, holy morn!
  Draw forth the cheerful day from night;
  O Father! touch the east, and light
The light shone when hope was born!
                    —ALFRED LORD TENNYSON
                    from *Christmas Classics*

ALFRED LORD TENNYSON (1809–1892)—The fourth child in a family of twelve, Alfred was fathered by a disgruntled clergyman. His father was known to exhibit rage and alcoholism, as did each of his children in time. This experience of suffering along with his brother's early death certainly impacted Tennyson's dark writings. Tennyson had the opportunity to attend Cambridge where he began his writing career. While there, his brother was institutionalized after a mental breakdown, and Tennyson grew in fear that he might do the same. After an unsuccessful business deal, Tennyson fell into debt and depression. He courted a young woman, Emily Sellwood, and he finally married her after a long courtship in 1850. The timely success of *In Memoriam*, published that same year, ensured Tennyson's appointment as Poet Laureate, succeeding William Wordsworth. In 1883 Tennyson accepted a peerage, the first poet to be so honored strictly on the basis of literary achievement. Tennyson died in 1892 and was interred in Poet's Corner of Westminster Abbey.

Jesus Is An Esteemed Name

According to Josephus, there are eleven men in the Old Testament with the name Joshua, the Hebrew translation of Jesus. And no parents had ever called their children by that name until Moses created a name for a man who was formerly called Hoshea: "These are the names of the men whom Moses sent to spy out the land. And Moses called Hoshea the son of Nun, Joshua" (Num. 13:16 NKJV).

Now *Hoshea* means "salvation." And *Jehovah* means "Lord." So when Moses changed Hoshea's name to "Joshua," he gave him a name of redemption, a name that sounds like some sort of a savior. And he was, wasn't he?

Many Bible scholars consider Joshua of the Old Testament to be a picture of Christ. And, if you think about it, there are some striking points of comparison between the two. Joshua led the Israelites out of

the wilderness to the promised land. Jesus, as our Savior, brings us from the wilderness of sin into the spiritual promised land. In the Old Testament, Joshua led his people to conquer enemies who were protected by walled cities and huge giants. Jesus leads us to conquer the enemies of our soul. He enables us to fight victoriously against all of life's most difficult obstacles and its giants of temptation, trial, and testing. As our Joshua, Jesus leads us to the inheritance that God has for us.

Joshua's salvation was earthly and temporal, but the salvation that Jesus came to bring is heavenly and eternal, and it never needs to be purchased for us again. In fact, the writer of the book of Hebrews puts these two men together in a wonderful little statement in Hebrews 4:8 (NKJV): "For if Joshua had given them rest, then He would not afterward have spoken of another day."

In other words, if Joshua could have done the salvation work for the people, there would have been no need for another Joshua in terms of Jesus. But Joshua could only work in the material world; so there remained a need for the New Testament Jesus to be born, so that we could be saved from our sin.

—DAVID JEREMIAH
from "Thou Shalt Call His Name
Jesus" in *The Heart of Christmas*

Born of Woman

So that is his mother.
That little woman.
The gray-eyed perpetrator.

The boat in which years ago
he floated to the shore.

Out of which he struggled
into the world,
into non-eternity.

The bearer of the man
with whom I walk through fire.

So that is she, the only one
who did not choose him
ready-made, complete.

Herself she pressed him
into the skin I know,
bound him to the bones
hidden from me.

Herself she spied out
his gray eyes,
with which he looked at me.

So that is she, his alpha.
Why did he show her to me.

Born of woman.
So he too was born.
Born like all others.
Like me who will die.

The son of a real woman.
A newcomer from body's depths.
A wanderer to omega.

Threatened
by his own non-existence
from all sides
at every instant.

And his head
is a head banging against the wall
that yields but for the moment.

And his movements
are all attempts to dodge
the universal verdict.

I understood
he had already travelled half the way.

But he didn't tell me that,
no, he did not.

"This is my mother,"
was all he said to me.

—WISLAWA SZYMBORSKA
from *Sounds, Feelings, Thoughts*

Come Thou Redeemer of the Earth

Come, Thou Redeemer of the earth,
And manifest Thy virgin birth:
Let every age adoring fall;
Such birth befits the God of all.

Begotten of no human will,
But of the Spirit, Thou art still
The Word of God in flesh arrayed,
The promised Fruit to man displayed.

The virgin womb that burden gained
With virgin honor all unstained;
The banners there of virtue glow;
God in His temple dwells below.

Forth from His chamber goeth He,
That royal home of purity,

ARTHUR HUGHES (1857–1858)   *Birmingham Museums and Art Gallery*

THE ANNUNCIATION
Oil and pencil on canvas

JOSEPH MALLARD WILLIAM TURNER (1775-1851)   *Tate Gallery, London*

HOLY FAMILY

Oil on canvas 1022 x 1416 mm

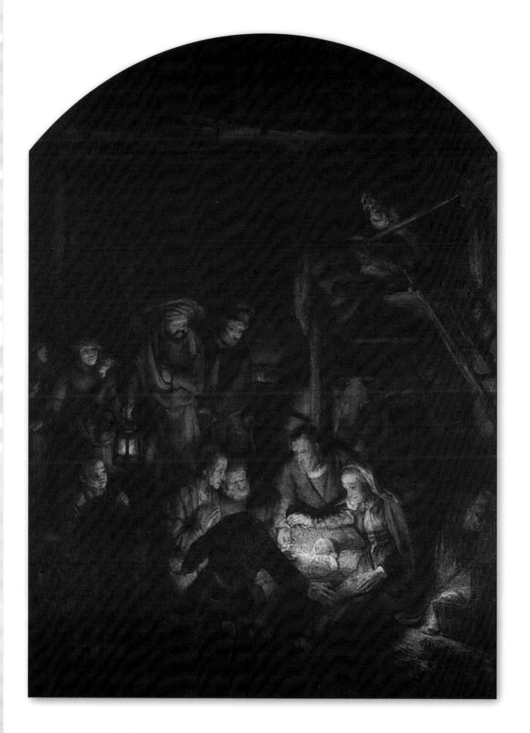

REMBRANDT (1646)   *National Gallery, London*

THE ADORATION OF THE SHEPHERDS
Canvas

MARC CHAGALL (1938-1942)

Museo Thyssen-Bornemisza

MADONNA OF THE VILLAGE

Oil on canvas 102.5 x 98 cm

GEORGES DE LA TOUR (1593–1652) *Louvre Museum*

CHRIST WITH ST. JOSEPH
IN THE CARPENTER'S SHOP
Canvas 1.37 x 1.02 m

REMBRANDT (c. 1666-69)   *National Museum, Stockholm Sweden*

SIMEON WITH THE CHRIST CHILD IN THE TEMPLE
Oil on canvas

A giant in twofold substance one,
Rejoicing now His course to run.

From God the Father He proceeds,
To God the Father back He speeds;
His course He runs to death and hell,
Returning on God's throne to dwell.

O equal to the Father, Thou!
Gird on Thy fleshly mantle now;
The weakness of our mortal state
With deathless might invigorate.

Thy cradle here shall glitter bright,
And darkness breathe a newer light,
Where endless faith shall shine
   serene,
And twilight never intervene.

All laud to God the Father be,
All praise, eternal Son, to Thee;
All glory, as is ever meet,
To God the Holy Paraclete.

—AMBROSE OF MILAN
from *Veni, Redemptor gentium*

The Burning Babe

As I in hoary winter's night stood shivering in the snow,
Surprised I was with sudden heat which made my heart
  to glow

And lifting up a fearful eye to view what fire was near,
A pretty Babe all burning bright did in the air appear,

Who scorched with excessive heat such floods of tears did
   shed
As though his floods should quench his flames which with
   were fed.

"Alas!" quoth he, "but newly born in firey heats, I fry,
Yet none approach to warm their hearts or feel my fire but I!

My faultless heart the furnace is, the fuel wounding
   thorns;
Love is the fire and sighs the smoke, the ashes shame and
   scorns;

The fuel Justice layeth on, and Mercy blows the coals;
The metal in this furnace wrought are men's defiled souls;

For which, as now on fire I am, to work them to their
   good,
So will I melt into a bath to wash them in my blood."

With that he vanished out of sight and swiftly shrunk away,
And straightway I called into mind that it was Christmas
   Day.

—ROBERT SOUTHWELL

Christmas Is a Simple Story

The Christmas story is serenely simple. It cannot be complicated
with philosophizing or with argument; it defies analysis and silences
calculation. It is as simple as the silent dawn, as unbelabored as the
bursting rose, as unsophisticated as a child's cry, as spontaneous as a
child's laughter.

God through the centuries has manifested Himself in diverse and
complex ways. We see an evidence of Him in the perfection of a mathe-

matical formula and in the order of a distant galaxy; we hear Him speak through the profound utterances of noble minds and in the erudite thoughts of great theologians. But Christmas is like none of these. Christmas is as simple as childhood and as beautiful.

When God made His most benevolent gesture of fatherly love, His giving of a Son, He wanted to be understood by all men. But no flaming chariot bore Jesus from highest heaven. No mighty cannonade announced His appearing. There were no bugles, no treading of armies, none of the grandeur and glory we should devise for so remarkable an event.

> *Christmas is as simple as childhood and as beautiful.*

Rather, silently and unobtrusively, Christ entered our world in the way each of us has come, as a weak and helpless child. Why? When surely legions of angels might have heralded His approach, why did God choose from the most obscure of villages the most unpretentious of maidens? Was it not that by sharing our nature, His Son would speak our language, understand our homes, sympathize with our heartaches, comprehend our hopes? Had He come in grandeur, He would have been for us an unapproachable object of wonder and awe. Had He come as a mighty conqueror, we should have honored Him, but we would also have feared Him . . .

> *To be Himself a star most bright*
> *To bring the wise men to His sight,*
> *To be Himself a voice most sweet*
> *To call the shepherds to His feet,*
> *To be a child—it was His will,*
> *That folk like us might find Him still.*
> —JOHN ERSKINE

And yet is there in all creation a more miraculous evidence of God's creatorship than a newborn baby? Is there in all the vast reaches of the universe a more wonderful expression of divine love than the child's first cry?

The divine messenger who announced to Mary the word of His coming said, "the power of the Most High will overshadow you; therefore

the child to be born will be called holy, the Son of God" (Luke 1:35). A holiness attends all births, and the promise which every newborn child brings to a mother's heart is an evidence of God's love.

Christ came into the world as a baby. He left the world thirty-three brief years later when He was in the vigor and beauty of noble and consecrated young manhood. From that day to this, there has been no more wonderful expression of God's heart than the promise of childhood and the fulfillment of maturity. All life has become more precious, more consecrated and less expendable because of Him who has shown us the possibilities that lie within our human nature.

Christmas is a simple story, divinely simple yet profoundly inspiring, showing what life may mean for each of us.

—CHARLES L. ALLEN and CHARLES L. WALLIS
from *Christmas In Our Hearts*

John 1:14 (1964)

The oriental histories* relate
That one king of those times, subject to
Splendor and tedium, would venture out alone
And, in secret, wander through the precincts

And lose himself in mobs of people with
Rough hands and unknown names;
Today, like that Emir of Believers,
Harun,† God wants to be with men

And is born of a mother, like the birth
Of dynasties that decompose to dust,
And the whole world will be given up to him,

---

*The Oriental histories are the stories of the Arabian nights.
†Harun al-Rashid.

Air, water, bread, tomorrows, lily, stone,
And afterwards the blood of martyrdom,
The mocking, and the nails, and the beam.

—JORGE LUIS BORGES
from *Selected Poems*

What Child Is This?
(Greensleeves)

What Child is this, who, laid to rest,
On Mary's lap is sleeping?
Whom angels greet with anthems sweet,
While shepherds watch are keeping?
This, this is Christ, the King,
Whom shepherds guard and angels sing:
Haste, haste to bring him laud,
The Babe, the Son of Mary!

So bring Him incense, gold and myrrh,
Come peasant, king to own Him;
The King of Kings, salvation brings:
Let loving hearts enthrone Him.
Raise, raise the song on high,
The Virgin sings her lullaby:
Joy, joy for Christ is born
The Babe, the son of Mary!

—Traditional Carol

The Name of A King

Among all the names given to announce the coming of the Messiah, there are none like the descriptions found in Isaiah 9:6, where the

glorious fivefold name of Jesus Christ was recorded seven hundred years before He was born in a lowly manger. The names shone brilliantly against the dark background of a world that had lost its way. Light is come! A Son is given! Isaiah was allowed a look through the telescope of prophecy and saw a new day dawning. God spoke a promise of a new kingdom and a new kind of King, Jesus Christ:

> *For unto us a Child is born,*
> *Unto us a Son is given;*
> *And the government will be upon His shoulder.*
> *And His name will be called*
> *Wonderful, Counselor, Mighty God,*
> *Everlasting Father, Prince of Peace.*
> —ISAIAH 9:6 NKJV

We must first notice several basics about this prophecy. The words clearly predict that He would be physically birthed; He would become a man in incarnation. It stated, "Unto us a Son is given," and indeed, Jesus was Son of Abraham, Son of David, Son of man, and Son of God.

Furthermore, this Son would be given as a sacrifice. I recall a story from World War II of a man whose leg had to be amputated. The doctor said to him, "We're going to have to take your leg." The man replied, "No sir. I am giving my leg for my country." The perspective changes the whole situation. Jesus made His perspective clear when He said, "No one takes My life from Me. I lay it down willingly."

The prophetic verse continues, "The government will be upon His shoulder." All authority would be granted to Him. This Son who was given would rise to become the Regent of the universe. Not only does He have authority over the government of all creation, the planet, and all the ages, but He can be Lord over each individual as well. Jesus would not come to take part in our lives; He would come to take over our lives.

During this season of the year like no other, we should take time to search our hearts and sincerely examine who is on the throne of our

will. Every time we try to control our own lives, everything ends up in a mess. Let the government of your own heart be upon Christ's shoulder.

—RON PHILLIPS
from "Call Him Wonderful" in *The Spirit of Christmas*

Lauda Sion Salvatorem

Light of lights! All gloom dispelling,
Thou didst come to make thy dwelling
Here within our world of sight.
Lord, in pity and in power,
Thou didst in our darkest hour
Rend the clouds and show thy light.

Praise to thee in earth and heaven
Now and evermore be given,
Christ, who art our sun and shield.
Lord, for us thy life thou gavest,
Those who trust in thee thou savest,
All thy mercy stands revealed.

—ST. THOMAS AQUINAS

ST. THOMAS AQUINAS (1225–1274)—Affectionately nicknamed "The Dumb Ox" by his classmates, Albert the Great prophesied that "this dumb ox will fill the world with his bellowing." Thomas Aquinas is perhaps the most influential theologian in the history of Christian theology. Educated under the Dominican friars at the University of Naples as well as in Paris and Cologne, he pursued a career in teaching and writing. The question of the thirteenth century was the issue of Aristotelian philosophy. How can the church synthesize the ideas of Augustine and Aristotle? Aquinas tackled these issues of nature and grace bringing together philosophy and theology, faith and reason. Alongside this lifelong endeavor Aquinas wrote extensively on Scripture, philosophical and theological treatises, the Eucharist, and about analogy. Many opposed his views and writings, and some of them were condemned shortly after his death. After his canonization as a saint, the opposition died down. Within the twentieth century, his fame has increased greatly after the Second Vatican Council.

In Excelsis Gloria

When Christ was born of Mary free
In Bethlehem in that fair citie,
Angels sungen with mirth and glee,
    In Excelsis Gloria!

Herdsmen beheld these angels bright
To them appeared with great light,
And said, God's son is born this night,
    In Excelsis Gloria!

This King is comen to save kind
[Even] in Scripture as we find,
[There] fore this song have we in mind,
    In Excelsis Gloria!

[Then, dear] Lord, for thy great grace
[Grant us] in bliss to see thy face,
Where we may sing to thee solace,
    In Excelsis Gloria!
            —from *Harleian MS. 5396*

The Divine Dawning

Slowly a light is beginning to dawn. I've begun to understand something I have known for a long time: You are still in the process of your coming. Your appearance in the form of a slave was only the beginning of your coming, a beginning in which you chose to redeem men by embracing the very slavery from which you were freeing them. And *you* can really achieve your purpose in this paradoxical way, because the paths that *you* tread have a real ending, the narrow passes which *you*

enter soon open out into broad liberty, the cross that *you* carry inevitably becomes a brilliant banner of triumph.

—KARL RAHNER

from *Encounters with Silence*

The Lamb

Little Lamb, who made thee?
Dost thou know who made thee?
Gave thee life, & bid thee feed,
By the stream & o'er the mead;
Gave thee clothing of delight,
Softest clothing, wooly, bright;
Gave thee such a tender voice,
Making all the vales rejoice?
    Little Lamb, who made thee?
    Dost thou know who made thee?

    Little Lamb, I'll tell thee,
    Little Lamb, I'll tell thee:
He is called by thy name,
For He calls Himself a Lamb.
He is meek, & he is mild;
He became a little child.
I a child, & thou a lamb,
We are called by his Name.
    Little Lamb God Bless Thee!
    Little Lamb God Bless Thee!

—WILLIAM BLAKE

WILLIAM BLAKE (1757–1827)—Born and raised in London, Blake, as a child, experienced visions and visitations from the angel Gabriel, the Virgin Mary, and various other historical figures. Blake married Catherine Boucher with whom he lived in poverty for much of his life. During his life, he wrote poetry, painted, engraved, illustrated, and printed his own books. His interest in legend was revived with the Romantics' rediscovery of the past, especially the Gothic and medieval. Today, Blake's works hang in the Tate Museum in London and his writings are read as British classics.

On the Incarnation

"God in human form—not, as in oriental religion, in animal form, monstrous, chaotic, remote and terrifying, nor in the conceptual forms of the absolute, metaphysical, inanimate, etc., nor yet in the Greek divine-human form of 'man in himself', but 'the man for other' and therefore the Crucified, the man who lives out of the transcendent."

—DIETRICH BONHOEFFER
from James W. Woefel's *Bonhoeffer's Theology*

The Incarnation Is No Compromise

The Incarnation required no compromise of Deity . . . . In times past, the mythical gods of the nations were no strangers to compromise. The Roman gods, the gods of the Grecian and Scandinavian legends, were gods that could easily compromise themselves and often did in the tales of mythical lore.

But the holy God who is God, and all else not God, our Father who art in heaven, could never compromise Himself. The Incarnation, the Word made flesh, was accomplished without any compromise of the holy Deity. The living God did not degrade Himself by this condescension. He did not in any sense make Himself to be less than God.

> *By the act of Incarnation He elevated mankind to Himself.*

He remained ever God and everything else remained not God. The gulf still existed even after Jesus Christ had become man and had dwelt among us. Instead of God degrading Himself when He became man, by the act of Incarnation He elevated mankind to Himself.

It is plain in the Athanasian Creed that the early church fathers were cautious at this point of doctrine. They would not allow us to believe that God, in the Incarnation, became flesh by a coming down of the Deity into flesh; but rather by the taking up of mankind into God.

Thus, we do not degrade God but we elevate man—and that is the wonder of redemption!

—A. W. TOZER

from *Christ The Eternal Son*

O Come Redeemer of Mankind

O come, Redeemer of mankind, appear,
Thee with full hearts the virgin born we greet;
Let every age with rapt amazement hear
That wondrous birth which for our God is meet.

Not by the will of man, or mortal seed,
But by the Spirit's breathed mysterious grace
The Word of God became our flesh indeed,
And grew a tender plant of human race.

Lo! Mary's virgin womb its burden bears;
Nor less abides her virgin purity;
In the King's glory see our nature shares;
Here in His temple God vouchsafes to be.

From His bright chamber, virtue's holy shrine
The royal Bridegroom cometh to the day;
Of twofold substance, human and divine,
As giant swift, rejoicing on His way.

Forth from His Father to the world He goes,
Back to the Father's face His way regains,
Far down to souls beneath His glory shows,
Again at God's right hand victorious reigns.

With the eternal Father equal, Thou,
Girt with our flesh dost triumph evermore,

Strengthening our feeble bodies here below
With endless grace from Thine own living store.

How doth Thy lowly manger radiant shine!
On the sweet breath of night new splendor grows;
So may our spirits glow with faith divine,
Where no dark cloud of sin shall interpose.

All praise and glory to the Father be,
All praise and glory to His only Son,
All praise and glory, Holy Ghost, to Thee,
Both now, and while eternal ages run.

—AMBROSE OF MILAN
from *Veni, Redemptor gentium*

Incarnation

"The Word became flesh," wrote John, "and dwelt among us, full of grace and truth" (John 1:14). That is what incarnation means. It is untheological. It is unsophisticated. It is undignified. But according to Christianity, it is the way things are.

All religions and philosophies which deny the reality or the significance of the material, the fleshly, the earthbound, are themselves denied. Moses at the burning bush was told to take off his shoes because the ground on which he stood was holy ground (Exodus 3:5), and incarnation means that all ground is holy ground because God not only made it but walked on it, ate and slept and worked and died on it. If we are saved anywhere, we are saved here. And what is saved is not some diaphanous distillation of our bodies and our earth, but our bodies and our earth themselves. Jerusalem becomes the New Jerusalem coming down out of heaven like a bride adorned for her husband (Revelation 21:2). Our bodies are sown perishable and raised imperishable (1 Corinthians 15:42).

One of the blunders religious people are particularly fond of making is the attempt to be more spiritual than God.

—Frederick Buechner
from *Wishful Thinking*

FREDERICK BUECHNER (1926–)—Born Carl Frederick Buechner in New York City, Buechner is a Presbyterian minister well-known for his contributions to literature. His first major literary work was *A Long Day's Dying*, published when Buechner was still in his early twenties. Throughout his life, Frederick Buechner was a recipient of numerous awards, including the O. Henry Prize for his short story "The Tiger" in 1955. His greatest literary achievement, however, came when he was nominated for the Pulitzer Prize for his novel *Godric*, which was published in 1980. Buechner continues writing both fiction and nonfiction even today.

Made Flesh

After the bright beam of hot annunciation
fused heaven with dark earth
his searing sharply-focused light
went out for a while
eclipsed in amniotic gloom:
his cool immensity of splendor
his universal grace
small-folded in a warm dim
female space—
the Word stern-sentenced
to be nine months dumb—
infinity walled in a womb
until the next enormity—the Mighty,
after submission to a woman's pains
helpless on a barn-bare floor
first-tasting bitter earth.

Now, I in him surrender
to the crush and cry of birth.

Because eternity
was closeted in time
he is my open door
to forever.
From his imprisonment my freedoms grow,
find wings.
Part of his body, I transcend this flesh.
From his sweet silence my mouth sings.
Out of his dark I glow.
My life, as his,
slips through death's mesh,
time's bars,
joins hands with heaven,
speaks with stars.

—LUCI SHAW
from *A Widening Light:*
Poems of the Incarnation

LUCI SHAW (1928–   )—Born in 1928 in London, England, Luci Shaw has lived in the U.S., Canada, and Australia. She co-founded and became president of Harold Shaw Publishers, and she currently holds an adjunct faculty position at Regents College in Vancouver. She has authored eight volumes of poetry, non-fiction prose books, and co-authored three books with her dear friend Madeleine L'Engle. She and her husband John Hoyte live in Bellingham, Washington.

CHAPTER SIX

The Gifts of the Magi

MATTHEW 2:1–12
¹*Now after Jesus was born in Bethlehem of Judea in the days of Herod the king, behold, wise men from the East came to Jerusalem, ²saying, "Where is He who has been born King of the Jews? For we have seen His star in the East and have come to worship Him." ³When Herod the king heard* this, *he was troubled, and all Jerusalem with him. ⁴And when he had gathered all the chief priests and scribes of the people together, he inquired of them where the Christ was to be born. ⁵So they said to him, "In Bethlehem of Judea, for thus it is written by the prophet:*

⁶   'But you, Bethlehem, *in* the land of Judah,
     Are not the least among the rulers of Judah;
     For out of you shall come a Ruler
     Who will shepherd My people Israel.'"

⁷*Then Herod, when he had secretly called the wise men, determined from them what time the star appeared. ⁸And he sent them to Bethlehem and said, "Go and search carefully for the young Child, and when you have found* Him, *bring back word to me, that I may come and worship Him also." ⁹When they heard the king, they departed; and behold, the star which they had seen in the East went before them, till it came and stood over where the young Child was. ¹⁰When they saw the star, they rejoiced with exceedingly great joy. ¹¹And when they had come into the house, they saw the young Child with Mary His mother, and fell down and worshiped Him. And when they had opened their treasures, they presented gifts to Him: gold, frankincense, and myrrh. ¹²Then, being divinely warned in a dream that they should not return to Herod, they departed for their own country another way.*

Moonless Darkness

Moonless darkness
stands between,
Past, O Past, no more be seen!
But the Bethlehem star may lead me
To the sight of Him who freed me
From the self that I have been.

Make me pure, Lord:
Thou art holy;
Make me meek, Lord:
Thou wert lowly;
Now beginning, and alway:
Now begin, on Christmas Day.

—GERARD MANLEY HOPKINS

The Adoration of the Kings

From the Nativity
which I have already celebrated
the Babe in its Mother's arms

the Wise Men in their stolen
splendor
and Joseph and the soldiery

attendant
with their incredulous faces
make a scene copied we'll say

from the Italian masters
but with a difference
the mastery

of the painting
and the mind the resourceful mind
that governed the whole

the alert mind dissatisfied with
what it is asked to
and cannot do

accepted the story and painted
it in brilliant
colors of the chronicler

the downcast eyes of the Virgin
as a work of art
for profound worship

—WILLIAM CARLOS WILLIAMS
from *Collected Poems of William*
Carlos Williams: 1939–1962, Vol. II

WILLIAM CARLOS WILLIAMS (1883–1963)—Born into a middle-class family who loved literature and the arts, William somewhat rejected the humanities in pursuit of science as he set his sights on becoming a physician at University of Pennsylvania. Ironically, it was during his studies there that his love for literature and writing began to flourish. In Pennsylvania, William met Ezra Pound. Pound became a lifelong friend and helped him develop his aesthetic of Magism. William did pursue a career as a physician in Rutherford for forty years while still writing. This vocation afforded him the opportunity to enter people's lives with a deep sense of empathy. Financially, this career gave him the leisure to write. Because he abandoned a traditional style of writing, his writings weren't fully appreciated until the 1950's Beat Movement. Just before he died, he was awarded the Pulitzer Prize.

The Jealousy of King Herod

Now the great place of all that country was Jerusalem—just as London is the great place in England—and at Jerusalem the King lived, whose name was King Herod. Some wise men came one day, from a country a long way off in the East, and said to the King "We have seen

a Star in the Sky, which teaches us to know that a child is born in Bethlehem who will live to be a man whom all people will love." When

> *"We don't know the whereabouts of the Child. But we think the Star will shew us."*

King Herod heard this, he was jealous, for he was a wicked man. But he pretended not to be, and said to the wise men, "Whereabouts is this child?" And the wise men said "We don't know. But we think the Star will shew us; for the Star has been moving on before us, all the way here, and is now standing still in the sky." Then Herod asked them to see if the Star would shew them where the child lived, and ordered them, if they found the child, to come back to him. So they went out, and the Star went on, over their heads a little way before them, until it stopped over the house where the child was. This was very wonderful, but God ordered it to be so.

When the Star stopped, the wise men went in, and saw the child with Mary, his Mother. They loved him very much, and gave him some presents. Then they went away. But they did not go back to King Herod; for they thought he was jealous, though he had not said so. So they went away, by night, back into their own country. And an Angel came, and told Joseph and Mary to take the child into a Country called Egypt, or Herod would kill him. So they escaped too, in the night— the father, the mother, and the child—and arrived there, safely.

—CHARLES DICKENS
from *The Life of Our Lord*

Hymn

Lord, when the wise men came from far
Led to thy cradle by a star,
Then did the shepherds too rejoice,
Instructed by thy angel's voice.
Blest were the wise men in their skill,
And shepherds in their harmless will.

Wise men, in tracing nature's laws,
Ascend unto the highest cause;
Shepherds with humble fearfulness
Walk safely, though their light be less.
Though wise men better know the way,
It seems no honest heart can stray.

There is no merit in the wise
But love, the shepherds' sacrifice.
Wise men, all ways of knowledge passed,
To the shepherds' wonder come at last.
To know can only wonder breed,
And not to know is wonder's seed.

A wise man at the altar bows,
And offers up his studied vows,
And is received. May not the tears,
Which spring too from a shepherd's fears,
And sighs upon his frailty spent,
Though not distinct, be eloquent?

'Tis true, the object sanctifies
All passions which within us rise,
But since no creature comprehends
The cause of causes, end of ends,
He who himself vouchsafes to know
Best pleases his creator so.

When then our sorrows we apply
To our own wants and poverty,
When we look up in all distress,
And our own misery confess,
Sending both thanks and prayers above,
Then, though we do not know, we love.

—SYDNEY GODOLPHIN
from *Jesus the Christ*

Journey of the Magi

"A cold coming we had of it,
  Just the worst time of the year
  For a journey, and such a long journey:
  The ways deep and the weather sharp,
  The very dead of winter."
And the camels galled, sore-footed, refractory,
Lying down in the melting snow.
There were times we regretted
The summer places on slopes, the terraces,
And the silken girls bringing sherbet.
Then the camel men cursing and grumbling
And running away, and wanting their liquor and
    women,
And the night-fires going out, and the lack
    of shelters,
And the cities hostile and the towns unfriendly
And the villages dirty and charging high prices:
A hard time we had of it.
At the end we preferred to travel all night,
Sleeping in snatches,
With the voices singing in our ears, saying
That this was all folly.

Then at dawn we came down to a temperate valley,
Wet, below the snow line, smelling of vegetation;
With a running stream and a water-mill beating
    the darkness,
And three trees on the low sky,
And an old white horse galloped away in the
    meadow.
Then we came to a tavern with vine-leaves over
    the lintel,

Six hands at an open door dicing for pieces of
   silver,
And feet kicking the empty wine-skins.
But there was no information, and so we continued
And arrived at evening, not a moment too soon
Finding the place; it was (you may say) satisfactory.

All this was a long time ago, I remember,
And I would do it again, but set down
This set down
This: were we led all that way for
Birth or Death? There was a Birth, certainly,
We had evidence and no doubt. I had seen birth
   and death;
But had thought they were different; this Birth was
Hard and bitter agony for us, like Death, our
   death.
We returned to our places, these Kingdoms,
But no longer at ease here, in the old dispensation,
With an alien people clutching their gods.
I should be glad of another death.

—T. S. ELIOT
from *Collected Poems 1909–1962*

The Wise Men

Step softly, under snow or rain,
   To find the place where men can pray;
The way is all so very plain
That we may lose the way.

Oh, we have learnt to peer and pore
   On tortured puzzles from our youth,
We know all the labyrinthine lore,

We are the three wise men of yore,
  And we know all things but the truth.

We have gone round and round the hill
  And lost the wood among the trees,
And learnt long names for every ill,
And served the mad gods, naming still
  The furies the Eumenides.

The gods of violence took the veil
  Of vision and philosophy,
The Serpent that brought all men bale,
He bites his own accursed tail,
  And calls himself Eternity.

Go humbly . . . it has hailed and snowed . . .
  With voices low and lanterns lit;
So very simple is the road,
  That we may stray from it.

The world grows terrible and white,
  And blinding white the breaking day;
We walk bewildered in the light,
For something is too large for sight,
  And something much too plain to say.

The Child that was ere worlds begun
  (. . . We need but walk a little way,
We need but see a latch undone . . .)
The Child that played with moon and sun
  Is playing with a little hay.

The house from which the heavens are fed,
  The old strange house that is our own,
Where trick of words are never said,

And Mercy is as plain as bread,
    And Honour is as hard as stone.

Go humbly, humble are the skies,
    And low and large and fierce the Star;
So very near the Manger lies
    That we may travel far.

Hark! Laughter like a lion wakes
    To roar to the resounding plain,
And the whole heaven shouts and shakes,
    For God Himself is born again,
And we are little children walking
    Through the snow and rain.

—G. K. CHESTERTON

G. K. CHESTERTON (1874–1936)—Though G. K. Chesterton considered himself a mere "rollicking journalist," he was actually a prolific and gifted writer in virtually every area of literature. A man of strong opinions and enormously talented at defending them, his exuberant personality nevertheless allowed him to maintain warm friendships with people—such as George Bernard Shaw and H. G. Wells—with whom he vehemently disagreed. Chesterton had no difficulty standing up for what he believed. He was one of the few journalists to oppose the Boer War. His 1922 *Eugenics and Other Evils* attacked what was at that time the most progressive of all ideas, the idea that the human race could and should breed a superior version of itself. In the Nazi experience, history demonstrated the wisdom of his once "reactionary" views. His poetry runs the gamut from the comic *The Logical Vegetarian* to dark and serious ballads. Chesterton died on the 14th of June, 1936 in Beaconsfield, Buckinghamshire.

Star Song

We have been having
epiphanies, like suns,
all this year long.
And now, at its close
when the planets

are shining through frost,
light runs like music
in the bones,
and the heart keeps rising
at the sound of any song.
An old magic flows
in the silver calling
of a bell,
rounding
high and clear,
flying, falling,
sounding
the death knell
of our old year,
telling the new appearing
of Christ, our Morning Star.

Now burst,
all our bell throats!
Toll,
every clapper tongue!
Stun the still night.
Jesus himself gleams through
our high heart notes
(it is no fable).
It is he whose light
glistens in each song sung
and in the true
coming together again
to the stable,
of all of us: shepherds,
sages, his women and men,
common and faithful,
wealthy and wise,

with carillon hearts
and suddenly, stars in our eyes.

> —Luci Shaw
> from *A Widening Light:*
> *Poems of the Incarnation*

The Three Kings of Cologne

A common conceit there is of the three Kings of Collein, conceived to be the wise men that travelled unto our Savior by the direction of the Star, Wherein (omitting the large Discourses of Baronius, Pineda, and Montacutius,) that they might be Kings, beside the Ancient Tradition and Authority of many Fathers, the Scripture also implieth: The Gentiles shall come to thy light, and Kings to the brightness of thy rising. The Kings of Tharsis and the Isles, the Kings of Arabia and Saba shall offer gifts; which places most Christians and many Rabbins interpret of the Messiah. Not that they are to be conceived potent Monarchs, or mighty Kings; but Toparks, Kings of Cities or narrow Territories; such as were the Kings of Sodom and Gomorrah, the Kings of Jericho and Ai, the one and thirty which Joshua subdued, and such as some conceive the Friends of Job to have been.

> *The Gentiles shall come to thy light, and Kings to the brightness of thy rising.*

But although we grant they were Kings, yet can we not be assured they were three. For the Scripture maketh no mention of any number; and the number of their presents, Gold, Myrrhe, and Frankincense, concludeth not the number of their persons; for these were the commodities of their Country, and such as probably the Queen of Sheba in one person had brought before unto Solomon. So did not the sons of Jacob divide the present unto Joseph, but are conceived to carry one for them all, according to the expression of their Father: Take of the best fruits of the land in your vessels, and carry down the man a present.

And therefore their number being uncertain, what credit is to be given unto their names, Gasper, Melchior, Balthazar, what to the charm thereof against the falling sickness, or what unto their habits, complexions, and corporal accidents, we must rely on their uncertain story, and received portraits of Collein.

Lastly, although we grant them Kings, and three in number, yet could we not conceive that they were Kings of Collein. For though Collein were the chief City of the Ubii, then called Ubiopolis, and afterwards Agrippina, yet will no History inform us there were three Kings thereof. Beside, these being rulers in their Countries, and returning home, would have probably converted their subjects; but according unto Munster, their conversion was not wrought until seventy years after by Maternus a disciple of Peter. And lastly, it is said that the wise men came from the East; but Collein is seated Westward from Jerusalem; for Collein hath of longitude thirty four degrees, but Jerusalem seventy two.

> *Having lost their Arabian titles they are crowned Kings of Collein.*

The ground of all was this. These wise men or Kings, were probably of Arabia, and descended from Abraham by Keturah, who apprehending the mystery of this Star, either by the Spirit of God, the prophesie of Balaam, the prophesie which Suetonius mentions, received and constantly believed through all the East, that out of Jury one should come that should rule the whole world: or the divulged expectation of the Jews from the expiring prediction of Daniel: were by the same conducted unto Judea, returned into their Country, and were after baptized by Thomas. From whence about three hundred years after, by Helena the Empress their bodies were translated to Constantinople. From thence by Eustathius unto Millane, and at last by Renatus the Bishop unto Collein: where they are believed at present to remain, their monuments shewn unto strangers, and having lost their Arabian titles, are crowned Kings of Collein.

—SIR THOMAS BROWNE
from *Pseudodoxia Epidemica*

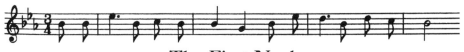

The First Noel

The first Noel the angel did say
Was to certain poor shepherds in fields as they lay;
In fields where they lay tending their sheep,
On a cold winter's night that was so deep.

Refrain
Noel, Noel, Noel, Noel,
Born is the King of Israel.

They looked up and saw a star
Shining in the east, beyond them far;
And to the earth it gave great light,
And so it continued both day and night.

Refrain

And by the light of that same star
Three Wise Men came from country far;
To seek for a King was their intent,
And to follow the star wherever it went.

Refrain

This star drew nigh to the northwest,
Over Bethlehem it took rest;
And there it did both stop and stay,
Right over the place where Jesus lay.

Refrain

Then did they know assuredly
Within that house the King did lie;
One entered it them for to see,
And found the Babe in poverty.

Refrain

Then entered in those Wise Men three,
Full reverently upon the knee,
And offered there, in His presence,
Their gold and myrrh and frankincense.

Refrain

Between an ox stall and an ass,
This Child truly there He was;
For want of clothing they did Him lay
All in a manger, among the hay.

Refrain

Then let us all with one accord
Sing praises to our heavenly Lord;
That hath made heaven and earth of naught,
And with His blood mankind hath bought.

Refrain

If we in our time shall do well,
We shall be free from death and hell;
For God hath prepared for us all
A resting place in general.

Refrain

"THE FIRST NOEL"—Probably the oldest popular carol in the English language, this song was handed down by custom over the centuries. It was harmonized and printed in 1833 in William Sandy's *Christmas Carols, Ancient, and Modern.* The music would have come from a French or English medieval shepherds' tune. "Noel," a French word probably derived from the Latin word "natalis" meaning "birth," is a shout of joy at the birth of Jesus. When the word found its way to England, it was spelled Nowell, and came to mean "Now all is well" because that is what the angels told the shepherds when Christ was born.

The Three Holy Kings
(Legend)

Once long ago when at the desert's edge
the Lord's hand spread open—
as if a fruit should deep in summer
proclaim its seed—
there was a miracle: across
vast distances a constellation formed
out of three kings and a star.

Three kings from On-the-Way
and the star Everywhere,
who all pushed on (just think!)
to the right a Rex and the left a Rex
toward a silent stall.

What was there that they *didn't* bring
to that stall of Bethlehem!
Each step clanked out ahead of them,
as the one who rode the sable horse
sat plush and velvet-snug.
And the one who walked upon his right
was like some man of gold,
and the one who sauntered on his left

with sling and swing
and jang and jing
from a round silver thing
that hung swaying inside rings,
began to smoke deep blue.
Then the star Everywhere laughed
so strangely over them,
and ran ahead and found the stall
and said to Mary:
I am bringing here an errantry
made up of many strangers.
Three kings with ancient might
heavy with gold and topaz
and dark, dim, and heathenish,—
but don't you be afraid.
They have all three at home
twelve daughters, not one son,
so they'll ask for use of yours
as sunshine for their heaven's blue
and comfort for their throne.
Yet don't straightaway believe: merely
some sparkle-prince and heathen-sheik
is to be your young son's lot.
Consider: the road is long.
They've wandered far, like herdsmen,
and meanwhile their ripe empire falls
into the lap of Lord knows whom.
And while here, warmly like westwind,
the ox snorts into their ear,
they are perhaps already destitute
and headless, for all they know.
So with your smile cast light
on that confusion which they are,
and turn your countenance
toward dawning with your child:
there in the blue lines lies

what each one left for you:
Emeralda and Rubinien
and the Valley of Turquoise.

—RAINER MARIA RILKE
from *The Book of Images*

There Came Wise Men From the East

The celebration of Christmas is always given a certain regal glamour by the story of the Wise Men, who, journeying long days and weary nights across waste land and desert, came at last to Bethlehem to pledge fealty to the newborn King Jesus. Theirs was the most complicated itinerary of all those who traveled to Bethlehem. Yet, long as their journey may have been, only a few pen strokes in a single chapter in Matthew chronicle their experiences. But how colorful is this story, and how much the Wise Men add to the drama of Christ's nativity!

They are called Wise Men because by profession and study they had mastered both the lore of books and the wisdom of the heavens; they were philosophers and astrologers. In that day astrologers observed the heavens in order to determine the will of God. The Wise Men had long accustomed themselves to look above the world of men for guidance from the Most High and their behavior was formed not by the foibles and folly of men but by the wisdom of God.

> *The Wise Men came at last to Bethlehem to pledge fealty to the newborn King Jesus.*

I imagine that those "kings of the east" were objects of ridicule and scorn when they first announced to their friends that they planned to make a long journey to a strange land to worship a new king. Many centuries before Noah had been laughed at when, in obedience to God, he fashioned an ark and prepared for a flood.

There are other thoughts which our imaginations kindle, for biographical information about the Wise Men is not available to us. No

names are recorded nor do we know from what countries they journeyed. Legend has, however, given us some grand and wonderful details. Legend says that they were kings of eastern monarchies. This is a reasonable presumption, for they brought royal gifts to the Child; they paused long enough at Herod's palace to pay their respects to the local ruler after the fashion of visiting potentates; and, finally, they came asking for One who would be King of the Jews, before whom they knelt. There is no particular reason for limiting their number to three; this number was probably based on the fact that three gifts were presented to Christ. An early tradition says that the kings traveled with a vast retinue of which seven thousand men were left beyond the Euphrates and more than a thousand continued on to Jerusalem. An ancient tradition also assigns names to the kings.

—CHARLES L. ALLEN and CHARLES L. WALLIS
from *Christmas in Our Hearts*

The Three Kings

Three Kings came riding from far away,
　　Melchior and Gaspar and Baltasar;
Three Wise Men out of the East were they,
And they travelled by night and they slept by day,
　　For their guide was a beautiful, wonderful star.

The star was so beautiful, large, and clear,
　　That all the other stars of the sky
Became a white mist in the atmosphere,
And by this they knew that the coming was near
　　Of the Prince foretold in the prophecy.

Three caskets they bore on their saddle-bows,
　　Three caskets of gold with golden keys;
Their robes were of crimson silk with rows

Of bells and pomegranates and furbelows,
    Their turbans like blossoming almond-trees.

And so the Three Kings rode into the West,
    Through the dusk of night, over hill and dell,
And sometimes they nodded with beard on breast,
And sometimes talked, as they paused to rest,
    With people they met at some wayside well.

"Of the child that is born," said Baltasar,
    "Good people, I pray you, tell us the news;
For we in the East have seen his star,
And have ridden fast, and have ridden far,
    To find and worship the King of the Jews."

And the people answered, "You ask in vain;
    We know of no king but Herod the Great!"
They thought the Wise Men were men insane,
As they spurred their horses across the plain,
    Like riders in haste, and who cannot wait.

And when they came to Jerusalem,
    Herod the Great, who had heard this thing,
Sent for the Wise Men and questioned them;
And said, "Go down unto Bethlehem,
    And bring me tidings of this new king."

So they rode away; and the star stood still,
    The only one in the gray of morn;
Yes, it stopped,—it stood still of its own free will,
Right over Bethlehem on the hill,
    The city of David, where Christ was born.
And the three kings rode through the gate and the guard,
    Through the silent street, till their horses turned

And neighed as they entered the great inn-yard;
But the windows were closed, and the doors were barred,
   And only a light in the stable burned.

And cradled there in the scented hay,
   In the air made sweet by the breath of kine,
The little child in the manger lay,
The child, that would be king one day
   Of a kingdom not human but divine.

His mother Mary of Nazareth
   Sat watching beside his place of rest,
Watching the even flow of his breath,
For the joy of life and the terror of death
   Were mingled together in her breast.

They laid their offerings at his feet:
   The gold was their tribute to a King,
The frankincense, with its odor sweet,
Was for the Priest, the Paraclete,
   The myrrh for the body's burying.

And the mother wondered and bowed her head,
   And sat as still as a statue of stone;
Her heart was troubled yet comforted,
Remembering what the Angel had said
   Of an endless reign and of David's throne.

Then the Kings rode out of the city gate,
   With a clatter of hoofs in proud array;
But they went not back to Herod the Great
For they knew his malice and feared his hate,
   And returned to their homes by another way.

—Henry Wadsworth Longfellow

The Star Still Guides

Most of us have viewed nativity scenes in many places and depicted in scores of ways. Some are expensive and elaborate; others are very simple. Mary, Joseph, the baby Jesus, a shepherd or two, and perhaps an angel or a couple of animals are gathered around a roughly hewn stable. Often missing, but in my mind mandatory, is the presence of the star: "When they heard the king, they departed; and behold, the star which they had seen in the East went before them, till it came and stood over where the young Child was. When they saw the star, they rejoiced with exceedingly great joy" (Matt. 2:9–10 NKJV).

The star stands out in significance as relevant and vital today as it was when God hung it in space. The Bible tells us that God commissioned a particular star to serve as a travel guide for a group of men from the East who had developed an interest in looking for a child to fulfill a prophecy:

> *But you, Bethlehem, in the land of Judah,*
> *Are not the least among the rulers of Judah;*
> *For out of you shall come a Ruler*
> *Who will shepherd My people Israel.*
> —MATTHEW 2:6 NKJV

King Herod had different plans for God's newly born Son. Guided by his scribes and chief priests, he was bent on destruction and rejected Christ's divinity. But God's way overturns the plans of earthly rulers.

That brilliantly shining star led to Bethlehem and Joseph, Mary, and Jesus: "When they had come into the house, they saw the young Child with Mary His mother, and fell down and worshiped Him. And when they had opened their treasures, they presented gifts to Him: gold, frankincense, and myrrh" (Matt. 2:11 NKJV).

There must have been an innate sense of awe in those wise men that the star had led them to Jesus. What an accurate travel guide its

brightness became to three travelers who set out without a contemporary direction finder, not knowing exactly where they were going. Within their hearts, they surely must have known that without the star, they would have been lost.

The Christmas star should be honored because it was put there by the God of the universe. After all, He spoke all the stars into place. It is also a symbol of God's gift of direction to us. It is His travel guide for seekers who will look and follow.

Marja, my dear wife, was a dispossessed waif in a war zone. But from before she was born, God had looked down and placed His arms of protection around her and led her, even as the wise men, toward the cross. The Lord promised, "You will seek Me and find Me, when you search for Me with all your heart" (Jer. 29:13 NKJV). The good news is that even those who may not realize they are seeking Him are still led by some significant sign or event to Jesus.

> *The Christmas star is a symbol of God's gift of direction to us.*

Many individuals relate miracles of how desperately lost they were in the dark world of sin and devastation when they came to faith in Jesus because another follower of the star shed light on their path. Is it so surprising? Daniel reminds us,

> *Those who are wise shall shine*
> *Like the brightness of the firmament,*
> *And those who turn many to righteousness*
> *Like the stars forever and ever.*
> —DANIEL 12:3 NKJV

Travel guides like the Bethlehem star should be honored as we think of Christmas. Faithful parents, friends, and strangers who pray for us, writers of the past and present who teach and lead, are Christmas travel guide stars. It is a challenge to be a faithful, earthbound star, always pointing to Jesus. After all, the greatest asset is the part of us that is the most like Jesus.

Some children who were performing in one of our pageants were asked what they wanted most for Christmas. One little girl from the inner city, who was wearing plain, secondhand clothes but had a radiant face, said, "I want my daddy who is here tonight to meet Jesus. Jesus could make him a good person." She asked nothing for herself, though her need was obvious; she looked beyond herself to her daddy. A contrasting study of economic status was another girl, decked out in the finery wealth provides, who sadly said, "I want Grandma to come to the altar. She doesn't even care about Jesus." These youngsters are proof that "a little child shall lead them." They may be unaware that they are travel guides, like the star, to light the way for their lost loved ones.

> *Children may be travel guides to light the way for their lost loved ones.*

The star led the wise men to Jesus. When they found Him, they worshiped and gave Him gifts. Gifts are the heart of Christmas to most people. When I think of what God has done for me and what He has done, not just in Phoenix First Assembly of God Church, but also at the Los Angeles International Church, I long to give gifts so great that their value cannot be equaled or exceeded—gifts that cannot be purchased.

One year our congregation gave more than $500,000 worth of gifts to needy children and families. More than 130,000 attended the various holiday performances. Their love and generosity were overwhelming and fueled my desire to give gifts that truly only God can give. Those gifts, not equated monetarily, have inestimable, eternal value.

A man who had been bound by drugs and the occult came to Christ in the Los Angeles International Church. He was asked to sing a song he had written for Christmas entitled, "He Is the Mender of Broken Hearts."

Members of the congregation in Los Angeles come from broken homes; they are ex-drug addicts, former prostitutes, and people who are displaced and hurting. Their praise, unlike the rather controlled expressions of the Phoenix Assembly, more resembles hoots, howls, and

whistles. When the soloist finished, the response was not unexpected. There was not a dry eye in the place, even among the most hardened persons.

As I placed my arm around the man, I told the audience he was blind, but his broken heart had been mended. He returned my embrace, and the man asked what he could give me for Christmas. I had no response. Walking later in the night, reflecting on that young man, I wished above all that I could restore his sight, but that was not mine to give.

What gifts beyond those that can be purchased, wrapped, and placed beneath a tree could be offered, not just to that soloist, but to all those we come in contact with every day? The wise men presented their gifts to Jesus. My desire is to present the gifts that Jesus has offered us all.

—TOMMY BARNETT
from *The Spirit of Christmas*

Wise Men

The story was told in Matthew's pen
Of visitors who were great, wise men.
They came from the eastern countries far,
Led by the light of the Christmas star.

Called by God, and guided by him
To the mother and child in Bethlehem.
The Magi knew that this was their King,
As songs of joy, to him, they did sing.

Though kings they were, and wealth possessed,
They humbly kneeled as the Savior's guest.
Bangles and beads and rich fabrics they wore,
And as His servants, fine gifts they bore . . .

A casket of gold for the Savior's birth.
Symbol of Jesus' infinite worth,
A vessel of Frankincense, perfume so sweet,
Was gently laid at the infant's feet.

Extracted from bushes all covered with thorns,
An urn filled with myrrh for the tiny newborn.
Spices and oils into balms would be made,
Then used for healing or maybe for trade.

What did they want? What was their price?
Only to witness the babe, Jesus Christ.
And when this was done, they returned to their lands
With peaceful hearts and prayerful hands.

Their story was told by night and by day
To all that would hear as they went on their way.
Accompanied by angels as by camels they trod.
And declared to all men, "He's the Son of God."

—SALLY MEYER

The Star

Bright spark, shot from a brighter place,
Where beams surround my Saviour's face,
Canst thou be any where
So well as there?

Yet, if thou wilt from thence depart,
Take a bad lodging in my heart;
For thou canst make a debtor,
And make it better.

First with thy fire-work burn to dust
Folly, and worse than folly, lust:
Then with thy light refine,
And make it shine:

So disengaged from sin and sickness,
Touch it with thy celestial quickness,
That it may hang and move
After thy love.

Then with our trinity of light,
Motion, and heat, let's take our flight
Unto the place where thou
Before didst bow.

Get me a standing there, and place
Among the beams, which crown the face
Of Him, who died to part
Sin and my heart:

That so among the rest I may
Glitter, and curl, and wind as they:
That winding is their fashion
Of adoration.

Sure thou wilt joy, by gaining me
To fly home like a laden bee
Unto that hive of beans
And garland-streams.

—GEORGE HERBERT

They Saw His Star

At the top of our Christmas trees most of us fix a star, for in the heavens, high over Bethlehem, there was a star.

The star is an especially meaningful symbol for Christmas. Stars

speak of other worlds; their radiance comes from afar and they testify to a realm beyond our earth. Christmas has just such a message for each of us. Above our busy lives, high over our varied activities and above our doubts and fears, there is a Spirit that presides and counsels, plans and guides.

God, like the stars He created, is eternal and steadfast.

Long before science gave to men exact ways of measuring celestial distances, for reckoning time, for finding directions on endless deserts and on vast oceans, men looked to the stars, and a sense of certainty came into their lives. The stars are constant and dependable; an astronomer can predict with surety their movements, ascertaining what position a particular star maintained a thousand years ago, and foretelling its movements during a thousand years to come. It is good to know that something is certain, something is steadfast. Human beings are fickle. Our steps turn at the slightest whim; our plans are altered by the weakest argument. But God, like the stars He created, is eternal and steadfast, the same yesterday, today, and forever. Like the stars in His heavens, God challenges our weakness by His dependability.

The stars are most clearly seen when it is night. When the earth is darkest, they shine with greatest brilliance. Just so, when we are overwhelmed by clouds of despondency and when our lives are shrouded in a night of fear, then we see most clearly the light of God's truth and the brightness of His all-comprehending love. Could the Almighty have chosen a more suitable or appropriate symbol for Christmas than a star?

The Wise Men were guided by a star. From their homes they traveled in its light. They did not know the way and they were not sure of their destination but they believed the star, for to them the star represented God's guiding hand. On the night of Christ's birth the Bethlehem star was high above the heads of every man. All men could have seen it, but the wise men followed it. In their hearts was a compelling faith that is a prerequisite for all star-led journeys. If we believe in God, He will guide our steps aright. When we trust Him,

He will make bright the way ahead. He who stands among us still is ". . . the bright morning star" (Revelation 22:16).

—CHARLES L. ALLEN and CHARLES L. WALLIS
from *Christmas in Our Hearts*

The Adoration of the Wise Men

Saw you never in the twilight,
   When the sun had left the skies,
Up in heaven the clear stars shining,
   Through the gloom like silver eyes?
So of old the wise men watching,
   Saw a little stranger star,
And they knew the King was given,
   And they follow'd it from far.

Heard you never of the story,
   How they cross'd the desert wild,
Journey'd on by plain and mountain,
   Till they found the Holy Child?
How they open'd all their treasure,
   Kneeling to that Infant King,
Gave the gold and fragrant incense,
   Gave the myrrh in offering?

Know ye not that lowly Baby
   Was the bright and morning star,
He who came to light the Gentiles,
   And the darken'd isles afar?
And we too may seek his cradle,
   There our heart's best treasures bring,
Love, and Faith, and true devotion,
   For our Saviour, God, and King.

—CECIL FRANCES ALEXANDER

Words for the Magi

'Shall I bring you wisdom, shall I bring you power?'
The first great stranger said to the child.
Then he noticed something he'd never felt before—
A wish in himself to be innocent and mild.

'Shall I bring you glory, shall I bring you peace?'
The second great stranger said when he saw
The star shine down on entire helplessness.
The gift that he offered was his sense of awe.

'Shall I show you riches' the third one began
Then stopped in terror because he had seen
A God grown-up and a tired tempted man.
'Suffering's my gift' he said
'That is what I mean.'

—ELIZABETH JENNINGS

The Other Wise Man
(Abridged)

You know the story of the Three Wise Men of the East, and how
they traveled from far away to offer their gifts at the manger cradle in
Bethlehem. But have you ever heard the story of the Other Wise Man,
who also saw the star in its rising, and set out to follow it, yet did not
arrive with his brethren in the presence of the young child Jesus? Of
the great desire of this fourth pilgrim, and how it was denied, yet
accomplished in the denial; of his many wanderings and the probations
of his soul; of the long way of his seeking and the strange way of his
finding the One whom he sought—I would tell the tale as I have heard
fragments of it in the Hall of Dreams, in the palace of the Heart of
Man.

I

In the days when Augustus Caesar was master of many kings and Herod reigned in Jerusalem, there lived in the city of Ecbatana, among the mountains of Persia, a certain man named Artaban. His house stood close to the outermost of the walls which encircled the royal treasury.

> *"The highest of all learning is the knowledge of the stars."*

From his roof he could look over the sevenfold battlements of black and white and crimson and blue and red and silver and gold, to the hill where the summer palace of the Parthian emperors glittered like a jewel in a crown . . . High above the trees a dim glow of light shone through the curtained arches of the upper chamber, where the master of the house was holding council with his friends.

He stood by the doorway to greet his guests . . . "Welcome!" he said, in his low pleasant voice, as one after another entered the room—"welcome, Abdus; peace be with you, Rhodaspes and Tigranes, and with you, my father, Abgarus" . . .

There were nine of the men . . . alike in the richness of their dress . . . marking them as Parthian nobles . . . They took their places around a small black altar at the end of the room . . . "You have come tonight," said he (Artaban), looking around the circle . . . "at my call . . . to renew your worship and rekindle your faith in the God of Purity . . . Hear me then" . . . said Artaban, "while I tell you of the new light and truth that have come to me through the most ancient of all signs. We have searched the secrets of Nature together, and studied the healing virtues of water and fire and the plants. We have read also the books of prophecy in which the future is dimly foretold in words that are hard to understand. But the highest of all learning is the knowledge of the stars. To trace their course is to untangle the threads of the mystery of life from the beginning to the end. If we could follow them perfectly, nothing would be hidden from us. But is not our knowledge of them still incomplete? Are there not many stars still beyond our horizon—lights that are known only to the dwellers in the far southland, among the spice trees of Punt and the gold mines of Ophir?" . . .

"It has been shown to me and to my three companions among the Magi—Casper, Melchior and Balthasar. We have searched the ancient tablets of Chaldea and computed the time. It falls in this year. We have studied the sky, and in the spring of the year we saw two of the greatest planets draw near together in the sign of the Fish, which is the house of Hebrews. We also saw a new star there, which shone for one night and then vanished . . . If the star shines again, they will wait ten days for me at the temple, and then we will set out together for Jerusalem, to see and worship the promised one who shall be born King of Israel. I believe the sign will come. I have made ready for the journey. I have sold my possessions, and bought these three jewels—a sapphire, a ruby and a pearl—to carry them as tribute to the King. And I ask you to go with me on the pilgrimage, that we may have joy together in finding the Prince who is worthy to be served."

While he was speaking he thrust his hand into the inmost fold of his girdle and drew out three great gems . . . and laid them on the outspread scrolls before him . . . But his friends looked on with strange and alien eyes. A veil of doubt and mistrust came over their faces . . .

At last Tigranes said: "Artaban, this is a vain dream. It comes from too much looking upon the stars and the cherishing of lofty thoughts. It would be wiser to spend the time in gathering money for the new fire temple at Chala. No king will ever rise from the broken race of Israel, and no end will ever come to the eternal strife of light and darkness. He who looks for it is a chaser of the shadows. Farewell." . . . So, one by one, they left the house of Artaban . . . and Artaban was left in solitude.

He gathered up the jewels and placed them on his girdle. For a long time he stood and

> *"I ask you to go with me on the pilgrimage, that we may find the Prince who is worthy to be served."*

watched the flame that flickered and sank upon the altar. Then he crossed the hall, lifted the heavy curtain, and passed out between the pillars of porphyry to the terrace on the roof.

Far over the eastern plain a white mist stretched like a lake. But where the distant peaks of Zagros serrated the western horizon the sky

was clear. Jupiter and Saturn rolled together like drops of lambent flame about to blend in one.

As Artaban watched them, a steel-blue spark was born out of the darkness beneath, rounding itself with purple splendors to a crimson sphere, and spiring upward through rays of saffron and orange into a point of white radiance. Tiny and infinitely remote, yet perfect in every part, it pulsated in the enormous vault as if the three jewels in the Magian's girdle had mingled and been transformed into a living heart of light.

He bowed his head. He covered his brow with his hands.

"It is the sign," he said. "The King is coming, and I will go to meet him."

II

All night long, Vasda, the swiftest of Artaban's horses, had been waiting, saddled and bridled, in her stall, pawing the ground impatiently and shaking her bit as if she shared the eagerness of her master's purpose, though she knew not its meaning.

Before the birds had fully roused to their strong, high, joyful chant of morning song . . . the Other Wise Man was in the saddle, riding swiftly along the highroad, which skirted the base of Mount Orontes, westward.

Artaban must indeed ride wisely and well if he would keep the appointed hour with the other Magi; for the route was a hundred and fifty parasangs, and fifteen was the utmost that he could travel in a day. But he knew Vasda's strength, and pushed forward without anxiety, making the fixed distance every day, though he must travel into the night, and in the morning long before sunrise . . .

> *"The King is coming, and I will go to meet him."*

Artaban pressed onward until he arrived, at nightfall on the tenth day, beneath the shattered walls of populous Babylon . . . Vasda was almost spent, and Artaban would gladly have turned into the city to find rest and refreshment for himself and her. But he knew that it was three hours' journey yet to the Temple of the Seven Spheres, and he must reach the place by

midnight if he would find his comrades waiting. So he did not halt, but rode steadily across the stubble fields . . .

As she passed into the shadow Vasda slackened her pace . . . Near the farther end of the darkness an access of caution seemed to fall upon her. She scented some danger or difficulty . . . At last she gave a quick breath of anxiety and dismay, and stood stock-still, quivering in every muscle, before a dark object in the shadow of the last palm tree.

> *The dim starlight revealed the form of a man lying across the road.*

Artaban dismounted. The dim starlight revealed the form of a man lying across the road. His humble dress and the outline of his haggard face showed that he was probably one of the Hebrews who still dwelt in great numbers around the city. His pallid skin, dry and yellow as parchment, bore the mark of the deadly fever which ravaged the marshlands in autumn. The chill of death was in his lean hand, and, as Artaban released it, the arm fell back inertly upon the motionless breast . . . But as he turned, a long faint, ghostly sigh came from the man's lips. The bony fingers gripped at the hem of the Magian's robe and held him fast.

Artaban's heart leaped to his throat, not with fear, but with a dumb resentment at the inopportunity of this blind delay.

How could he stay here in the darkness to minister to a dying stranger? . . . His companions would think he had given up the journey. They would go without him. He would lose his quest.

But if he went on now, the man would surely die. If Artaban stayed, life might be restored. His spirit throbbed and fluttered with the urgency of the crisis . . .

"God of truth and purity," he prayed, "direct me in the holy path, the way of wisdom which Thou only knowest."

Then he turned back to the sick man. Loosening the grasp of his hand, he carried him to a little mound at the foot of the palm tree . . .

At last the man's strength returned; he sat up and looked about him . . . "Who art thou?" he said, in the rude dialect of the country, "and why hast thou sought me here to bring back my life?"

"I am Artaban the Magian, of the city of Ecbatana, and I am going

to Jerusalem in search of one who is to be born King of the Jews, a great Prince and Deliverer of all men. I dare not delay any longer upon

> *Artaban covered his head in dispair.*

my journey, for the caravan that has waited for me may depart without me. But see, here is all that I have left of bread and wine, and here is a potion of healing herbs. When thy strength is restored thou canst find the dwellings of the Hebrews among the houses of Babylon."

The Jew raised up his hand solemnly to heaven.

"Now may the God of Abraham and Isaac and Jacob bless and prosper the journey. . . . I can tell thee where the Messiah must be sought. For our prophets have said that he should be born not in Jerusalem, but in Bethlehem of Judah. May the Lord bring thee in safety to that place, because thou hast had pity upon the sick."

It was already long past midnight. . . . Artaban rode swiftly around the hill. He dismounted and climbed to the highest terrace, looking out toward the west. . . .

At the edge of the terrace he saw a little cairn of broken bricks, and under them a piece of papyrus. He caught it up and read: "We have waited past the midnight, and can delay no longer. We go to find the King. Follow us across the desert."

Artaban sat down upon the ground and covered his head in dispair.

"How can I cross the desert," said he, "with no food and with a spent horse? I must return to Babylon, sell my sapphire, and buy a train of camels, and provision for the journey. I may never overtake my friends. Only God the merciful knows whether I shall not lose the sight of the King because I tarried to show mercy."

III

There was a silence in the Hall of Dreams, where I was listening to the story of the Other Wise Man. Through this silence I saw, but very dimly, his figure passing over the dreary undulations of the desert, high upon the back of his camel, rocking steadily like a ship over the waves . . . I followed the figure of Artaban moving steadily onward until he arrived at Bethlehem. And it was the third day after the three Wise Men had come to that place and had found Mary and Joseph, with the

young child, Jesus, and had laid their gifts of gold and frankincense and myrrh at his feet.

The Other Wise Man drew near, weary, but full of hope, bearing his ruby and his pearl to offer to the King. . . . The streets of the village seemed to be deserted, and Artaban wondered whether the men had all gone up to the hill pastures to bring down their sheep. From the open door of a cottage he heard the sound of a woman's voice singing softly. He entered and found a young mother hushing her baby to rest. She told him of the strangers from the far East who had appeared in the village three days ago, and how they said that a star had guided them to the place where Joseph of Nazareth was lodging with his wife and her new-born child, and how they had paid reverence to the child and given him many rich gifts.

"But the travelers disappeared again," she continued, "as suddenly as they had come. We were afraid at the strangeness of their visit. We could not understand it. The man of Nazareth took the child and his mother, and fled away that same night secretly, and it was whispered that they were going to Egypt. Ever since, there has been a spell upon the village; something evil hangs over it. They say the Roman soldiers are coming from Jerusalem to force a new tax from us, and the men have driven the flocks and herds far back among the hills, and hidden themselves to escape it."

> *The man of Nazareth took the child and his mother, and fled away secretly.*

The young mother laid the baby in its cradle, and rose to minister to the wants of the strange guest that fate had brought into her house. She set food before him. . . . Artaban accepted it gratefully; and, as he ate, the child fell into a happy slumber, and murmured sweetly in its dreams, and a great peace filled the room.

But suddenly there came the noise of a wild confusion in the streets of the village, a shrieking and wailing of women's voices, a clangor of brazen trumpets and clashing of swords, a desperate cry: "The soldiers! The soldiers of Herod! They are killing our children."

The young mother's face grew white with terror. She clasped her child to her bosom, and crouched motionless in the darkest corner of

the room, covering him with the folds of her robe, lest he should wake and cry.

But Artaban went quickly and stood in the doorway of the house. . . .

The soldiers came hurrying down the street with bloody hands and dripping swords. At the sight of the stranger in his imposing dress they hesitated with surprise. The captain of the band approached the threshold to thrust him aside. But Artaban did not stir. . . . He held the soldier silently for an instant, and then said in a low voice:

"I am all alone in this place, and I am waiting to give this jewel to the prudent captain who will leave me in peace."

He showed the ruby, glistening in the hollow of his hand like a great drop of blood.

The captain was amazed at the splendor of the gem. . . . He stretched out his hand and took the ruby.

"March on!" he cried to his men; "there is no child here. The house is empty." . . .

Artaban re-entered the cottage. He turned his face to the east and prayed:

"God of truth, forgive my sin! I have said a thing that is not, to save the life of a child. And two of my gifts are gone. I have spent for man that which was meant for God. Shall I ever be worthy to see the face of the King?"

But the voice of the woman, weeping for joy in the shadow behind him, said very gently:

"Because thou hast saved the life of my little one, may the Lord bless thee and keep thee; the Lord make His face to shine upon thee and be gracious unto thee; the Lord lift up His countenance upon thee and give thee peace."

IV

Again there was a silence in the Hall of Dreams, deeper and more mysterious than the first interval, and I understood that the years of Artaban were flowing very swiftly under the stillness, and I caught only a glimpse, here and there, of the river of his life shining through the mist that concealed its course.

I saw him moving among the throngs of men in populous Egypt,

seeking everywhere for traces of the household that had come down from Bethlehem, and finding them under the spreading sycamore trees of Heliopolis, and beneath the walls of the Roman fortress of New Babylon beside the Nile—traces so faint and dim that they vanished before him continually. . . .

"May the Lord make His face to shine upon thee and be gracious unto thee."

So I saw the Other Wise Man again and again, traveling from place to place, and searching among the people of Dispersion, with whom the little family from Bethlehem might, perhaps have found refuge. . . . He visited the oppressed and the afflicted in the gloom of subterranean prisons, and the crowded wretchedness of slave markets, and the weary toil of galley ships. In all this populous and intricate world of anguish, though he found none to worship, he found many to help. He fed the hungry, and clothed the naked, and healed the sick, and comforted the captive. . . .

It seemed almost as if he had forgotten his quest. . . .

V

Three-and-thirty years of the life of Artaban had passed away, and he was still a pilgrim and a seeker after light. . . .

Worn and weary and ready to die, but still looking for the King, he had come for the last time to Jerusalem. . . . It seemed as if he must make one more effort, and something whispered in his heart that, at last, he might succeed.

It was the season of the Passover. The city was thronged with strangers. The children of Israel, scattered in far lands, had returned to the Temple for the great feast, and there had been a confusion of tongues in the narrow streets for many days.

Artaban joined a group of people from his own country, Parthian Jews who had come up to keep the Passover, and inquired of them the cause of the tumult, and where they were going.

"We are all going," they answered, "to the place called Golgotha, outside the city walls, where there is to be an execution. Have you not heard what has happened? Two famous robbers are to be crucified, and with them another, called Jesus of Nazareth, a man who has done many

wonderful works among the people, so that they love him greatly. But the priests and elders have said that he must die, because he gave himself out to be the Son of God. And Pilate has sent him to the cross because he said that he was the 'King of the Jews.'"

> *Twice the gift which he had consecrated to the worship of religion had been drawn to the service of humanity.*

How strangely these familiar words fell upon the tired heart of Artaban! They had led him for a lifetime over land and sea. And now they came to him mysteriously, like a message of despair. The King had arisen, but he had been born in Bethlehem thirty-three years ago, at whose birth the star had appeared in heaven, and of whose coming the prophets had spoken?

Artaban's heart beat unsteadily with that troubled, doubtful apprehension which is the excitement of old age. But he said within himself: "The ways of God are stranger than the thoughts of men, and it may be that I shall find the King, at last, in the hands of his enemies, and shall come in time to offer my pearl for his ransom before he dies."

So the old man followed the multitude with slow and painful steps toward the Damascus gate of the city. Just beyond the entrance of the guardhouse a troop of Macedonian soldiers came down the street, dragging a young girl with torn dress and disheveled hair. As the Magian paused to look at her with compassion, she broke suddenly from the hands of the tormentors, and threw herself at his feet, clasping him around the knees. She had seen his white cap and the winged circle on his breast.

"Have pity on me," she cried, "and save me, for the sake of the God of Purity! I also am a daughter of the true religion which is taught by the Magi. My father was a merchant of Parthia, but he is dead, and I am seized for his debts to be sold as a slave. Save me from worse than death!"

Artaban trembled.

It was the old conflict in his soul, which had come to him in the palm grove of Babylon and in the cottage at Bethlehem—the conflict

between the expectation of faith and the impulse of love. Twice the gift which he had consecrated to the worship of religion had been drawn to the service of humanity. This was the third trial, the ultimate probation, the final and irrevocable choice.

Was it his great opportunity, or his last temptation? He could not tell. One thing only was clear in the darkness of his mind—it was inevitable. And does not the inevitable come from God?

One thing only was sure to his divided heart—to rescue this helpless girl would be a true deed of love. And is not love the light of the soul?

He took the pearl from his bosom. Never had it seemed so luminous, so radiant, so full of tender, living luster. He laid it in the hand of the slave.

"This is thy ransom, daughter! It is the last of my treasures which I kept for the King."

While he spoke, the darkness of the sky deepened, and shuddering tremors ran through the earth heaving convulsively like the breast of one who struggles with mighty grief.

The walls of the houses rocked to and fro. Stones were loosened and crashed into the street. Dust clouds filled the air. The soldiers fled in terror, reeling like drunken men. But Artaban and the girl whom he had ransomed crouched helpless beneath the wall of the Praetorium.

What had he to fear? What had he to hope? He had given away the last remnant of his tribute for the King. He had parted with the last hope of finding him. The quest was over, and it had failed. But even in that thought, accepted and embraced, there was peace. . . . He knew that all was well, because he had done the best that he could from day to day. He had been true to the light that had not been given to him. . . . He had not seen the revelation of

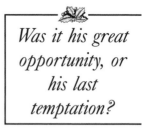

Was it his great opportunity, or his last temptation?

"life everlasting, incorruptible and immortal." But he knew that even if he could live his earthly life over again, it could not be otherwise than it had been.

One more lingering pulsation of the earthquake quivered through the ground. A heavy tile, shaken from the roof, fell and struck the old

man on the temple. He lay breathless and pale, with his gray head resting on the young girl's shoulder, and the blood trickling from the wound. As she bent over him, fearing that he was dead, there came a voice through the twilight, very small and still, like music sounding from a distance, in which the notes are clear but the words are lost. The girl turned to see if someone had spoken from the window above them, but she saw no one.

Then the old man's lips began to move, as if in answer, and she heard him say in the Parthian tongue:

"Not so, my Lord! For when saw I thee an hungered and fed thee? Or thirsty, and gave thee drink? When saw I thee a stranger, and took thee in? Or naked, and clothed thee? When saw I thee sick or in prison, and came unto thee? Three-and-thirty years have I looked for thee; but I have never seen thy face, nor ministered to thee, my King."

He ceased, and the sweet voice came again. And again the maid heard it, very faint and far away. But now it seemed as though she understood the words:

"Verily I say unto thee, Inasmuch as thou hast done it unto one of the least of these my brethren, thou hast done it unto me."

A calm radiance of wonder and joy lighted the pale face of Artaban like the first ray of dawn on a snowy mountain peak. A long breath of relief exhaled gently from his lips.

His journey was ended. His treasures were accepted. The Other Wise Man had found the King.

—HENRY VAN DYKE
from *A New Christmas Treasury*

A Song of Gifts to God

When the first Christmas presents came, the straw where
    Christ was rolled
Smelt sweeter than their frankincense, burnt brighter than
    their gold,

And a wise man said, 'We will not give; the thanks would
    be but cold.'

'Nay,' said the next. 'To all new gifts, to this gift or another,
Bends the high gratitude of God; even as He now, my
    brother,
Who had a Father for all time, yet thanks Him for a Mother.

'Yet scarce for Him this yellow stone or prickly smells and
    sparse,
Who holds the gold heart of the sun that fed these timber
    bars,
Nor any scentless lily lives for One that smells the stars.'

Then spake the third of the Wise Men, the wisest of the
    three:
'We may not with the widest lives enlarge His liberty,
Whose wings are wider than the world. It is not He, but we.

'We say not He has more to gain, but we have more to lose.
Less gold shall go astray, we say, less gold, if thus we
    choose,
Go to make harlots of the Greeks and hucksters of the
    Jews.

'Less clouds before colossal feet redden in the under-light,
To the blind gods from Babylon less incense burn tonight,
To the high beasts of Babylon, whose mouths make mock of
    right.'

Babe of the thousand birthdays, we that are young yet
    grey,
White with the centuries, still can find no better thing to
    say,

We that with sects and whims and wars have wasted
   Christmas Day.

Light Thou Thy censer, to Thyself, for all our fires are dim,
Stamp Thou Thine image on our coins, for Caesar's face
   grows grim,
And a dumb devil of pride and greed has taken hold of him.

We bring Thee back great Christendom, churches and
   towns and towers,
And if our hands are glad, O God, to cast them down like
   flowers,
'Tis not that they enrich Thine hands, but they are saved
   from ours.

—G. K. CHESTERTON

The Star in the East

Many plants and flowers are featured in our remembrance of Christ's nativity. An ancient tale relates that at the hour of our Lord's birth the trees in the forests burst into bloom and the birds began to sing. Among the most familiar Christmas greenery are the mistletoe, the holly, evergreen trees, and ivy. Flowers which have in various places in Christendom been associated with this season are cherry blossoms, rosemary, and the Christmas rose.

The favorite Christmas plant is the poinsettia, whose gorgeous red bracts or leaves surround an almost inconspicuous yellow flower. The normal period of maturity of poinsettias is in midwinter, and so they flourish at a season when their colors of bright red and green seem especially appropriate.

Poinsettias are named for the Hon. Joel Roberts Poinsett, onetime congressman and a member of President Van Buren's Cabinet. He

served for a time as our minister to Mexico. While he represented the American people in Mexico, he continued his great interests in plants and flowers. He was especially attracted to the flaming leaves of poinsettias, a plant which grows in profusion in both Mexico and Central America.

When Mr. Poinsett returned to his home in South Carolina, he spent much time trying to cultivate these beautiful plants in a strange climate. His careful efforts were rewarded, and his achievement has given us one of our most beloved Christmas flowers.

Not much is now remembered concerning Mr. Poinsett's long political career, but we may feel certain that his continuing love of flowers indicates that he was a man who loved all of God's marvelous creations. His gift to us of the poinsettia surely is as splendid and as inspiring a contribution to our Christmas celebrations as the gifts of music and art from other men whose minds were also dedicated to the Babe of Bethlehem.

The poinsettia is a plant of exquisite beauty. It also symbolizes for many of us the shining star that led the steps of the Wise Men. This association of the fiery leaves of the poinsettia with the star of Bethlehem makes it an especially meaningful adornment for our churches and homes.

As the Magi of old were guided along strange roads to the crib of our Lord, so have Christians of every generation been directed through their pilgrimages in life. The hand of the Eternal may bring is to green pastures and still waters, and beyond to the valleys of many shadows, for always "the steps of a good man are ordered by the Lord . . ." (Psalms 37:23).

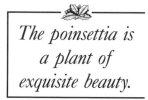

The poinsettia is a plant of exquisite beauty.

Stars speak of other worlds. Their radiance comes from afar. They testify to a realm beyond our earth. Christmas, too, had just such a message for each of us. Above our busy lives, high over our many activities, and above our doubts and fears, there is a Spirit which presides and counsels, plans and guides. Above us all is God in whom we move and have our being.

Stars are constant and dependable. They bring to our thoughts this additional spiritual truth: God is eternal and steadfast. Astronomers can predict with accuracy movements of stars. They can tell what were the positions of particular stars thousands of years ago, and they can foretell their movements for thousands of years into the future. Our human lives are fickle; our steps turn at the slightest whim; our plans are altered by the weakest arguments. How good it is to know that God is the same yesterday, today, and forever! Like the stars high in His heavens, God challenges our inconstancy by His dependability.

> *When the earth is darkest, the stars are brightest. When our lives are shrouded in fear, we see most clearly the light of God's truth.*

Stars also shine most clearly at night. When the earth is darkest, the stars are brightest. Stars remind is that when we are overwhelmed by clouds of despondency and when our lives are shrouded in nights of fear, then we see most clearly the light of God's truth and the brightness of His all-comprehending love.

The Wise Men followed the star, and they found the Christ. They were not sure of their destination. But they believed the star, for to them the star represented God's guiding hand. And their faith was rewarded. The star of Bethlehem was high above the heads of all men, but only the Wise Men followed it. In their hearts there was confidence. Faith in the heart is prerequisite for all star-led journeys. If we believe in God, He will lead us. When we trust Him, He will show us the way to Christ.

Zacharias prophesied of the Christ Child: ". . . the dayspring from on high hath visited us, To give light to them that sit in darkness and in the shadow of death, to guide our feet into the way of peace" (Luke 1:78–79). Jesus is "the bright and morning star" (Revelation 22:16), and in Him we may find our bearings through life and eternity.

—CHARLES L. ALLEN and CHARLES L. WALLIS
from *Christmas in Our Hearts*

The Magi

Now as at all times I can see in the mind's eye,
In their stiff, painted clothes, the pale unsatisfied ones
Appear and disappear in the blue depth of the sky
With all their ancient faces like rain-beaten stones,
And all their helms of silver hovering side by side,
And all their eyes still fixed, hoping to find once more,
Being by Calvary's turbulence unsatisfied,
The uncontrollable mystery on the bestial floor.

—WILLIAM BUTLER YEATS

Christmas Memories

Without a doubt, the best time of the year for shared memories is Christmas. Some of my happiest memories, both as a child and as an adult, have been rooted in the Christmas season. I remember the year my father went to the bank and bought twenty new, crisp one dollar bills; back in the days when a dollar would buy a meal. He attached a Merry Christmas note to each dollar and handed them out; one apiece to the newsboy, the shoeshine man, the postman, and seventeen others. He was merely thanking them for being his friends.

Another memory occurred many years later. My wife, two children, and I had boarded a plane for Kansas City to spend the holidays with my parents. When I stepped off the plane and into the terminal, I instantly caught sight of my six-foot-four-inch father towering over the crowd. There was a twinkle in his eyes and a smile on his face, and Mom, of course, was aglow with excitement. Her family had come home for Christmas. That scene is videotaped in my mind today. Now those good people are gone, and only the memory lingers on.

During the Christmas season, I hope your own times of excitement

and sharing and fellowship will leave you with a special gift—memories that will last a lifetime.

—JAMES DOBSON
from *Home with a Heart*

JAMES DOBSON—Founder and President of Focus on the Family, James Dobson is best known for his dedication to the preservation of the home. His educational organization consists of 60 different ministries, and he is heard on more than 4,000 radio facilities around the world. His background as a licensed psychologist for more than 25 years gives credence to his writings on marriage, family, and children. Currently, he holds a position on faculty at the University of Southern California School of Medicine. At the same time, he is actively involved in advising governmental leaders on family matters. He and his wife, Shirley, live in Colorado Springs.

From the Eastern Mountains

From the eastern mountains, pressing on, they come,
Wise men in their wisdom, to His humble home;
Stirred by deep devotion, hasting from afar,
Ever journeying onward, guided by a star.

Light of life that shineth ere the worlds began,
Draw Thou near, and lighten every heart of man.

There their Lord and Savior meek and lowly lay,
Wondrous Light that led them onward on their way,
Ever now to lighten nations from afar,
As they journey homeward by that guiding star.

Refrain

Thou Who in a manger once hast lowly lain,
Who dost now in glory o'er all kingdoms reign,

Gather in the heathen who in lands afar
Ne'er have seen the brightness of Thy guiding star.

Refrain

Onward through the darkness of the lonely night
Shining still before them with Thy kindly light.
Guide them, Jew and Gentile, homeward from afar,
Young and old together, by Thy guiding Star.

Refrain

Until every nation, whether bond or free,
'Neath Thy starlit banner, Jesus follows Thee.
O'er the distant mountains to that heavenly home,
Where nor sin nor sorrow evermore shall come.

Refrain

Gather in the outcasts, all who've gone astray,
Throw Thy radiance o'er them, guide them on their
    way.
Those who never knew Thee, those who've wandered
    far,
Guide them by the brightness of Thy guiding star . . .

                 —GODFREY THRING

The Gift

As the wise men of old brought gifts
guided by a star
to humble birthplace

of the god of love,
   the devils
      as an old print shows
retreated in confusion.

What could a baby know
   of gold ornaments
or frankincense and myrrh,
   of priestly robes
      and devout genuflections?
But the imagination
   knows all stories
      before they are told
and knows the truth of this one
   past all defection.

The rich gifts
   so unsuitable for a child
      though devoutly proffered,
stood for all that love can bring.
   The men were old
      how could they know

of a mother's needs
   or a child's
      appetite?

But as they kneeled
   the child was fed.
      They saw it
and gave praise!
   A miracle

had taken place,
   hard gold to love,
a mother's milk!
   before
      their wondering eyes.

The ass brayed
   the cattle lowed.
      It was their nature.

All men by their nature give praise.
   It is all
      they can do.
         —WILLIAM CARLOS WILLIAMS
           from *Collected Poems of William*
           Carlos Williams, 1939–1962, Vol. II

The Gift of the Magi

One dollar and eighty-seven cents. That was all. And sixty cents of it was in pennies. Pennies saved one and two at a time by bulldozing the grocer and the vegetable man and the butcher until one's cheeks burned with the silent imputation of parsimony that such close dealing implied. Three times Della counted it. One dollar and eighty-seven cents. And the next day would be Christmas.

There was clearly nothing to do but flop down on the shabby little couch and howl. So Della did it. Which instigates the moral reflection that life is made up of sobs, sniffles, and smiles, with sniffles predominating.

While the mistress of the home is gradually subsiding from the first stage to the second, take a look at the home. A furnished flat at $8 per week. It did not exactly beggar description, but it certainly had that word on the lookout for the mendicancy squad.

In the vestibule below was a letter-box into which no letter would go, and an electric button from which no mortal finger could coax a ring. Also appertaining thereunto was a card bearing the name "Mr. James Dillingham Young."

The "Dillingham" had been flung to the breeze during a former period of prosperity when its possessor was being paid $30 per week.

> *Only $1.87 to buy a present for Jim. Her Jim.*

Now, when the income was shrunk to $20, though, they were thinking seriously of contracting to a modest and unassuming D. But whenever Mr. James Dillingham Young came home and reached his flat above he was called "Jim" and greatly hugged by Mrs. James Dillingham Young, already introduced to you as Della. Which is all very good.

Della finished her cry and attended to her cheeks with the powder rag. She stood by the window and looked out dully at a gray cat walking a gray fence in a gray backyard. Tomorrow would be Christmas Day, and she had only $1.87 with which to buy Jim a present. She had been saving every penny she could for months, with this result. Twenty dollars a week doesn't go far. Expenses had been greater than she had calculated. They always are. Only $1.87 to buy a present for Jim. Her Jim. Many a happy hour she had spent planning for something nice for him. Something fine and rare and sterling—something just a little bit near to being worthy of the honor of being owned by Jim.

There was a pier-glass between the windows of the room. Perhaps you have seen a pier-glass in an $8 flat. A very thin and very agile person may, by observing his reflection in a rapid sequence of longitudinal strips, obtain a fairly accurate conception of his looks. Della, being slender, had mastered the art.

Suddenly she whirled from window and stood before the glass. Her eyes were shining brilliantly, but her face had lost its color within twenty seconds. Rapidly she pulled down her hair and let it fall to its full length.

Now, there were two possessions of the James Dillingham Youngs in which they both took a mighty pride. One was Jim's gold watch that

had been his father's and his grandfather's. The other was Della's hair. Had the queen of Sheba lived in the flat across the airshaft, Della would have let her hair hang out the window some day to dry just to depreciate Her Majesty's jewels and gifts. Had King Solomon been the janitor, with all his treasures piled up in the basement, Jim would have pulled out his watch every time he passed, just to see him pluck at his beard from envy.

So now Della's beautiful hair fell about her rippling and shining like a cascade of brown waters. It reached below her knee and made itself almost a garment for her. And then she did it up again nervously and quickly. Once she faltered for a minute and stood still while a tear or two splashed on the worn red carpet.

On went her old brown jacket; on went her old brown hat. With a whirl of skirts and with the brilliant sparkle still in her eyes, she fluttered out the door and down the stairs to the street.

Where she stopped the sign read: "Mne. Sofronie. Hair Goods of All Kinds." One flight up Della ran, and collected herself, panting. Madame, large, too white, chilly, hardly looked the "Sofronie."

"Will you buy my hair?" asked Della.

"I buy hair," said Madame. "Take yer hat off and let's have a sight at the looks of it."

Down rippled the brown cascade.

"Twenty dollars," said Madame, lifting the mass with a practised hand.

"Give it to me quick," said Della.

>
> *Della's beautiful hair fell about her rippling and shining like a cascade of brown waters.*

Oh, and the next two hours tripped by on rosy wings. Forget the hashed metaphor. She was ransacking the stores for Jim's present.

She found it at last. It surely had been made for Jim and no one else. There was no other like it in any of the stores, and she had turned all of them inside out. It was a platinum fob chain simple and chaste in design, properly proclaiming its value by substance alone and not by meretricious ornamentation—as all good things should do. It was even worthy of The Watch. As soon as she saw it she knew that it must be

Jim's. It was like him. Quietness and value—the description applied to both.

Twenty-one dollars they took from her for it, and she hurried home with the 87 cents. With that chain on his watch, Jim might be properly anxious about the time in any company. Grand as the watch was, he sometimes looked at it on the sly on account of the old leather strap that he used in place of a chain.

When Della reached home her intoxication gave way a little to prudence and reason. She got out her curling irons and lighted the gas and went to work repairing the ravages made by generosity added to love. Which is always a tremendous task, dear friends—a mammoth task.

> *"Please God, make him think I am still pretty."*

Within forty minutes, her head was covered with tiny, close-lying curls that made her look wonderfully like a truant schoolboy. She looked at her reflection in the mirror long, carefully, and critically.

"If Jim doesn't kill me," she said to herself, "before he takes a second look at me, he'll say I look like a Coney Island chorus girl. But what could I do—oh! what could I do with a dollar and eighty-seven cents?"

At 7 o'clock the coffee was made and the frying-pan was on the back of the stove hot and ready to cook the chops.

Jim was never late. Della doubled the fob chain in her hand and sat on the corner of the table near the door that he always entered. Then she heard his step on the stair away down on the first flight, and she turned white for just a moment. She had a habit for saying little silent prayers about the simplest everyday things, and now she whispered: "Please God, make him think I am still pretty."

The door opened and Jim stepped in and closed it. He looked thin and very serious. Poor fellow, he was only twenty-two—and to be burdened with a family! He needed a new overcoat and he was without gloves.

Jim stopped inside the door, as immovable as a setter at the scent of quail. His eyes were fixed upon Della, and there was an expression

in them that she could not read, and it terrified her. It was not anger, nor surprise, nor disapproval, nor horror, nor any of the sentiments that she had been prepared for. He simply stared at her fixedly with that peculiar expression on his face.

Della wriggled off the table and went for him. "Jim, darling," she cried, "don't look at me that way. I had my hair cut off and sold because I couldn't have lived through Christmas without giving you a present. It'll grow out again—you won't mind, will you? I just had to do it. My hair grows awfully fast. Say 'Merry Christmas!' Jim, and let's be happy. You don't know what a nice—what a beautiful, nice gift I've got for you."

> *"Maybe the hairs of my head were numbered, but nobody could ever count my love for you."*

"You've cut off your hair?" asked Jim, laboriously, as if he had not arrived at that patent fact yet even after the hardest mental labor.

"Cut it off and sold it," said Della. "Don't you like me just as well, anyhow? I'm me without my hair, ain't I?"

Jim looked about the room curiously.

"You say your hair is gone?" he said, with an air almost of idiocy.

"You needn't look for it," said Della. "It's sold, I tell you—sold and gone, too. It's Christmas Eve, boy. Be good to me, for it went for you. Maybe the hairs of my head were numbered," she went on with sudden serious sweetness, "but nobody could ever count my love for you. Shall I put the chops on, Jim?"

Out of his trance Jim seemed quickly to wake. He enfolded his Della. For ten seconds let us regard with discreet scrutiny some inconsequential object in the other direction. Eight dollars a week or a million a year—what is the difference? A mathematician or a wit would give you the wrong answer. The magi brought valuable gifts, but that was not among them. This dark assertion will be illuminated later on.

Jim drew a package from his overcoat pocket and threw it upon the table.

"Don't make any mistake, Dell," he said, "about me. I don't think there's anything in the way of a haircut or a shave or a shampoo that

could make me like my girl any less. But if you'll unwrap that package you may see why you had me going a while at first."

White fingers and nimble tore at the string and paper. And then an ecstatic scream of joy; and then, alas! a quick feminine change to hysterical tears and wails, necessitating the immediate employment of all the comforting powers of the lord of the flat.

For there lay The Combs—the set of combs, side and back, that Della had worshipped long in a Broadway window. Beautiful combs, pure tortoise shell, with jewelled rims—just the shade to wear in the beautiful vanished hair. They were expensive combs, she knew, and her heart had simply craved and yearned over them without the least hope of possession. And now, they were hers, but the tresses that should have adorned the coveted adornments were gone.

> *There lay The Combs—the beautiful combs, pure tortoise shell, with jewelled rims.*

But she hugged them to her bosom, and at length she was able to look up with dim eyes and a smile and say: "My hair grows so fast, Jim!"

And then, Della leaped up like a little singed cat and cried, "Oh, oh!"

Jim had not yet seen his beautiful present. She held it out to him eagerly upon her open palm. The dull precious metal seemed to flash with a reflection of her bright and ardent spirit.

"Isn't it a dandy, Jim? I hunted all over town to find it. You'll have to look at the time a hundred times a day now. Give me your watch. I want to see how it looks on it."

Instead of obeying, Jim tumbled down on the couch and put his hands under the back of his head and smiled.

"Dell," said he, "let's put our Christmas presents away and keep 'em a while. They're too nice to use just at present. I sold the watch to get the money to buy your combs. And now suppose you put the chops on."

The magi, as you know, were wise men—wonderfully wise men—who brought gifts to the Babe in the manger. They invented the art of giving Christmas presents. Being wise, their gifts were no doubt wise

ones, possibly bearing the privilege of exchange in case of duplication. And here I have lamely related to you the uneventful chronicle of two foolish children in a flat who most unwisely sacrificed for each other the greatest treasures of their house. But in a last word to the wise of these days, let it be said that of all who give gifts, these two were the wisest. O all who give and receive gifts, such as they are wisest. Everywhere they are wisest. They are the magi.

—O. HENRY

O. HENRY (1862–1910)—William Sidney Porter, better known as "O. Henry," was born in North Carolina and trained to be a licensed pharmacist. Primarily for health reasons, William soon had to move to Texas where he worked on a sheep ranch. It was here that he derived his pen name from the frequent calling of the cat, "Oh, Henry." After holding and losing several jobs, William was accused of embezzling funds from his employment at a bank. Leaving his wife and child, he fled to New Orleans and Honduras. Upon his return, he was arrested and imprisoned in Ohio. During this period, his writing flourished. He emerged from prison with his pen name to protect his identity. By the end of his life, he had published over 300 short stories and had gained the title of America's favorite short story writer. Throughout his life he struggled with alcoholism, and he died in New York City virtually penniless.

CHAPTER SEVEN

As Shepherds Watched Their Flocks

LUKE 2:8–20

⁸*Now there were in the same country shepherds living out in the fields, keeping watch over their flock by night. ⁹And behold, an angel of the Lord stood before them, and the glory of the Lord shone around them, and they were greatly afraid. ¹⁰Then the angel said to them, "Do not be afraid, for behold, I bring you good tidings of great joy which will be to all people. ¹¹"For there is born to you this day in the city of David a Savior, who is Christ the Lord." ¹²"And this will be the sign to you: You will find a Babe wrapped in swaddling cloths, lying in a manger." ¹³And suddenly there was with the angel a multitude of the heavenly host praising God and saying:*

¹⁴   "Glory to God in the highest,
    And on earth peace, goodwill toward men!"

¹⁵*So it was, when the angels had gone away from them into heaven, that the shepherds said to one another, "Let us now go to Bethlehem and see this thing that has come to pass, which the Lord has made known to us." ¹⁶And they came with haste and found Mary and Joseph, and the Babe lying in a manger. ¹⁷Now when they had seen Him, they made widely known the saying which was told them concerning this Child. ¹⁸And all those who heard it marveled at those things which were told them by the shepherds. ¹⁹But Mary kept all these things and pondered them in her heart. ²⁰Then the shepherds returned, glorifying and praising God for all the things that they had heard and seen, as it was told them.*

As Shepherds Watched Their Flocks

While he was asleep, some Shepherds who were watching Sheep in the Fields, saw an Angel from God, all light and beautiful, come moving over the grass towards Them. At first they were afraid and fell down and hid their faces. But it said "There is a child born to-day in the City of Bethlehem near here, who will grow up to be so good that God will love him as his own son; and he will teach men to love one another, and not to quarrel and hurt one another; and his name will be Jesus Christ; and people will put that name in their prayers, because they will know God loves it, and will know that they should love it too." And then the Angel told the Shepherds to go to that Stable, and look at that little child in the Manger. Which they did; and they kneeled down by it in its sleep, and said "God bless this child!"

—CHARLES DICKENS
from *The Life of Our Lord*

Shepherds, Rejoice! Lift Up Your Eyes

"Shepherds, rejoice! lift up your eyes,
And send your fears away;
News from the regions of the skies,
Salvation's born today.

"Jesus, the God Whom angels fear,
Comes down to dwell with you;
Today He makes His entrance here,
But not as monarchs do.

"No gold nor purple swaddling bands,
Nor royal shining things;
A manger for His cradle stands,
And holds the King of kings.

"Go, shepherds where the Infant lies,
And see His humble throne
With tears of joy in all your eyes,
Go, shepherds, kiss the Son."

Thus Gabriel sang, and straight around
The heav'nly armies throng;
They tune their harps to lofty sound,
And thus conclude the song:

"Glory to God that reigns above!
Let peace surround the earth!
Mortals shall know their Maker's love,
At their Redeemer's birth."

Lord, and shall angels have their songs,
And men no tunes to raise?
O may we lose our useless tongues
When they forget to praise.

Glory to God that reigns above,
That pitied us forlorn;
We join to sing our Maker's love,
For there's a Savior born.

—Isaac Watts
from *Horae Lyrica*

Annunciation to the Shepherds from Above

Look up, you men. Men at the fire there, you
familiar with the sky's unbounded ways,
star-readers, hither! Look, I am a new
uprising star. My being is one blaze,
so filled with light the firmament is too

small now to hold me and my powerful rays,
for all its depth. Do let my splendour throw
its beams right into you: oh the dark sight,
the gloomy hearts, destinies black as night
that you're brim-full of. Shepherds, I am so
alone in you. Yet, now, there's room for me.
Weren't you astonished: the big bread-fruit-tree
was casting shadow. Well, that shade *I* threw.
O you undaunted, if you only knew
how even now upon each gazing face
the future shines. Much will be taking place
in that clear light. To you I can speak out,
you have discretion; straight souls, free from doubt,
you hear tongues everywhere. Warmth speaks and rain,
wind, birds' flight, what you are; no one sound is
more than another, and no vanities
fatten themselves. You don't detain
things in that interval the breast, to be
tormented there. As his own ecstasy
streams through an angel, earthliness can make
its way through you. And should a thornbush take
fire suddenly, the Infinite could still
call to you from it; Cherubim would fill,
if any deigned to walk where your flocks graze,
those hearts of yours with no alarmed surprise:
you'd fall upon your faces and give praise,
and name this earth still and not Paradise.

But all this was. A new thing dawns to-day
for which the round earth seeks to grow more wide.
What is a thornbush now: God feels his way
into a virgin's womb. I am the ray
thrown by her inwardness, which is your guide.

—RAINER MARIA RILKE
Translated by J. B. Leishman from *Selected Works*
of Rainer Maria Rilke: Poetry, Vol. II

Rise Up, Shepherd, and Follow

There's a star in the East on Christmas morn,
Rise up, shepherd, and follow.
It will lead to the place where the Christ was born,
Rise up shepherd, and follow.

Refrain
Follow, follow, rise up, shepherd, and follow.
Follow the Star of Bethlehem,
Rise up, shepherd, and follow.

If you take good heed to the angel's words,
Rise up, shepherd, and follow.
You'll forget your flocks, you'll forget your herds,
Rise up, shepherd, and follow.

Refrain

—African-American Spiritual

Shepherds at the Grange

Shepherds at the grange,
　Where the Babe was born,
Sang with many a change,
　Christmas carols until morn.

—HENRY WADSWORTH LONGFELLOW

Angels We Have Heard on High

Angels we have heard on high
Sweetly singing o'er the plains,
And the mountains in reply
Echoing their joyous strains.

Refrain
Gloria, in excelsis Deo!
Gloria, in excelsis Deo!

Shepherds, why this jubilee?
Why your joyous strains prolong?
What the gladsome tidings be
Which inspire your heavenly song?

Refrain

Come to Bethlehem and see
Christ Whose birth the angels sing;
Come, adore on bended knee,
Christ the Lord, the newborn King.

Refrain

See Him in a manger laid,
Whom the choirs of angels praise;
Mary, Joseph, lend your aid,
While our hearts in love we raise.

Refrain

Words: Traditional French Carol (*Les Anges dans nos Campagnes*). Translated from French to English by James Chadwick (1813–1882); appeared in *Crown of Jesus*, 1862

A Christmas Carol

I

The shepherds went their hasty way,
  And found the lowly stable-shed
Where the Virgin-Mother lay:
  And now they checked their eager tread.
For to the Babe, that at her bosom clung,
A mother's song the Virgin-Mother sung.

II

They told her how a glorious light,
  Streaming from a heavenly throng,
Around them shone, suspending night!
  While sweeter than a mother's song,
Blest Angels heralded the Saviour's birth,
Glory to God on high! and Peace on Earth.

III

She listened to the tale divine,
  And closer still the Babe she prest;
And while she cried, the Babe is mine!
  The milk rushed faster to her breast:
Joy rose within her, like a summer's morn;
Peace, Peace on Earth! the Prince of Peace is born.

IV

Thou Mother of the Prince of Peace,
  Poor, simple, and of low estate!
That strife should vanish, battle cease,
  O why should this thy soul elate?
Sweet music's loudest note, the poet's story,—
Didst thou ne'er love to hear of fame and glory?

V

And is not War a youthful king,
    A stately hero clad in mail?
Beneath his footsteps laurels spring;
    Him Earth's majestic monarchs hail
Their friend, their playmate! and his bold bright eye
Compels the maiden's love-confessing sigh.

VI

"Tell this in some more courtly scene,
    To maids and youths in robes of state!
I am a woman poor and mean,
    And therefore is my soul elate.
War is a ruffian, all with guild defiled,
That from the aged father tears his child!

VII

"A murderous fiend, by fiends adored,
    He kills the sire and starves the son;
The husband kills, and from her board
    Steals all his widow's toil had won;
Plunders God's world of beauty; rends away
All safety from the night, all comfort from the day.

VIII

"Then wisely is my soul elate
    That strife should vanish, battle cease:
I'm poor and of a low estate,
    The Mother of the Prince of Peace.
Joy rises in me, like a summer's morn:
Peace, Peace on Earth! the Prince of Peace is born."

—SAMUEL COLERIDGE
from *Poems of Coleridge*

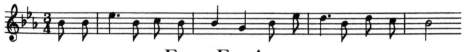

From Far Away

From far away we come to you,
   The snow in the street, and the wind on the door,
To tell of great tidings, strange and true.
   Minstrels and maids, stand forth on the floor.
From far away we come to you,
   To tell of great tidings, strange and true.

For as we wandered far and wide,
   The snow in the street, and the wind on the door,
What hap do you deem there should us betide?
   Minstrels and maids, stand forth on the floor.

Under a bent when the night was deep,
   The snow in the street, and the wind on the door,
There lay three shepherds, tending their sheep.
   Minstrels and maids, stand forth on the floor.

"O ye shepherds, what have ye seen,
   The snow in the street, and the wind on the door,
To stay your sorrow and heal your teen?"
   Minstrels and maids, stand forth on the floor.

"In an ox stall this night we saw,
   The snow in the street, and the wind on the door,
A Babe and a maid without a flaw.
   Minstrels and maids, stand forth on the floor.

"There was an old man there beside;
   The snow in the street, and the wind on the door,

His hair was white and his hood was wide.
　　Minstrels and maids, stand forth on the floor.

"And as we gazed this thing upon,
　　The snow in the street, and the wind on the door,
Those twain knelt down to the little one.
　　Minstrels and maids, stand forth on the floor.

"And a marvellous song we straight did hear,
　　The snow in the street, and the wind on the door,
That slew our sorrow and healed our care."
　　Minstrels and maids, stand forth on the floor.

News of a fair and marvellous thing,
　　The snow in the street, and the wind on the door,
Nowell, Nowell, Nowell, we sing.
　　Minstrels and maids, stand forth on the floor.

　　　　　　　　　　　　　　　　—Old English Carol

The Three Poor Shepherds

According to the carol, *The First Nowell,* and many legends, the Angel spake to 'three poor shepherds.' Other sources, however, give the number as four. Their names, Misael, Achael, Cyriacus, and Stephanus, were, together with the names of the three Kings, used as a charm in the Middle Ages to cure the bites of snakes and other venomous reptiles. In the seventh of the Chester Mysteries the shepherds, three in number, have the more homely names of Harvey, Tudd, and Trowle. By birth and habits they are the yokels of Cheshire or Lancashire. Trowle's gift to Jesus is 'a pair of his wife's old hose.'

　　　　　　　　　　　　　—Sir Thomas Browne
　　　　　　　　　　　　　from *A Christmas Companion*

The Shepherd's Hymn

Come, we shepherds, whose blest sight
  Hath met Love's moon in nature's night;
Come, lift we up our loftier song,
  And wake the sun that lies too long!

Gloomy night embraced the place
  Where the noble Infant lay.
The Babe looked up and showed His face;
  In spite of the darkness, it was day.
  It was Thy day, Sweet! and did rise,
  Not from the East, but from Thine eyes.

We saw Thee in Thy balmy nest,
  Young dawn of our eternal Day!
We saw Thine eyes break from their east
  And chase the trembling shades away.
  We saw Thee; and we blest the sight;
  We saw Thee by Thine own sweet light.

Poor world (said I), what wilt thou do
  To entertain this starry Stranger?
Is this the best thou canst bestow?
  A cold, and not too cleanly, manger?
  Contend, the powers of Heaven and Earth,
  To fit a bed for this huge birth!

—RICHARD CRASHAW
from *"A Hymn Sung as by
the Shepherds"*

In the Lonely Midnight

In the lonely midnight on the wintry hill,
Shepherds heard the angels singing, "Peace, good will."
Listen, O ye weary, to the angels' song,
Unto to you the tidings of great joy belong.

Though in David's city angels sing no more,
Love makes angel music on earth's darkest shore;
Though no heavenly glory meet your wondering eyes,
Love can make your dwelling bright as paradise.

Though the Child of Mary, sent from heaven on high,
In His manger cradle may no longer lie,
Love is King forever, though the proud world scorn;
If ye truly seek Him, Christ your King is born.

—THEODORE C. WILLIAMS

Dawning Fair, Morning Wonderful

Dawning fair, morning wonderful,
When the infant Christ was born;
Tidings brought by humble shepherds,
Child beloved, Child adored,
Child beloved, Child adored.

—Traditional Carol

There Were Shepherds

The shepherds of Bethlehem did not have far to travel. The wise
men followed the dusty caravan routes that led from their eastern

countries, but the shepherds did not need to travel by day and night along strange and sometimes dangerous roads. Christmas came to them. Christ was born in their home town and to see Him, the shepherds walked along familiar streets.

High above the roads of Bethlehem the shepherds were tending their sheep, a task often dull and monotonous. One night must have seemed the same as a thousand others. Occasionally there would be a stir among the sheep, and the shepherds would move among the flocks to see if there was trouble, returning to the open fire where they would try to keep warm as they again listened to the yarns and tales which herdsmen had told each other for generations. These common shepherds were doing their duty, as they understood it, by protecting their sheep and earning a meager subsistence for their families.

Then into the midst of their routine lives came a glowing, amazing experience. God pierced the shadows of their common task with a light not of this world and with a message for the ages. Angels sang of wonderful good news and the shepherds went in haste to Bethlehem.

Our lives are like that, too. In our daily living unexpected wonders constantly appear. Here we are, doing our duty with what faithfulness we can muster, and then suddenly life glows. The unexpected happens, our lives take on new dimensions. Never again do our days seem quite so plain.

> *Any day may become a special day if we have the heart to see its wonders.*

The shepherds did not question that God had actually manifested Himself to them, for they immediately left the mountainside and hurried into the streets they had walked since childhood. An ordinary day had become extraordinary, and now a town they had known so long became more than commonplace, too. Probably in their hearts those shepherds many times had envied those who journeyed from strange, exotic places and had longed for the day when they too might travel to the golden lands beyond the horizon.

But on Christmas Eve no such wanderlust lingered in their minds.

God had come to them. Their home town seemed wonderfully alive with a glory they had never seen before.

Two things stand out in the story of the shepherds. First, any day may become a special day if we have the heart to see its wonders. Second, any town will become more than marvelous to the man who seeks for evidences of God's presence along the most familiar byways.

—CHARLES L. ALLEN and CHARLES L. WALLIS
from *Christmas In Our Hearts*

Peaceful the Wondrous Night

Peaceful the wondrous night,
Peaceful and holy,
Under the silv'ry light,
Gleaming afar.
Faithfully watching there,
Shepherds so lowly,
Over the hills so fair,
Saw glory's star.

Refrain
Hail to the starry night,
Sparkling with glory;
Angels on wings of light,
Thronging the sky.
Hail to that starry night!
Wondrous its story:
Jesus the Prince of Light,
Came from above.

Come with that shepherd band,
Come to the manger;

Join in the chorus grand,
Glory to God!
Worship the holy Child,
Wonderful Stranger,
Give to the Undefiled,
Glory and laud.

Refrain

Sweet favor, thus to bow,
Love's treasure bringing,
Gratefully yielding now,
Life's joyful praise.
Hear form the heav'nly height,
Glad echoes ringing,
Blessing and pow'r and might,
Through endless days.

Refrain

—ELIZA E. HEWITT

The Shepherds Had an Angel

The shepherds had an angel,
The wise men had a star;
But what have I, a little child,
To guide me home from far,
Where glad stars sing together,
And singing angels are?

Lord Jesus is my Guardian
So I can nothing lack;

The lambs lie in His bosom
Along life's dangerous track:
The wilful lambs that go astray
He, bleeding, brings them back.

Those shepherds thro' the lonely night
Sat watching by their sheep,
Until they saw the heav'nly host
Who neither tire nor sleep,
All singing glory, glory,
In festival they keep.

Christ watches me, His little lamb,
Cares for me day and night,
That I may be His own in heav'n,
So angels clad in white
Shall sing their Glory, glory,
For my sake in the height.

Lord, bring me nearer day by day,
Till I my voice unite,
And sing my Glory, glory,
With angels clad in white,
All Glory, glory, giv'n to Thee,
Thro' all the heav'nly height.

—Christina G. Rossetti

Shepherd

While shepherds careful vigil kept o'er lambs in fields
of green.
The sky took on a brilliant glow and lit the grassy
scene.

In dread they looked upon the star that rose anew that
night.

Then angels came to calm their fears and tell of the
heavenly light.

In word and song they shared the news of the babe who
was their king.

They sang of peace and love and joy, and the good will
he would bring.

The keepers of the flocks arose and followed the
heavenly beam,

But not to gleaming palace walls as it would surely
seem.

It led them to an earthen stall where cattle and goats
were kept.

And in the manger soft and warm, the little Jesus slept.

Tears filled up their tired eyes and ran down wind
burned cheeks.

They had found the promised one, for whom the world
still seeks.

Though they were watchers of the flocks, tenders of
lamb and ewe,

He was the keeper of God's flock, HE was the
shepherd true.

—SALLY MEYER

Come, All Ye Shepherds

Come, all ye shepherds, ye children of earth,
Come ye, bring greetings to yon heavenly birth,
For Christ the Lord to all men is given,
To be our Savior sent down from heaven:
Come, welcome Him!

Hasten then, hasten to Bethlehem's stall,
There to see heaven descend to us all.
With holy feeling, there humbly kneeling,
We will adore Him, bow down before Him,
Worship the King.

Angels and shepherds together we go
Seeking the Savior from all earthly woe;
While angels, winging, His praise are singing,
Heaven's echoes ringing, peace on earth bringing,
Good will to men.

—Bohemian folk song
Translated by Mari Ruef Hofer

We Have Christmas in Our Neighbor

There are some of us . . . who think to ourselves, "If I had only been there! How quick I would have been to help the Baby. I would have washed His linen. How happy I would have been to go with the shepherds to see the Lord lying in the manger!" Yes, we would. We say that because we know how great Christ is, but if we had been there at that time, we would have done no better than the people of Bethlehem . . . Why don't we do it now? We have Christ in our neighbor.

—MARTIN LUTHER

MARTIN LUTHER (1483–1546)—The Father of the Reformation began as a monk in the Order of St. Augustine with a Doctor of Theology. Luther is most famous for nailing his 95 Theses to the door of the church in Wittenberg at midnight on All Saints' Day 1517. He was a prolific writer whose writings and commentaries are still widely read today. Luther preached justification by faith alone, the reduction of sacraments to Scripture and Baptism, and the ability to pray to God without the aid of a priest. In a word, he began the Protestant movement. Though Luther was called to numerous Councils for questioning and was excommunicated from the Catholic Church, he stayed true to his beliefs. In doing so, his following experienced the freedom in Christ Jesus.

Christians, Awake, Salute the Happy Morn

Christians, awake, salute the happy morn
Whereon the Savior of the world was born.
Rise to adore the mystery of love
Which hosts of angels chanted from above,
With them the joyful tidings first begun
Of God incarnate and the virgin's Son.

Then to the watchful shepherds it was told,
Who heard th'angelic herald's voice, "Behold,
I bring good tidings of a Savior's birth
To you and all the nations of the earth;
This day hath God fulfilled His promised Word;
This day is born a Savior, Christ the Lord."

He spoke; and straightaway the celestial choir
In hymns of joy, unknown before, conspire;
The praises of redeeming love they sang,
And heav'n's whole orb with alleluias rang.
God's highest glory was their anthem still
Peace on the earth and unto men good will.

To Bethl'hem straight th'enlightened shepherds ran
To see the wonder God had wrought for man
And found, with Joseph and the blessed maid,
Her Son, the Savior, in a manger laid;
Then to their flocks, still praising God, return,
And their glad hearts with holy rapture burn.

Like Mary let us ponder in our mind
God's own wondrous love in saving lost mankind!
Trace we the Babe, who hath retrieved our loss,
From His poor manger to His bitter cross,

Tread in His steps, assisted by His grace,
Till man's first heav'nly state again takes place.

Then may we hope, th'angelic hosts among,
To sing, redeemed, a glad triumphal song.
He that was born upon this joyful day
Around us all His glory shall display.
Saved by His love, incessantly we sing
Eternal praise to heav'n's almighty King.

—JOHN BYROM

Hark! The Herald Angels Sing

Hark! the herald angels sing
Glory to the new-born King!
Peace on earth and mercy mild,
God and sinners reconciled.

Joyful all ye nations rise,
Join the triumph of the skies,
With the angelic host proclaim
Christ is born in Bethlehem!

Hail the heaven-born Prince of Peace!
Hail the Sun of Righteousness!
Light and life to all he brings,
Risen with healing in his wings.

Mild, he lays his glory by;
Born, that man no more may die,
Born to raise the sons of earth,
Born to give them second birth.

—CHARLES WESLEY

Christmas II

The shepherds sing; and shall I silent be?
  My God, no hymn for Thee?
My soul's a shepherd too; a flock it feeds
  Of thoughts, and words, and deeds.
The pasture is Thy word: the streams, Thy grace
  Enriching all the place.
Shepherd and flock shall sing, and all my powers
  Outsing the daylight hours.
Then will we chide the sun for letting night
  Take up his place and right:
We sing one common Lord; wherefore he should
  Himself the candle hold.
I will go searching, till I find a sun
  Shall stay, till we have done;
A willing shiner, that shall shine as gladly,
  As frost-nipped suns look sadly.
Then will we sing, and shine all our own day,
  And one another pay:
His beams shall cheer my breast, and both so
    twine,
Till ev'n His beams sing, and my music shine.

—George Herbert

Go Tell It on the Mountain

Go, tell it on the mountain,
Over the hills and everywhere
Go, tell it on the mountain,
That Jesus Christ is born.

While shepherds kept their watching
Over silent flocks by night
Behold throughout the heavens
There shone a holy light.

Refrain

The shepherds feared and trembled,
When lo! above the earth
Rang out the angels chorus
That hailed the Savior's birth.

Refrain

Down in a lowly manger
The humble Christ was born
And God sent us salvation
That blessed Christmas morn.

Refrain

—JOHN W. WORK, JR.

"GO TELL IT ON THE MOUNTAIN"—This more modern American carol is a Negro spiritual, a religious folksong that originated with slaves in the Southeastern United States. After the slaves were freed, a man named William Francis Allen first collected their songs in 1868 in a book called *Slave Songs of the United States*. In the following decade, a group called the "Jubilee Singers" became popular in Nashville, Tennessee. They sang in choir lofts and on concert stages across the country, spreading the spiritual among the people. "Go Tell It on the Mountain" in its simplicity and directness, became one of the most popular Negro spirituals associated with Christmas.

A Christmas Prayer

O God our loving Father, help us
Rightly to remember the birth of Jesus,
that we may share in the song of the angels,

the gladness of the shepherds,
and the worship of the wise men.

Close the door of hate, and open
the door of love all over the world.
Deliver us from evil by the blessing
that Christ brings, and teach us
to be merry with clear hearts.

May the Christmas morning make us happy
to be Thy children and the Christmas
evening bring us to our beds with
grateful thoughts, forgiving and
forgiven, for Jesus' sake. Amen.

—ROBERT LOUIS STEVENSON

ROBERT LOUIS STEVENSON (1850–1894)—With a grandfather known as the greatest builder of lighthouses in Britain and a father as a joint-engineer to the Board of Northern Lighthouses, Stevenson was born into a family of affluence. Throughout his childhood, however, Robert suffered from tuberculosis that plagued him throughout his life. With many hours bedridden, Robert composed many short stories. In spite of these talents, Robert went on to be a lawyer in Scotland. Due to his health, he traveled to warmer climates where his vast and exciting experiences offered him much material for his poetry, fiction, and travel books. Instead of practicing law, Robert committed himself to writing and traveling the South Seas. Stevenson died of a brain hemorrhage in Vailima, Samoa.

The Child and the Shepherd

O tell me, gentle shepherd,
Gentle shepherd, gentle shepherd,
O tell me what the angels sang
In the early Christmas morn.
O tell me what the angels sang
In the early Christmas morn.

O listen, happy children,
Happy children, happy children,
While I tell you what the angels sang
In the early Christmas morn.
"Fear ye not, I bring good tidings,
For today the Lord is born!"

O tell me, gentle shepherd,
Gentle shepherd, gentle shepherd,
What the great bright host of angels sang,
All out in the fields so still.
What the great bright host of angels sang,
All out in the fields so still.

I will tell you, Christian children,
Christian children, Christian children,
What the great bright host of angels sang,
All out in the fields so still:
"Glory in the highest, glory!
Peace on earth, to all goodwill!"

Let us keep, then, happy Christmas,
Happy Christmas, happy Christmas,
Children, shepherds, folks, and angels
All the blest song repeating still:
"Glory in the highest, glory!
Peace on earth, to all goodwill!"

—FRANK SEWALL

The Truce of Christmas

Passionate peace is in the sky—
And in the snow in silver sealed
The beasts are perfect in the field,

And men seem men so suddenly—
  (But take ten swords and ten times ten
  And blow the bugle in praising men;
  For we are for all men under the sun;
  And they are against us every one;
  And misers haggle and madmen clutch,
  And there is peril in praising much,
  And we have the terrible tongues uncurled
  That praise the world to the sons of the world.)

The idle humble hill and wood
Are bowed upon the sacred birth,
And for one little hour the earth
Is lazy with the love of good—
  (But ready are you, and ready am I,
  If the battle blow and the guns go by;
  For we are for all men under the sun,
  And they are against us everyone;
  And the men that hate herd all together,
  To pride and gold, and the great white feather,
  And the thing is graven in star and stone
  That the men who love are all alone.)

Hunger is hard and time is tough,
But bless the beggars and kiss the kings;
For hope has broken the heart of things,
And nothing was ever praised enough.
  (But hold the shield for a sudden swing
  And point the sword when you praise a thing,
  For we are for all men under the sun,
  And they are against us every one;
  And mime and merchant, thane and thrall
  Hate us because we love them all;
  Only till Christmastide go by
  Passionate peace is in the sky.)

—G. K. CHESTERTON

While Shepherds Watched Their Flocks

While shepherds watched their flocks by night,
All seated on the ground,
The angel of the Lord came down,
And glory shone around,
And glory shone around.

"Fear not!" said he, for mighty dread
Had seized their troubled mind.
"Glad tidings of great joy I bring
To you and all mankind
To you and all mankind.

"To you, in David's town, this day
Is born of David's line
A Savior, who is Christ the Lord,
And this shall be the sign.
And this shall be the sign.

"The heavenly Babe you there shall find
To human view displayed,
All meanly wrapped in swathing bands,
And in a manger laid,
And in a manger laid."

Thus spake the seraph and forthwith
Appeared a shining throng
Of angels praising God on high,
Who thus addressed their song,
Who thus addressed their song:

"All glory be to God on high,
And to the Earth be peace;
Good will henceforth from heaven to men
Begin and never cease,
Begin and never cease!"

—NAHUM TATE

"WHILE SHEPHERDS WATCHED THEIR FLOCKS BY NIGHT"—
This carol, as does "Joy to the World," has music from a piece from
G. F. Handel, his opera *Siroe, King of Persia.* Included among the
"Shepherd Carols" in which average men (as shepherds) have a part
to play in the greatest story ever told. The lyrics to this carol are by
Rev. Nahum Tate, who was inspired by eight verses from the second
chapter of Luke, beginning "And there were in the same country shepherds abid-
ing in the field, keeping watch over their flock by night." He was born in 1652 in
Ireland, son of a clergyman. He became England's poet-laureate after writing
many plays and also the royally-sanctioned "New Version of the Psalms of David,"
which is to this day the Authorized Version used by the Church of England in its
prayer book. This particular hymn was included in a supplement on his Psalm
collection, first published in 1703.

CHAPTER EIGHT

The Flight into Egypt and the Massacre

MATTHEW 2:13–18

¹³Now when they had departed, behold, an angel of the Lord appeared to Joseph in a dream, saying, "Arise, take the young Child and His mother, flee to Egypt, and stay there until I bring you word; for Herod will seek the young Child to destroy Him." ¹⁴When he arose, he took the young Child and His mother by night and departed for Egypt, ¹⁵and was there until the death of Herod, that it might be fulfilled which was spoken by the Lord through the prophet, saying, "Out of Egypt I called My Son."

¹⁶Then Herod, when he saw that he was deceived by the wise men, was exceedingly angry; and he sent forth and put to death all the male children who were in Bethlehem and in all its districts, from two years old and under, according to the time which he had determined from the wise men. ¹⁷Then was fulfilled what was spoken by Jeremiah the prophet, saying:

¹⁸ "A voice was heard in Ramah,
  Lamentation, weeping, and great mourning,
  Rachel weeping for her children,
  Refusing to be comforted,
  Because they are no more."

All Hail, Ye Little Martyr Flowers

All hail, ye little martyr flowers,
Sweet rosebuds cut in dawning hours!
When Herod sought the Christ to find
Ye fell as bloom before the wind.

First victims of the martyr bands,
With crowns and palms in tender hands,
Around the very altar, gay
And innocent, ye seem to play.

What profited this great offense?
What use was Herod's violence?
A Babe survives that dreadful day,
And Christ is safely borne away.

All honor, laud, and glory be,
O Jesus, virgin born, to Thee;
All glory, as is ever meet
To Father and to Paraclete.

—AURELIUS PRUDENTIUS
from *Salvete Flores Martyrum*
Translated by John A. L. Riley

The Massacre of the Innocents

A carpenter among carpenters, Joseph had finished eating his lunch, and he and his companions still had some free time before the overseer gave the signal to get back to work. Joseph could sit for a while, stretch out and take a nap or indulge in pleasant thoughts, imagine himself on the open road, wandering the countryside amid the hills of Samaria or, better still, looking down from a great height on the village of Nazareth, which he sorely missed. His soul rejoiced as he told himself that this long separation would soon be over and he would be on his way with only the morning star in the sky, singing praises to the Lord who protects our homes and guides our footsteps. Startled, he opened his eyes, afraid that he had dozed off and missed the overseer's signal, but he had only been daydreaming, his companions were still there, some chatting, others taking a nap, and the jovial mood of the overseer suggested that he might give his workers the rest of the day off. The

sun is overhead, sharp gusts of wind drive the smoke from the sacrificial fires in the opposite direction. In this ravine, which looks onto the site where a hippodrome is under construction, not even the gabbling of the vendors in the Temple can be heard. The machine of time appears to have come to a halt, as if it too were awaiting a signal from the mighty overseer of universal space and time. Joseph suddenly became uneasy, after feeling so happy only a moment ago. He looked around him and saw the same familiar building site, to which he had grown accustomed in recent weeks, slabs of stone and wooden planks, a thick layer of white dust everywhere, and sawdust that never seemed to dry. He tried to find some explanation for this unexpected gloom, it was probably the natural reaction of a man who had to leave his work unfinished, even if this particular job was not his responsibility and he had every reason for leaving. Rising to his feet, Joseph tried to calculate how much time was left. The overseer did not even turn to glance in his direction, so Joseph decided to take one last look at the section of the building on which he had worked, to bid farewell, as it were, to the timbers he had planed and the joists he

> *The machine of time appears to have come to a halt.*

had fitted, if they could possibly be identified, for where is the bee that can claim, This honey was made my me.

After taking a good look around, Joseph was heading back to the site when he paused for a moment to admire the city on the opposite slope, built up in stages, with stones baked to the color of bread. The overseer must have given the signal by now, but Joseph was in no hurry, he gazed at the city, waiting for who knows what. The minutes passed and nothing happened. Joseph muttered to himself, Well, I might as well get back to work, when he heard voices on the path below the spot where he was standing, and, leaning over the stone wall, he saw three soldiers. They must have been walking along the path and decided to stop for a break, two of them were resting on their lances and listening to the third man, who looked older and was probably their officer, although it was not easy to tell the difference unless you were familiar with the various uniforms and knew the significance of the many insignia, stripes, and braids denoting rank. The words, which

Joseph could barely make out, sounded like a question, something like, And when will that be, and one of the younger men answered in a clear voice, At the beginning of the third hour, when everyone is indoors. Whereupon the other soldier asked, How many of us are being dispatched, only to be told, I don't know yet but enough men to surround the village. Has an order been given to kill all of them. No, not all of them, only those under the age of three. It's difficult to tell a two-year-old from a four-year-old. And how many will that make, the second soldier wanted to know. According to the census, the officer told them, there must be around twenty-five. Joseph's eyes widened as if they could grasp this conversation better than his ears could, and he trembled from head to foot, because it was clear that these soldiers were talking about killing people. People, what people, he asked himself, bewildered and distressed, No, no, not people, or rather, people, but children. Children under the age of three, the officer in charge said, or perhaps it was one of the junior soldiers, but where, where could this be. Joseph could not very well lean over the wall and ask, Is there a war going on. He felt his legs shaking. He could hear one of the men say gravely, though with relief, How fortunate for us and our children that we don't live in Bethlehem. Does anyone know why they've chosen

> *Joseph trembled from head to foot.*

to kill the children of Bethlehem, one of the soldiers asked. No, the commander didn't say and I'll wager he doesn't know himself, the order came from the king, and that's all we need to know. Tracing a line on the ground with his lance, as if dividing and parceling out destiny, the other soldier said, Wretched are we who not only practice the evil that is ours by nature but must also serve as an instrument of evil for those who abuse their power. But these words went unheard by Joseph, who had stolen away from his vantage point, cautiously at first and then in a mad rush, like a frightened goat, scattering pebbles in all directions as he ran. Unfortunately, without Joseph's testimony, we have reason to doubt the authenticity of this soldier's philosophical remark, both in form and content given the obvious contradiction between the aptness of the sentiment and the humble station of the person who expressed it.

Delirious, bumping into everything, overturning fruit stalls and bird cages, even a money changer's table, and oblivious to the cries of fury from the vendors in the Temple, Joseph is concerned only that his child's life is in danger. He cannot imagine why anyone would want to do such a thing, he is desperate, he chose to father a child and now someone wants to take it from him, one desire is as valid as another, to do and undo, to tie and untie, to create and destroy. Suddenly he stops, realizing the risk he is running if he continues in this reckless flight, the Temple guards might appear and arrest him, he is surprised they have not already been alerted by the up-

> *Joseph is concerned only that his child's life is in danger.*

roar. Dissembling as best he can, like a louse taking refuge in the seams of a garment, he disappears into the crowd and instantly becomes anonymous, the only difference being that he walks a little faster than others, but this is hardly noticed amid the labrynth of people. He knows he must not run until he reaches the city gate, but he is distressed at the thought that the soldiers may already be on their way, ominously armed with lance, dagger, and unprovoked hatred. If they are traveling on horseback, he will never catch up with them, and by the time he gets there, his son will be dead, poor child, sweet little Jesus. At this moment of deepest anguish a foolish thought occurs to him, he remembers his wages, the week's wages he stands to lose, and such is the power of these vile material things that, without exactly coming to a halt, he slows down just long enough to ponder whether he can rescue both his money and his child's life. Quick as it surfaced, this unworthy thought disappears, leaving no sense of shame, that feeling which often, but not often enough, proves our most reliable guardian angel.

Joseph finally puts the city behind him. There are no soldiers on the road for as far as the eye can reach, no crowds gathered as one might expect them to for a military parade, but the most reassuring sight of all is that of children playing innocent games, with none of the wild enthusiasm they display when flags, drums, and horns go marching by. If any soldiers had passed this way, there would be no boys in sight, they would have followed the detachment at least to the first bend in the road, as is the time-honored custom, and perhaps one child, his

heart set on becoming a soldier someday, accompanied them on their mission and so learned the fate that awaited him, namely to kill or be killed. Now Joseph can run as fast as he likes, he takes advantage of the slope, is hampered only by his tunic, which he hitches up over his knees. As in a dream, he has the agonizing sensation that his legs cannot keep up with the rest of his body, with his heart, head, and eyes, and his hands, eager to offer protection, are so painfully slow in their movement. Some people stop on the road and shake their heads disapprovingly at this undignified performance, for these people are known for their composure and noble bearing. The explanation for Joseph's extraordinary behavior in their eyes is not that he is running to save his child's life but that he is Galilean, one of a lot with no real breeding, as has often been observed. He has already passed Rachel's tomb, and that good woman could never have suspected that she would have so much cause to weep for her children, to cover the nearby hills with her cries and lamentations, to claw at her face, tear out her hair, and then beat her bare skull.

Before he comes to the first houses on the outskirts of Bethlehem, Joseph leaves the main road and goes cross-country. I am taking a shortcut, he would reply if we were to question this sudden change of direction, a route that might be shorter but is certainly much less comfortable. Taking care not to encounter any laborers at work in the fields, and hiding behind boulders whenever he sees a shepherd, Joseph makes for the cave where his wife is not expecting him at this hour and his son. fast asleep, is not expecting him at all. Halfway up the slope of the last hill, from where he can already see the dark chasm of the grotto, Joseph is assailed by a terrible thought, suppose his wife has gone to the village, taking the child with her, nothing more natural, knowing what women are, than for her to take advantage of being on her own to make a farewell visit to Salome and several families with whom she has become acquainted in recent weeks, leaving Joseph to thank the owners of the cave with all due formality. He sees himself running through the streets and knocking on every door. Is my wife here? It would be foolish to inquire anxiously. Better, Is my son here, in case some woman, carrying a child in her arms, for

> *"I am taking a shortcut."*

example, should ask, on seeing him distressed, Is something wrong. No, nothing, he would reply, Nothing at all, it's just that we have to set off at first light and we still haven't packed. The village, seen from here, with its identical roof terraces, reminds Joseph of the building site, stones scattered everywhere until the workers assemble them, one on top of another, to erect a watchtower, an obelisk to commemorate some victory, or a wall for lamentations. A dog barks in the distance, others bark in response, but the warm evening silence continues to hover over the village like a blessing about to lose its effect, like a wisp of a cloud on the point of vanishing This pause was short-lived. In one last spurt the carpenter reached the entrance to the cave and called out, Mary are you there. She called in reply, and Joseph realized that his legs were weak, probably from all the running, but also from the sheer relief of knowing his child was safe. Inside the cave Mary was chopping vegetables for the evening meal, the

"What are those screams?"

child asleep in the manger. Joseph collapsed on the ground but was soon back on his feet, We must leave, we must get out of this place. Mary looked at him in dismay, Are we leaving, she asked, Yes, this very minute, But you said, Be quiet and start packing while I harness the donkey. Aren't we going to eat first. No, we'll eat something on the way. But it will soon be dark and we might get lost, whereupon Joseph lost his temper, Be quiet, woman, I've already told you we're leaving, so do as I say. Tears sprang to Mary's eyes, this was the first time her husband had ever raised his voice to her. Without another word she began gathering their scant possessions. Be quick, be quick, he kept repeating as he saddled the donkey and tightened the straps and crammed whatever came to hand into the baskets, while Mary looked on dumbfounded at this husband she barely recognized. They were ready to leave, the only thing left to be done now was put out the fire with earth. Joseph signaled to his wife to wait until he took a look outside.

The ashen shadows of twilight merged heaven and earth. The sun had not yet set, but the heavy mist, while too high to obscure the surrounding fields, kept the sunlight from them. Joseph listened carefully, took a few steps, his hair on end. A scream came from the village,

so shrill that it scarcely sounded human, its echo resounding from hill to hill, and it was followed by more screams and wailing, which could be heard everywhere. These were not weeping angels lamenting human misfortune, these were the voices of men and women maddened by grief beneath an empty sky. Slowly, afraid of being heard, Joseph stepped back to the cave, and collided with Mary, who had disregarded his warning. She was trembling. What are those screams, she asked, but he pushed her back inside without replying and hastily began throwing earth on the fire. What are those screams, Mary asked a second time, invisible in the darkness, and Joseph eventually answered, People are being put to death. He paused and then added in a whisper, Children, by order of Herod, his voice breaking into a dry sob, That's why I said we should leave. There was muffled sound of clothing and hay being disturbed, Mary was lifting her child from the manger and pressing him to her bosom, Sweet little Jesus, who would want to harm you, her words drowned in tears. Be quiet, said Joseph, don't make a sound, perhaps the soldiers won't find this place, they've been ordered to kill all the children in Bethlehem under the age of three. How did you find out. I overheard it in the Temple and that's why I ran back. What do we do now. We're on the outskirts of the village, the soldiers aren't likely to look inside these caves, they've been ordered to carry out a house-to-house search, so let's hope no one reports us and we're spared. He took another cautious look outside, the screaming had stopped, nothing could be heard now except a wailing chorus, which gradually subsided. The massacre of the innocents had ended.

—JOSE SARAMAGO
from *The Gospel According to
Jesus Christ*

JOSE SARAMAGO (1922–   )—Born in the village of Azinhaga in 1922, Saramago's parents emigrated to Lisbon, Portugal when he was three years old. Though he completed secondary studies, he did not continue due to a lack of finances. Saramago held jobs as a mechanical locksmith, designer, publisher, translator, and journalist. Since 1976, he has devoted his time exclusively to his literary work. In 1998, Saramago won the Nobel Prize for literature.

The Carnal and the Crane

As I pass'd by a river side,
  And there as I did reign,
In argument I chanced to hear
  A Carnal and a Crane.

The Carnal said unto the Crane,
  If all the world should turn,
Before we had the Father,
  But now we have the Son!

From whence does the Son come?
  From where and from what place?
He said, In a manger,
  Between an ox and ass!

I pray thee, said the Carnal,
  Tell me before thou go,
Was not the mother of Jesus
  Conceived by the Holy Ghost?

She was the purest Virgin,
  And the cleanest from sin;
She was the handmaid of our Lord,
  And mother of our King.

Where is the golden cradle
  That Christ was rocked in?
Where are the silken sheets
  That Jesus was wrapt in?

A manger was the cradle
  That Christ was rocked in;

The provender the asses left
  So sweetly he slept on.

There was a star in the West land,
  So bright did it appear
Into King Herod's chamber,
  And where King Herod were.

The Wise Men soon espied it,
  And told the king on high,
A princely babe was born that night
  No king could e'er destroy.

If this be true, King Herod said,
  As thou tellest unto me,
This roasted cock that lies in the dish
  Shall crow full fences three.

The cock soon freshly feathered was
  By the work of God's own hand,
And then three fences crowed he
  In the dish where he did stand.

Rise up, rise up, you merry men all,
  See that you ready be,
All children under two years old
  Now slain they all shall be.

Then Jesus, ah! and Joseph,
  And Mary, that was so pure,
They travelled into Egypt,
  As you shall find it sure.

And when they came to Egypt's land,
  Amongst those fierce wild beasts,

Mary, she being weary,
Must needs sit down to rest.

Come sit thee down, says Jesus,
Come sit thee down by me,
And thou shalt see how these wild beasts
Do come and worship me.

First came the lovely lion,
Which Jesu's grace did spring,
And of the wild beasts in the field,
The lion shall be the king.

We'll choose our virtuous princes,
Of birth and high degree,
In every sundry nation,
Where'er we come and see.

Then Jesus, ah! and Joseph,
And Mary, that was unknown,
They travelled by a husbandman,
Just while his seed was sown.

God speed thee, man! said Jesus,
Go fetch thy ox and wain,
And carry home thy corn again,
Which thou this day hast sown.

The husbandman fell on his knees,
Even before his face;
Long time hast thou been looked for,
But now thou are come at last.

And I myself do now believe
Thy name is Jesus called;

Redeemer of mankind thou art,
Though undeserving all.

The truth, man, thou has spoken,
Of it thou may'st be sure,
For I must lose my precious blood
For thee and thousands more.

If any one should come this way,
And inquire for me alone,
Tell them that Jesus passed by,
As thou thy seed did sow.

After that there came King Herod,
With his train so furiously,
Inquiring of the husbandman,
Whether Jesus passed by.

Why, the truth it must be spoke,
And the truth it must be known,
For Jesus passed by this way
When my seed was sown.

—Traditional Carol

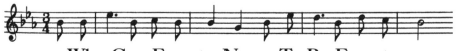

Who Can Forget—Never To Be Forgot

Who can forget—never to be forgot—
The time, that all the world in slumber lies,
When, like the stars, the singing angels shot
To earth, and heaven awaked all his eyes,
To see another sun at midnight rise.
On earth? Was never sight of pareil fame
For God before, man like himself did frame,
But God himself now like a mortal man became.

A Child he was, and had not learnt to speak,
That with his word the world before did make;
His mother's arms him bore, he was so weak,
That with one hand the vaults of heaven could shake;
See how small room my infant Lord doth take
   Whom all the world is not enough to hold!
   Who of his years, or of his age hath told?
Never such age so young, never a child so old.

And yet but newly he was infanted,
And yet already he was sought to die;
Yet scarcely born, already banished;
Not able yet to go, and forced to fly:
But scarcely fled away, when by and by,
   The tyran's sword with blood is all defiled,
   And Rachel, for her sons, with fury wild,
Cries, "O thou cruel king, and O my sweetest Child!"

Egypt his nurse became, where Nilus springs,
Who, straight to entertain the rising sun,
The hasty harvest in his bosom brings;
But now for drought the fields were all undone,
And now with waters all is overrun:
   So fast the Cynthian mountains pour'd their snow,
   When once they felt the sun so near them glow,
That Nilus Egypt lost, and to a sea did grow.

The angels carolled loud their song of peace;
The cursed oracles were strucken dumb;
To see their Shepherd, the poor shepherds press;
To see their King, the kingly sophies come;
And them to guide unto his Master's home,
   A star comes dancing up the Orient,
   That springs for joy over the strawy tent,
Where gold, to make their prince a crown, they all present.

                    —Traditional English Carol

Coventry Carol

Lully, lullay, Thou little tiny Child,
By, by, lully, lullay.

O sisters too, how may we do,
For to preserve this day
This poor Youngling for Whom we sing
By, by, lully, lullay?

Herod the king, in his raging,
Charged he hath this day
His men of might, in his own sight,
All young children to slay.

That woe is me, poor Child for Thee!
And ever morn and day
For Thy parting neither say nor sing,
By, by, lully, lullay.

Lully, lullay, Thou little tiny Child,
By, by, lully, lullay.

"COVENTRY CAROL"—Also known as "Lully Lullay" and the "Covenant Carol," it is a lullaby from 15th or 16th century English theater. In those days various guilds would perform "mystery plays" that re-enacted Christmas scenes from the Bible. They were written in English, instead of Latin, and instead of being done in churches, were performed publicly on bi-leveled "Pageant Wagons" The lower level served as a curtained dressing chamber. This was a sort of street theater in which the topic matter of the play would relate to the particular guild that performed it (for example, the building of the ark was performed by the ship-builders). The Coventry Carol was included in the *Pageant of the Shearmen and Tailors*. Although the composer is unknown, the text was written in 1534 by Robert Croo. In the play itself, the women of Bethlehem sing this lullaby just before Herod's soldiers come onstage to slaughter their children.

On the Flight into Egypt and the Massacre of the Innocents

The flight into Egypt led to a very memorable event. Seeing that the Wise Men had not returned to him, the alarm and jealousy of Herod assumed a still darker and more malignant aspect. He had no means of identifying the royal infant of the seed of David, and least of all would he have been likely to seek for him in the cavern stable of the village khan. But he knew that the child whom the visit of the Magi

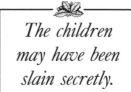

The children may have been slain secretly.

had taught him to regard as a future rival of himself or of his house was yet an infant at the breast; and as Eastern mothers usually suckle their children for two years, he issued his fell mandate to slay all the children of Bethlehem and its neighbourhood "from two years old and under." Of the method by which the decree was carried out we know nothing. The children may have been slain secretly, gradually, and by various forms of murder; or, as has been generally supposed, there may have been one single hour of dreadful butchery. The decrees of tyrants like Herod are usually involved in a deadly obscurity; they reduce the world to a torpor in which it is hardly safe to speak above a whisper. But the wild wail of anguish which rose from the mothers thus cruelly robbed of their infant children could not be hushed, and they who heard it might well imagine that Rachel, the great ancestress of their race, whose tomb stands by the roadside about a mile from Bethlehem, once more, as in the pathetic image of the prophet, mingled her voice with the mourning and lamentation of those who wept so inconsolably for their murdered little ones.

To us there seems something inconceivable in a crime so atrocious; but our thoughts have been softened by eighteen centuries of Christianity, and such deeds are by no means unparalleled in the history of heathen despots and of the ancient world. Infanticide of a deeper dye than this of Herod's was a crime dreadfully rife in the days of the Empire; and the Massacre of the Innocents, as well as the motives

which led to it, can be illustrated by several circumstances in the history of this very epoch. Suetonius, in his Life of Augustus, quotes from the life of the Emperor by his freedman Julius Marathus, a story to the effect that shortly before his birth there was a prophecy in Rome that a king over the Roman people would soon be born. To obviate this danger to the Republic, the Senate ordered that all the male children born in that year should be abandoned or exposed; but the Senators whose wives were pregnant took means to prevent the ratification of the statute, because each of them hoped that the prophecy might refer to his own child. Again, Eusebius quotes from Hegesippus, a Jew by birth, a story that Domitian, alarmed by the growing power of the name of Christ, issued an order to destroy all the descendants of the house of David. Two grandchildren of St. Jude—"the Lord's brother"—were still living, and were known as the Desposyni. They were betrayed to the Emperor by a certain Jocatus, and other Nazaraean heretics, and were brought into the imperial presence; but when Domitian observed that they only held the rank of peasants, and that their hands were hard with manual toil, he dismissed them in safety with a mixture of pity and contempt.

Although doubts have been thrown on the Massacre of the Innocents, it is profoundly in accordance with all that we know of Herod's character. The master-passions of that able but wicked prince were a most unbounded ambition, and, a most excruciating jealousy. His whole career was red with the blood of murder. He had massacred priests and nobles; he had decimated the Sanhedrin; he had caused the High Priest, his brother-in-law, the young and noble Aristobulus, to be drowned in pretended sport before his eyes; he had ordered the strangulation of his favourite wife, the beautiful Asmonaean princess Mariamne, though she seems to have been the only

> *The wild wail of anguish which rose from the mothers.*

human being whom he passionately loved. His sons Alexander, Aristobulus, and Antipater—his uncle Joseph—Antigonus and Alexander, the uncle and father of his wife—his mother-in-law Alexandra—his kinsman Cortobanus—his friends Dositheus and Gadias, were but a few of the multitudes who fell victims to his sanguinary, suspicious, and guilty

terrors. His brother Pheroras and his son Archelaus barely and narrowly escaped execution by his orders. Neither the blooming youth of the prince Aristobulus, nor the white hairs of the king Hyrcanus, had protected them from his fawning and treacherous fury. Deaths by strangulation, deaths by burning, deaths by being cleft asunder, deaths by secret assassination, confessions forced by unutterable torture, acts of insolent and inhuman lust, mark the annals of a reign which was so cruel that, in the energetic language of the Jewish ambassadors to the Emperor Augustus, "the survivors during his lifetime were even more miserable than the sufferers." And as in the case of Henry VIII, every dark and brutal instinct of his character seemed to acquire fresh intensity as his life drew towards its close. Haunted by the spectres of his murdered wife and murdered sons, agitated by the conflicting furies of remorse and blood, the pitiless monster, as Josephus calls him, was seized in his last days by a black and bitter ferocity, which broke out against all with whom he came in contact. There is no conceivable difficulty in supposing that such a man—a savage barbarian with a thin veneer of corrupt and superficial civilisation— would have acted in the exact manner which St. Matthew describes; and the belief in the fact receives independent confirmation from various sources. "On Augustus being informed," says Macrobius, "that among the boys under two years of age whom Herod ordered to be slain in Syria, his own son also had been slain," "It is better," said he, "to be Herod's pig (ûn) than his son (uìòn)." Although Macrobius is a late writer, and made the mistake of supposing that Herod's son Antipater, who was put to death about the same time as the Massacre of the Innocents, had actually perished in that massacre, it is clear that the form in which he narrates the bon mot of Augustus, points to some dim reminiscence of this cruel slaughter.

> *He was a savage barbarian with a thin veneer of corrupt and superficial civilisation.*

Why then, it has been asked, does Josephus make no mention of so infamous an atrocity? Perhaps because it was performed so secretly that he did not even know of it. Perhaps because, in those terrible days, the murder of a score of children, in consequence of a transient

suspicion, would have been regarded as an item utterly insignificant in the list of Herod's murders. Perhaps because it was passed over in silence by Nikolaus of Damascus, who, writing in the true spirit of those Hellenising courtiers, who wanted to make a political Messiah out of a corrupt and blood-stained usurper, magnified all his patron's achievements, and concealed or palliated all his crimes. But the more probable reason is that Josephus, whom, in spite of all the immense literary debt which we owe to him, we can only regard as a renegade and a sycophant, did not choose to make any allusion to facts which were even remotely connected with the life of Christ. The single passage in which he alludes to Him is interpolated, if not wholly spurious, and no one can doubt that his silence on the subject of Christianity was as deliberate as it was dishonest.

But although Josephus does not distinctly mention the event, yet every single circumstance which he does tell us about this very period of Herod's life supports its probability. At this very time two eloquent Jewish teachers, Judas and Matthias, had incited their scholars to pull down the large golden eagle which Herod had placed above the great gate of the Temple. Josephus connects this bold attempt with premature rumours of Herod's death; but Lardner's conjecture that it may have been further encouraged by the Messianic hopes freshly kindled by the visit of the Wise Men, is by no means impossible. The attempt, however, was defeated, and Judas and Matthias, with forty of their scholars, were burned alive. With such crimes as this before him on every page, Josephus might well have ignored the secret assassination of a few unweaned infants in a little village. Their blood was but a drop in that crimson river in which Herod was steeped to the very lips. It must have been very shortly after the murder of the Innocents that Herod died. Only five days before his death he had made a frantic attempt at suicide, and had ordered the execution of his eldest son Antipater. His death-bed, which once more reminds us of Henry VIII, was accompanied by circumstances of peculiar horror, and it has been noticed that the

> *Their blood was but a drop in that crimson river in which Herod was steeped to the very lips.*

loathsome disease of which he died is hardly mentioned in history, except in the case of men who have been rendered infamous by an atrocity of persecuting zeal. On his bed of intolerable anguish, in that splendid and luxurious palace which he had built for himself under the palms of Jericho, swollen with disease and scorched by thirst—ulcerated externally and glowing inwardly with a "soft slow fire"—surrounded by plotting sons and plundering slaves, detesting all and detested by all—longing for death as a release from his tortures, yet dreading it as the beginning of worse terrors—stung by remorse, yet still unslaked with murder—a horror to all around him, yet in his guilty conscience a worse terror to himself—devoured by the premature corruption of an anticipated grave—eaten of worms as though visibly smitten by the finger of God's wrath, after seventy years of successful villany—the wretched old man, whom men had called the Great, lay in savage frenzy awaiting his last hour. As he knew

> *St. Luke passed over Herod's death in silence.*

that none would shed one tear for him, he determined that they should shed many for themselves, and issued an order that, under pain of death, the principal families in the kingdom and the chiefs of the tribes should come to Jericho. They came, and then, shutting them in the hippodrome, he secretly commanded his sister Salome that at the moment of his death they should all be massacred. And so, choking as were with blood, devising massacres in its very delirium, the soul of Herod passed forth into the night.

In purple robes, with crown and sceptre and precious stones, the corpse was placed upon its splendid bier, and accompanied with military pomp and burning incense to its grave in the Herodium, not far from the place where Christ was born. But the spell of the Herodian dominion was broken, and the people saw how illusory had been its glittering fascination. The day of Herod's death was, as he had foreseen, observed as a festival. His will was disputed; his kingdom disintegrated; his last order was disobeyed; his sons died for the most part in infamy and exile; the curse of God was on his house, and though, by ten wives and many concubines, he seems to have had nine sons and five daughters, yet within a hundred years the family of the heirodoulos of Ascalon had perished by disease or violence, and there was no living descendant to perpetuate his name.

If the intimation of Herod's death was speedily given to Joseph, the stay in Egypt must have been too short to influence in any way the human development of our Lord. This may perhaps be the reason why St. Luke passes it over in silence.

It seems to have been the first intention of Joseph to fix his home in Bethlehem. It was the city of his ancestors, and was hallowed by many beautiful and heroic associations. It would have been easy to find a living there by a trade which must almost anywhere have supplied the simple wants of a peasant family. It is true that an Oriental rarely leaves his home, but when he has been compelled by circumstances to do so, he finds it comparatively easy to settle elsewhere. Having once been summoned to Bethlehem, Joseph might find a powerful attraction in the vicinity of the little town to Jerusalem; and the more so since it had recently been the scene of such memorable circumstances. But, on his way, he was met by the news that Archelaus ruled in the room of his father Herod. The people would only too gladly have got rid of the whole Idumaean race: at the worst they would have preferred Antipas to Archelaus. But Augustus had unexpectedly decided in favour of Archelaus, who, though younger than Antipas, was the heir nominated by the last will of his father and as though anxious to show that he was the true son of that father, Archelaus, even before his inheritance had been confirmed by Roman authority, "had," as Josephus scornfully remarks, "given to his subjects a specimen of his future virtue, by ordering a slaughter of 3,000 of his own countrymen at the Temple." It was clear that under such a government there could be neither hope nor safety; and Joseph, obedient once more to an intimation of God's will, seeking once more the original home of himself and Mary, "turned aside into the parts of Galilee," where, in remote obscurity, sheltered by poverty and insignificance, the Holy Family might live secure under the sway of another son of Herod—the equally unscrupulous, but more indolent and indifferent Antipas.

—FREDERIC FARRAR, Dean of Canterbury Cathedral
from *The Life of Christ*

The Murder of the Innocents

. . . But when this cruel Herod found that the wise men did not come back to him, and that he could not, therefore, find out where this child, Jesus Christ, lived, he called his soldiers and captains to him, and told them to go and Kill all the children in his dominions that were not more than two years old. The wicked men did so. The mothers of the children ran up and down the streets with them in their arms trying to save them, and hide them in caves and cellars, but it was of no use. The soldiers with their swords killed all the children they could find. This dreadful murder was called the Murder of the Innocents. Because the little children were so innocent.

King Herod hoped that Jesus Christ was one of them. But He was not, as you know, for He had escaped safely into Egypt. And he lived there, with his father and mother, until Bad King Herod died.

—CHARLES DICKENS
from *The Life of Our Lord*

Glory to Thee, O Lord

Glory to Thee, O Lord,
Who, from this world of sin,
By cruel Herod's ruthless sword
Those precious ones didst win.

Baptized in their own blood,
Earth's untried perils o'er,
They passed unconsciously the flood,
And safely gained the shore.

Glory to Thee for all
The ransomed infant band,

Who, since that hour have heard Thy call,
And reached the quiet land.

O that our hearts within,
Like theirs, were pure and bright,
O that as free from stain of sin
We shrank not from Thy sight.

Lord, help us every hour
Thy cleansing grace to claim;
In life to glorify Thy power,
In death to praise Thy name.

—EMMA L. TOKE

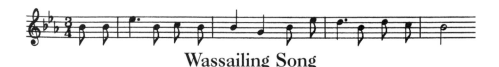

Wassailing Song

We wish you merry Christmas, also a glad New Year;
We come to bring you tidings to all mankind so dear;
We come to tell that Jesus was born in Bethl'em town,
And now he's gone to glory and pityingly looks down
  On us poor wassailers,
  As wassailing we go;
  With footsteps sore
  From door to door
We trudge through sleet and snow.

A manger was his cradle, the straw it was his bed,
The oxen were around him within that lowly shed'
No servants waited on him with lords and ladies gay;
But now he's gone to glory and unto him we pray.
    Us poor wassailers, &c.

His mother loved and tended him and nursed him at
      her breast,

And good old Joseph watched them both the while
    they took their rest;
And wicked Herod vainly sought to rob them of their
    child,
By slaughtering the Innocents in Bethlehem undefiled.
        But us poor wassailers, &c.

Now, all good Christian people, with great concern
    we sing,
These tidings of your Jesus, the Saviour, Lord and
    King;
In poverty he passed his days that riches we might
    share,
And of your wealth he bids you give and of your
    portion spare.
        To us poor wassailers, &c.

Your wife shall be a fruitful vine, a hus'sif good and
    able;
Your children like the olive branches round about
    your table;
Your barns shall burst with plenty and your crops
    shall be secure
If you will give your charity to us who are so poor.
        Us poor wassailers, &c.

And now no more we'll sing to you because the hour
    is late,
And we must trudge and sing our song at many
    another gate;
And so we'll wish you once again a merry Christmas
    time,
And pray God bless you while you give good silver
    for our rhyme.
        Us poor wassailers, &c.

Night Flight into Egypt

Joseph tossed and turned, trying to be quiet so as not to wake Mary, but unable to settle down and sleep. Seldom in his life had he experienced the frustration of sleeplessness. He had always worked hard, and at the end of the day he reveled in the satisfying tiredness that came with a job well done. When the lamp went out, Joseph slept, and woke refreshed with each new dawn.

Only twice in recent memory had he lain awake until the early hours of morning: in Bethlehem, the night their son was born, and nine months before that, those few days of agony before the angel had appeared to him in a restless dream, instructing him to take Mary as his wife.

> *Was God trying to tell him something now?*

Was God trying to tell him something now?

Joseph got up and tiptoed away from the bed. Mary stirred slightly, mumbled in her sleep, and then began to snore softly once again. He passed by his son's little bed—the boy had long since outgrown the cradle Joseph had made—and looked down at the chubby face. In sleep, the child looked serene and peaceful. Quite a difference from the energetic toddler who kept both of them running from daylight till dark.

The lad's eyes opened, and he reached his arms up.

"Abba!"

Joseph reached down and caressed his head. "Yes, my son," he soothed. "Abba's here. Go back to sleep, now."

But Jesus would not be dissuaded. "Abba!" he insisted.

"All right, all right." Joseph lifted Jesus out of his crib, wrapped him in his blanket, and took him over near the fire. Holding the boy in one arm, he stirred the embers of the fire and put on a little more wood. The flames danced to life, reflecting in the child's dark eyes. When the fire was burning, Joseph sat down in a chair and began to rock.

"Let the redeemed of the Lord say so," he sang softly, "whom God

has delivered from the hands of their enemies . . ." Jesus's eyelids began to droop. His hand grasped Joseph's finger, and within a few moments his breathing grew even.

Why, Joseph wondered, *can I not sleep in peace even as he does?* Was it because of the money, the treasures brought by the wise men who had come to do homage to the child? It wasn't a fortune, exactly, but it was far more than Joseph had ever possessed. And with money came increased responsibility—and, perhaps, a few sleepless nights.

But he didn't think so. He and Mary had already agreed that the gifts should be saved for the future, for the uncertainties that could not be anticipated. In the meantime, their lives would go on in the simplicity they were accustomed to. Joseph would continue his carpentry, the work he loved so much. They would stay in Nazareth. Nothing would change.

> *What a blood-chilling, terrifying dream!*

The heat of the fire seeped into his bones, and the warmth from Jesus's little body soaked into his chest. Joseph found his own eyes growing heavy, but still he sat there, holding his son, staring into the flames.

"Take the child and his mother, and flee to Egypt, and remain there until I tell you."

The voice startled Joseph, and he looked around. The house was dark, the fire a little dimmer, and he still held the sleeping child in his arms. Had he imagined it? He strained his ears, but all he heard was the gentle crackling of the flames.

"Take the child and his mother, and flee to Egypt, and remain there until I tell you," the voice repeated. *"For Herod is about to search for the child, to destroy him."*

An image passed before Joseph's eyes—the King standing on a dais as his soldiers paraded by with the naked sons of his neighbors and friends impaled upon their swords. The soldiers were waving the infant bodies like triumphal flags, and Herod was laughing. A gruesome, horrible scene . . .

Joseph awoke with a start. The fire had died, and he was shivering. What a blood-chilling, terrifying dream! He shook his head to try to rid himself of the memory, but still it remained.

This was no ordinary nightmare. It was a warning.

He clutched little Jesus tighter to his chest, and the boy stirred in protest and began to whine.

"Joseph?" Mary sat up on the sleeping mat and pushed her hair out of her eyes. "Is everything all right?"

He wanted to reassure her, to say, *Yes, Mary, everything's fine; go back to sleep.* But everything wasn't fine, and he knew it. Crazy as it seemed, there was only one thing to do.

"Get up, Mary." He went to her and laid his son on the sleeping mat beside her.

"It isn't daylight yet, is it?" she mumbled. "Come back to bed."

"No, it's still dark. But we have to leave—now!" As he moved about the house, lighting lamps and gathering supplies, Joseph told her about the message that had come in his dream. "Herod is going to try to kill our son, and we can't let that happen."

In an instant, Mary was on her feet. She dressed, threw extra clothes into a bag, and packed bread, wine, and cheese for the journey. "Egypt?" she repeated. "We're going to Egypt? But how will we live?"

"We'll manage. God will provide, and—"

He heard a crash, and turned. Jesus, now wide awake, sat in the center of a cache of gold coins, playing with them and laughing. Somehow he had toddled over to the table, climbed up on it, and pulled down from a shelf the small chest Balthasar had brought to honor the child.

Joseph grinned. "It looks as if God has already provided."

"The gifts! I had almost forgotten!"

He nodded. "I didn't think of them, either. But God didn't forget."

By the time dawn broke, Joseph, Mary, and Jesus were well into the hills of Judea and making their way south

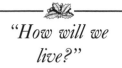

"How will we live?"

and east toward Egypt. An extended journey lay ahead of them, days of camping in the desert, taking refuge in towns along the way. But at least they had enough money to sustain them. They would make it—Joseph believed that with all his heart. And someday, when it was safe to return, they would come home again.

A rumbling in the valley below arrested Joseph's attention. "Look!"

he told Mary, and nodded at the scene below them. "Herod's soldiers, hundreds of them, on horseback, coming from Jerusalem!"

Mary shifted on the donkey's back and gripped Jesus in her arms. "I didn't think it would happen so quickly. We got out just in time."

They stood there staring, watching until the King's troops vanished in a cloud of dust.

But little Jesus didn't notice the soldiers. He had eyes only for the morning. "Abba!" he squealed, jabbing a chubby finger toward the east. "Pretty!"

The sun was rising into a bank of clouds, painting the eastern sky with a panorama of color—red, gold, purple, blue. One shaft of sunlight pierced the clouds, directing them, it seemed, toward Egypt.

> *A rumbling in the valley below arrested Joseph's attention.*

Joseph scooped his son off the donkey's back and held him close. "Abba!" the child repeated, pointing to the sun.

"Abba," Joseph echoed. The Father who loved them and protected them. The Parent who watched over them all, provided for their needs, gave them direction. The God who would never forsake them.

"Yes," he repeated. "Abba is here."

Then he settled his son on the donkey with Mary, and they began the long trek toward Egypt.

—PENELOPE STOKES
from *The Miracle of the Christmas Child*

Flight by Night

There is an epilogue to the high drama of the Christmas story. It brings the story of the angel's song, the wise men's visit and the joy of Mary's heart back to the rough realities of the world in which we live. The epilogue is tragic, and perhaps only those who have been ruthlessly uprooted by fear and prejudice in our day can fully appreciate the flight of Joseph, Mary, and the Child into Egypt. St. Matthew relates tersely

the blunt facts: "Now when they [the Wise Men] had departed, behold an angel of the Lord appeared to Joseph in a dream and said, 'Rise, take the child and his mother, and flee to Egypt, and remain there till I tell you; for Herod is about to search for the child, to destroy him.' And he rose and took the child and his mother by night, and departed to Egypt, and remained there until the death of Herod . . ." (Matthew 2:13–15).

> *It is strange how life so often dashes us from the heights of joy to the lowlands of despair.*

Herod, whose life and actions anticipated the cruel despotism of our generation, had sought to obtain from the Wise Men information about Him who was born to be King of the Jews. The Wise Men, led by God, returned to their homes without informing Herod. Herod's wrath waxed hot. He ordered the slaying of all children, lest the One among them might some day challenge his authority. But God once more revealed His will to Joseph, and the holy family departed, under the cloak of darkness, for refuge in a foreign land.

It is strange how life so often dashes us from the heights of joy to the lowlands of despair, from the mountaintops of vision to the valleys of sorrow. This was the bewildering experience of the holy family. One night a star stood high above them, but the next night every shadow was potentially dangerous; from behind a rock or a tree might step one of Herod's informers.

But the Lord God, whom Joseph had obeyed all of his life and whom Mary had loved with a constant faithfulness, did not abandon them in their hour of danger. Very often, in the years that followed, Mary told her Child of the ways in which God always attends His children in their great need. That Child's faith in God never was to waver in an hour of trouble when His friends left nor in an hour of trial when He stood alone with God. We naturally trust God when life moves smoothly, when the waters of experience are untroubled, when the wind brushes gently against our cheeks. But trust in God is even more needful when dangers threaten and when calamity falls with a heavy

thud upon our lives. Mary and Joseph knew that God was with them in the stable, and they knew too that they were within His encircling love when they followed the rough road of escape to Egypt.

The Herod of the Christmas chronicle is Herod the Great, who fought his way to power with a strong arm and a clever head. He was zealous and fanatic; fear and suspicion were his masters. He was a despot who cajoled his subjects and ultimately persecuted members of his own family. His was the order which put to death his wife Mariamne and two of their sons. History has given him the benevolent title of "Herod the Great" because he was an empire builder, but he passed to his children a legacy of craftiness and passion. His second son, Herod Antipas, was tetrarch when Jesus was crucified.

"But when Herod died . . ." (Matthew 2:19). The words have the dull, cold, impersonal character of rock. How final are the words which mark Herod's passing in the pages of Scripture. It is like a great sigh of relief. It marks the end of a tyrannical rule. The folly of man had spent itself.

Joseph then took his family into Galilee and once again, he returned to his Nazareth home. There ". . . the child grew and became strong, filled with wisdom; and the favor of God was upon him" (Luke 2:40).

—CHARLES L. ALLEN and CHARLES L. WALLIS
from *Christmas in Our Hearts*

Rest on the Flight into Egypt

These, who late so breathlessly had flown
from the scene where blood of infants flowed,
oh, to what a greatness they had grown,
imperceptibly, upon the road.

Scarcely had their furtive backward glancing
melted anguish, dissipated dread,
when they brought, on their gray mule advancing,
danger to whole towns that lay ahead;

for when they, in this huge land so small,
neared strong temples where the heathen prayed,
idols there, as if they'd been betrayed,
grew demented, crashed down, one and all.

Who could have supposed that all this mad
rage would greet their coming on the scene?
And they feared themselves, this power they had,
while the babe alone remained serene.

Yet, they had to sit down and recover
for a little, where a tree spread wide.
When—the tree that silently hung over
came, as though to serve them, to their side,

bowing down. That very tree, whose wreath
has until eternity the sleeping
Pharoah's brow entrusted to its keeping,
stooped. Felt other crowns' new green up-leaping.
And they sat, as in a dream, beneath.

> —RAINER MARIA RILKE
> Translated by J. B. Leishman
> from *Selected Works of Rainer
> Maria Rilke: Poetry, Vol. II*

The Suffering Servant

He was wounded for our transgressions.
—ISAIAH 53:5

Jesus' life began in the midst of persecution and peril. He came on
a mission of love and mercy, sent by the Father. An angel announced
His conception and gave Him His name. The heavenly host sang a
glorious anthem at His birth. By the extraordinary star, the very heavens

indicated His coming. He was the most illustrious child ever born—the holy child of Mary, the divine Son of God.

Yet no sooner did He enter our world than Herod decreed His death and labored to accomplish it. Warned of God in a dream, Joseph fled Bethlehem at night, taking Mary and the baby Jesus to Egypt until Herod's death finally made it safe to return.

The Son of the eternal Father, He entered time and was made in the likeness of man. He assumed our human nature with all its infirmities, and weakness, and capacity for suffering. He came as a child of the poorest parents. His entire life was one long pathway of humiliation.

Now He is in Heaven, no longer limited by time and space. And some day He will come again—this time in glory—to take us to Himself.

—BILLY GRAHAM
from *Hope for Each Day*

CHAPTER · NINE

The Home in Nazareth

MATTHEW 2:19–23

¹⁹But when Herod was dead, behold, an angel of the Lord appeared in a dream to Joseph in Egypt, ²⁰saying, "Arise, take the young Child and His mother, and go to the land of Israel, for those who sought the young Child's life are dead." ²¹Then he arose, took the young Child and His mother, and came into the land of Israel. ²²But when he heard that Archelaus was reigning over Judea instead of his father Herod, he was afraid to go there. And being warned by God in a dream, he turned aside into the region of Galilee. ²³And he came and dwelt in a city called Nazareth, that it might be fulfilled which was spoken by the prophets, "He shall be called a Nazarene."

Twelfth Night

It has always been King Herod that I feared;
   King Herod and his kinsmen, ever since . . .
I do not like the colour of your beard;
   I think that you are wicked, and a prince.

I keep no stable . . . how your horses stamp! . . .
   If you are wise men, you will leave me soon;
I have been frightened by a thievish tramp
   Who counted bloody silver in the moon.

You get no lodging underneath these roofs,
   No, though you pay in frankincense and myrrh;
Your harness jangles with your horses' hooves;
   Be quiet; you will wake him if you stir.

This is no church for Zoroastrians,
    Nor resting-place for governors from Rome;
Oh, I have knowledge of your secret plans;
    Your faces are familiar; go home.

And you, young captain of the lion stare,
    Subdue your arrogance to this advice;
You should forbid your soldiery to swear,
    To spit at felons, and to play at dice.

You have perceived, above the chimney ledge,
    Hanging inverted by Saint David's harp,
His sword from heaven, with the double edge
    Which, for your service, is no longer sharp.

He sleeps, like some ingenuous shepherd boy
    Or carpenter's apprentice, but his slim
And wounded hands shall never more destroy
    Another giant; do not waken him.

The counterpane conceals the deeper wound
    Which lately I have washed with vinegar;
Now let this iron bar be importuned;
    I say you shall not speak to him of war.

—ELINOR WYLIE
from *Collected Poems*

The Visited Planet

Sorting through the stack of cards that arrived at our house last Christmas, I note that all kinds of symbols have edged their way into the celebration. Overwhelmingly, the landscape scenes render New England towns buried in snow, usually with the added touch of a horse-drawn sleigh. On other cards, animals frolic: not only reindeer

but also chipmunks, raccoons, cardinals, and cute gray mice. One card shows an African lion reclining with a foreleg draped affectionately around a lamb.

Inside, the cards stress sunny words like love, goodwill, cheer, happiness, and warmth. It is a fine thing, I suppose, that we honor a sacred holiday with such homey sentiments. And yet when I turn to the gospel accounts of the first Christmas, I hear a very different tone, and sense mainly disruption at work. . . .

In the birth stories of Luke and Matthew, only one person seems to grasp the mysterious nature of what God has set in motion: the old man Simeon, who recognized the baby as the Messiah, instinctively understood that conflict would surely follow. "This child is destined to cause the falling and rising of many in Israel, and to be a sign that will be spoken against . . ." he said, and then made the prediction that a sword would pierce Mary's own soul. Somehow Simeon sensed that though on the surface little had changed—the autocrat Herod still ruled, Roman troops were still stringing up patriots, Jerusalem still overflowed with beggars—underneath, everything had changed. A new force had arrived to undermine the world's powers. . . .

> *Underneath, everthing had changed.*

The earliest events in Jesus' life, though, give a menacing preview of the unlikely struggle now under way. Herod, King of the Jews, enforced Roman rule at the local level, and in an irony of history we know Herod's name mainly because of the massacre of the innocents. I have never seen a Christmas card depicting that state-sponsored act of terror, but it too was a part of Christ's coming. Although secular history does not refer to the atrocity, no one acquainted with the life of Herod doubts him capable. He killed two brothers-in-law, his own wife Mariamne, and two of his own sons. Five days before his death, he ordered the arrest of many citizens and decreed that they be executed on the day of his death, in order to guarantee a proper atmosphere of mourning in the country. For such a despot, a minor extermination procedure in Bethlehem posed no problem.

Scarcely a day passed, in fact, without an execution under Herod's regime. The political climate at the time of Jesus' birth resembled that

of Russia in the 1930s under Stalin. Citizens could not gather in public meetings. Spies were everywhere. In Herod's mind, the command to slaughter Bethlehem's infants was probably an act of utmost rationality, a rearguard action to preserve the stability of his kingdom against a rumored invasion from another . . .

And so, Jesus the Christ entered the world amid strife and terror, and spent his infancy hidden in Egypt as a refugee. Matthew notes that local politics even determined where Jesus would grow up. When Herod the Great died, an angel reported to Joseph it was safe for him to return to Israel, but not to the region where Herod's son Archelaus had taken command. Joseph moved his family instead to Nazareth in the north, where they lived under the domain of another of Herod's sons, Antipas, the one Jesus would call "that fox," and also the one who would have John the Baptist beheaded.

A few years later, the Romans took over direct command of the southern province that encompassed Jerusalem, and the cruelest and most notorious of these governors was a man named Pontius Pilate. Well-connected, Pilate had married the granddaughter of Augustus Caesar. According to Luke, Herod Antipas and

Spies were everywhere.

the Roman governor Pilate regarded each other as enemies until the day fate brought them together to determine the destiny of Jesus. On that day they collaborated, hoping to succeed where Herod the Great had failed; by disposing of the strange pretender and thus preserving the kingdom.

From beginning to end, the conflict between Rome and Jesus appeared to be entirely one-sided. The execution of Jesus would put an apparent end to any threat, or so it was assumed at the time. Tyranny would win again. It occurred to no one that his stubborn followers just might outlast the Roman Empire. . . .

As I read the birth stories about Jesus, I cannot help but conclude that though the world may be tilted toward the rich and powerful, God is tilted toward the underdog. "He has brought down rulers from their thrones but lifted up the humble. He has filled the hungry with good things but sent the rich away empty," said Mary in her Magnificat. . . .

I wonder what Mary thought about her militant hymn during her harrowing years in Egypt. For a Jew, Egypt evoked bright memories of a powerful God who had flattened a pharaoh's army and brought liberation; now Mary fled there, desperate, a stranger in a strange land hiding from her own government. Could her baby, hunted, helpless, on the run, possibly fulfill the lavish hopes of his people?

Even the family's mother-tongue summoned up memories of their underdog status: Jesus spoke Aramaic, a trade language closely related to Arabic, a stinging reminder of the Jews' subjection to foreign empires.

> *Could her baby, hunted, helpless, on the run, possibly fulfill the lavish hopes of his people?*

Some foreign astrologers (probably from the region that is now Iraq) had dropped by to visit Jesus, but these men were considered "unclean" by Jews of the day. Naturally, like all dignitaries, they had checked first with the ruling king in Jerusalem, who knew nothing about a baby in Bethlehem. After they saw the child and realized who he was, these visitors engaged in an act of civil disobedience: they deceived Herod and went home another way, to protect the child. They had chosen Jesus' side against the powerful.

Growing up, Jesus' sensibilities were affected most deeply by the poor, the powerless, the oppressed—in short, the underdogs. Today theologians debate the aptness of the phrase "God's preferential option for the poor" as a way of describing God's concern for the underdog. Since God arranged the circumstances in which to be born on planet earth—without power or wealth, without rights, without justice—his preferential options speak for themselves. . . .

There is one more view of Christmas I have never seen on a Christmas card, probably because no artist, not even William Blake, could do it justice. Revelation 12 pulls back the curtain to give us a glimpse of Christmas as it must have looked from somewhere far beyond Andromeda: Christmas from the angels' viewpoint.

The account differs radically from the birth stories in the Gospels. Revelation does not mention shepherds and an infanticidal king; rather,

it pictures a dragon leading a ferocious struggle in heaven. A woman clothed with the sun and wearing a crown of twelve stars cries out in pain as she is about to give birth. Suddenly, the enormous red dragon enters the picture, his tale sweeping a third of the stars out of the sky and flinging them to the earth. He crouches hungrily before the woman, anxious to devour her child the moment it is born. At the last second, the infant is snatched away to safety, the woman flees into the desert, and all-out cosmic war begins.

—PHILIP YANCEY
from *The Jesus I Never Knew*

PHILIP YANCEY—Currently the editor-at-large of *Christianity Today* and the author of 15 books, Yancey is a prominent writer in Christian literature. Though he once served as an editor of *Campus Life Magazine,* he devotes most of his time now as a freelance writer. His books have won eight gold medallion awards and have sold more than five million copies. His *The Jesus I Never Knew,* from which this excerpt is derived, won the 1996 Book of the Year. He lives with his family in the mountains of Colorado.

Where Shall We Find Him

When the Wise Men had come to Jerusalem, they asked, "Where is he that is born King of the Jews? for we have seen his star in the east, and are come to worship him" (Matthew 2:2). Whom did they ask? We do not know. The Scriptures are silent at this point.

We do know that their travel to Bethlehem had been on no magic carpet and that no automobile association sped them on their way again. *But they did find Bethlehem.* Someone in that teeming capital city of Judea gave them the answer they sought.

Perhaps some youngster, whose eyes had been lured by an unknown celestial light, pointed them toward Bethlehem, five short miles as the crow flies to the south. Or perhaps a man in the flower of youth and, like them, a knight of spiritual adventuring and derring-do, agreed to accompany them. Or perhaps a man of advancing years, his sight too

dim now to read the heavens, recalled having read in the ancient scroll of Micah a messianic promise to which his heart still clung: "But thou, Bethlehem Ephratah, though thou be little among the thousands of Judah, yet out of thee shall he come forth unto me that is to be ruler in Israel; whose goings forth have been from old, from everlasting" (Micah 5:2).

Someone, no doubt an obscure passerby, knew the answer, and so the Wise Men continued on the last lap of their pilgrimage.

In the days which followed, men were ever seeking Jesus. Certain of the Jews asked of the brethren of Jesus, "Where is he?" (John 7:11). The neighbors of the man born blind, whose sight Jesus restored, questioned him concerning the One who had anointed his eyes with healing, and then they asked concerning the Healer, "Where is he?" (John 9:12). To Philip the Greeks said with insistence, "Sir, we would see Jesus" (John 12:21). After having found Jesus in a solitary sanctuary

> *Is there any hope at all that we may find Christ?*

of prayer, the disciples exclaimed to their Master, "All men seek for thee" (Mark 1:37). At the door of the tomb on the first Easter morning, an angel said to the faithful women, "Fear not ye: for I know that ye seek Jesus. . ." (Matthew 28.5).

Even as He was sought after during His ministry in the flesh, so do men today seek to find Him. Where shall we find Him? At this season we are especially reminded that within the whole span of life there is no more important question.

Some wise men of our generation have wondered aloud whether He really can be found. Edwin Arlington Robinson in his poem "Credo" laments:

> *I cannot find my way: there is no star*
> *In all the shrouded heavens anywhere.*

And Archibald MacLeish in *J.B.*, his twentieth-century redaction of the story of Job, bemoans a spiritual climate that hangs heavily over our day:

The candles in churches are out.
The lights have gone out in the sky.

Is there any hope at all that we may find Christ? Will our searching bring us to Him?

Herod missed seeing the Child, but the Wise Men and the shepherds were not disappointed in their quests. There is a chance that we shall miss Him altogether. It could be that we shall become so encumbered in our multitude of Yuletime activities that we shall be exhausted before we get to Bethlehem. Or maybe we shall let others search for Him for us, and await whatever word they may bring back. This is what Herod did, and the Wise Men bypassed him on their journey home. Or our hard hearts may be so flooded with doubt and skepticism that we shall hesitate to believe with our minds what our spirits affirm.

> *He may be our constant Companion and everliving Friend.*

Of this we may be certain: if we fail to find Christ in this season of joyous faith, we shall have little more than a synthetic Christmas. What a tragedy to exchange cards, gifts, and greetings, but not to know the radiance of stardust!

To be sure, we shall not now find Him in a crib. He was a Child for only a handful of fleeting years. Nor shall we find Him walking along some hallowed pathway in Palestine. He long since passed from the familiar shores of Galilee. Nor shall we gaze at Him upon a cross or within the dark recesses of a tomb. The cross claimed Him for a narrow day, and the tomb could not bind Him.

Of none other whose name is inscribed upon the annals of history is it said that, having been raised from the dead, He dieth no more. ". . . death hath no more dominion over him" (Romans 6:9). The testimony and witness of Christianity is that Christ, though slain by spiritual astigmatism and malignant hate, defied death, and rose to everlasting life.

This is a mystery which befuddles our power of explanation and

interpretation. Yet, upon this truth, vindicated in the experience of many generations of believers, is established the gospel and the glory of our faith.

And of none other who has shared the garments of mortal flesh is it affirmed that He is a living Personality who may be our constant Companion and everliving Friend.

By faith Christ lives within our hearts, His Spirit is closer to us than our own hands and feet. He has assured us, "I am with you alway . . ." (Matthew 28:20). Paul wrote, ". . . I live; yet not I, but Christ liveth in me . . ." (Galatians 2:20). ". . . we dwell in him, and he in us . . ." (1 John 4:13). Katharine Lee Bates telescopes a vast truth into four brief lines:

> *Not the Christ in the manger,*
> *Not the Christ on the Cross;*
> *But the Christ in the soul,*
> *When all but love is lost.*

This is the supreme and redeeming word which the Christmas message should bring home to each of us: not that we must still seek a Babe in a crib He outgrew, nor a Teacher who has now moved from the classrooms of Galilee, nor an exhausted Saviour stretched upon a cross, nor a Leader wrapped in the soft linens of death, but rather ". . . Christ in you, the hope of glory" (Colossians 1:27).

—CHARLES L. ALLEN and CHARLES L. WALLIS
from *Christmas In Our Hearts*

Making a Home in Nazareth

When King Herod was dead, an angel came to Joseph again, and said he might now go to Jerusalem, and not be afraid for the child's sake. So Joseph and Mary, and her Son Jesus Christ (who are commonly called The Holy Family) traveled towards Jerusalem; but hearing on

the way that King Herod's son was the new King, and fearing that he, too, might want to hurt the child, they turned out of the way, and went to live in Nazareth. They lived there, until Jesus Christ was twelve years old.

—Charles Dickens
from *The Life of Our Lord*

CHARLES DICKENS (1812–1870)—Born in the heart of the industrial era, Charles Dickens' life is loosely delineated in his *David Copperfield*. He wrote many novels over the course of his life of which many were published as a series in periodicals. From the 1840's, he spent much time travelling and campaigning against many of the social evils of his time. In addition, he gave talks, readings, wrote pamphlets, plays, letters, and traveled extensively abroad. He also lectured in America for a time. Toward the end of his travels, he collapsed in a performance and experienced a stroke shortly thereafter. Dickens had asked that when he died he be buried "in an inexpensive, unostentatious, and strictly private manner." Here, in his writings on the story of Jesus in *The Life of Our Lord*, his faith is exhibited as he rewrites the narrative solely for his children. Later, this book was published so that all children might know the life and teachings of Jesus Christ.

CHAPTER · TEN

Simeon and Anna
Proclaim the Christ Child

UKE 2:25–38
²⁵And behold, there was a man in Jerusalem whose name was Simeon, and this man was just and devout, waiting for the Consolation of Israel, and the Holy Spirit was upon him. ²⁶And it had been revealed to him by the Holy Spirit that he would not see death before he had seen the Lord's Christ. ²⁷So he came by the Spirit into the temple. And when the parents brought in the Child Jesus, to do for Him according to the custom of the law, ²⁸he took Him up in his arms and blessed God and said:

> ²⁹ "Lord, now You are letting Your servant depart in peace,
>   According to Your word;
> ³⁰ For my eyes have seen Your salvation
> ³¹ Which You have prepared before the face of all peoples,
> ³² A light to bring revelation to the Gentiles,
>   And the glory of Your people Israel."

³³And Joseph and His mother marveled at those things which were spoken of Him. ³⁴Then Simeon blessed them, and said to Mary His mother, "Behold, this Child is destined for the fall and rising of many in Israel, and for a sign which will be spoken against ³⁵"(yes, a sword will pierce through your own soul also), that the thoughts of many hearts may be revealed."

³⁶Now there was one, Anna, a prophetess, the daughter of Phanuel, of the tribe of Asher. She was of a great age, and had lived with a husband seven years from her virginity; ³⁷and this woman was a widow of about eighty-four years, who did not depart from the temple, but served God with fastings and prayers night and day. ³⁸And coming in that instant she gave thanks to the Lord, and spoke of Him to all those who looked for redemption in Jerusalem.

A Song for Simeon

Lord, the Roman hyacinths are blooming in bowls and
The winter sun creeps by the snow hills;
The stubborn season has made stand.
My life is light, waiting for the death wind,
Like a feather on the back of my hand.
Dust in the sunlight and memory in corners
Wait for the wind that chills toward the dead land.

Grant us thy peace.
I have walked many years in this city,
Kept faith and fast, provided for the poor,
Have taken and given honour and ease.
There went never any rejected from my door.
Who shall remember my house, where shall live my
    children's children
When the time of sorrow is come?
They will take to the goat's path, and the fox's home,
Fleeing from the foreign faces and the foreign swords.

Before the time of cords and scourges and
    lamentation Grant us thy peace.
Before the stations of the mountain of desolation,
Before the certain hour of maternal sorrow,
Now at this birth season of decease,
Let the Infant, the still unspeaking and unspoken
    Word, Grant Israel's consolation
To one who has eighty years and no tomorrow.

According to thy word.
They shall praise Thee and suffer in every generation
With glory and derision,
Light upon light, mounting the saints' stair.

Not for me the martyrdom, the ecstasy of thought
   and prayer,
Not for me the ultimate vision.
Grant me thy peace.
(And a sword shall pierce thy heart, Thine also).
I am tired with my own life and the lives of those
   after me,
I am dying in my own death and the deaths of those
   after me.
Let thy servant depart,
Having seen thy salvation.

—T. S. ELIOT
from *Collected Poems*

T. S. ELIOT (1888–1965)—Born into a distinguished family of Puritan descendents, Eliot returned to his roots in Massachusetts beginning his undergraduate studies at Harvard University. Upon this completion, he pursued graduate work at Harvard, Sorbonne, Marburg, and Oxford. During this time he met both Ezra Pound and Vivian Haigh-Wood. The former became a lifelong friend and the latter his first wife. T. S. Eliot and his wife lived in London where he taught while writing reviews and composing poetry. Unfortunately, their marriage struggled to survive through various issues. Though he quit teaching to pursue banking, his passion for writing and editing continued. Unfortunately, mental illnesses plagued both him and his wife, and both spent time in mental institutions. It was there that he wrote *The Wasteland*. Shortly thereafter, Eliot was appointed for the Charles Eliot Norton professorship at Harvard and subsequently lectured at major universities throughout the United States. He later remarried Valerie Fletcher and had a happier and healthier marriage. In 1948 Eliot received both the Nobel Prize for Literature and the Order of Merit by George VI, augmenting his stature as a celebrated literary figure which he maintained until his death in 1965. Eliot is buried in Poet's Corner of Westminster Abbey.

The Ancients

The old man awoke to find himself in that in-between time when darkness has not fully given way to dawn. He lay there and watched for a few minutes as the shapes around him, gray and shrouded, gradually, imperceptibly, began to take on form and color.

"Simeon," he muttered to himself as he lifted his aching body off the sleeping mat, "you need more rest. More rest." Perhaps he would not go to the temple this morning. He would say his prayers like a faithful son of Israel and save his rusty knees the walk into town.

Why, he wondered, did people sleep less and less as they grew older? It seemed to him that an ancient body would need more hours of restoration, not fewer. It was something he fully intended to speak to the Almighty about when the two of them came face to face. He hoped it would be soon.

> *He, after all, would live to see the Chosen One.*

He shuffled to the ewer and bowl that sat on a table at the edge of the room and splashed his face with cold water. *Soon,* he thought—a ritual morning prayer these past few years, as his body grew wearier and stiffer by the day. *Soon, O God of the Universe, Lord Almighty. Soon.*

Years ago, God had revealed to Simeon through the Spirit that he would not die until he had beheld the Messiah face to face. At the time, Simeon had thought himself the most blessed among men—he, after all, would live to see the Chosen One. But as the years dragged by and no Messiah was forthcoming, Simeon began to wonder. He never doubted the voice of the Almighty—God had spoken too clearly to allow for any misgivings. But he had begun to believe that the promise was an evidence of God's mysterious sense of humor: how long would the Lord have to keep him alive to see the prophecy fulfilled? As long as Methuselah—or longer?

Simeon dressed, draped his prayer shawl over his head, and went outside to present his morning litany. The sun was rising through broken clouds, and the air held a chill. He steeled himself against a shiver and began to pray: "Blessed art thou, Lord of the Universe, Creator of heaven and earth . . ."

Simeon halted, arrested by the incredible beauty of the sunlight shafting through the clouds over the bright white buildings of Jerusalem. It almost looked as if God were reaching out from the heavens, pointing down to the very place where he stood.

Then a voice whispered in his mind: *This is the day.*

"This is the day that the Lord has made; let us rejoice and be glad

in it," Simeon murmured, continuing to pray as his mind progressed through the Psalm. "Blessed is the one who comes in the name of the Lord . . ."

This is the day, the voice repeated. *The One who comes in the name of the Lord comes today.*

"The Lord is God, and has given us light," Simeon persisted.

The Light has dawned, the voice whispered. *The new day is at hand. This is the day.*

Suddenly the truth pierced through to Simeon's mind. *This is the day. The Light has dawned. The One who comes in the name of the Lord comes today.* His heart began to race, and despite the chill of the morning, a bead of sweat formed across his neck and trickled down his spine. *Today?*

He muttered a hurried "Omaine," trusted God to understand his haste, and rushed inside the house to retrieve his cloak. He had to get to the temple. Now.

When he reached the temple, a circumcision was already in progress. Simeon watched as a young girl and her powerfully-built husband presented their infant boy for the ritual. The girl, he noticed, turned her head aside when the cut was made, cringing when her son began to cry. The man stood silent and reverent, watching. When the ceremony was finished, the father scooped the tiny babe up in his massive arms and comforted him, then handed him to his mother.

> *Who was he to resist the nudging of the Spirit?*

Simeon smiled. A nice little family—obviously poor, but faithful. How it warmed his old heart to see the younger generation being true to their heritage, true to their God! He looked past them, his eyes scanning the temple for some sign of the Anointed One. He would no doubt be a person of some importance, easily recognizable . . .

Blessed is the One who comes in the name of the Lord.

Simeon frowned. Surely God could not mean the bawling infant of this poverty-stricken couple? He shook his head. No. *Blessed is the One who comes,* the voice repeated. *Blessed. Blessed.*

Well. This was not at all what Simeon had envisioned, but who was

he to resist the nudging of the Spirit? He walked forward and looked down into the face of the child.

The baby had grown quiet, calmed by his mother's nearness. Tears still streaked his round little face, but his eyes opened in an expression of wonder. Without warning, Simeon's heart melted and he reached out a quivering hand toward the baby's head.

Anna stayed in the temple night and day.

"His name is Jesus," the young mother said quietly. "Would you like to hold him?"

Simeon opened his arms and gathered the infant to his breast. At the first touch, a jolt went through him, like liquid warmth filling his veins and pumping strength and renewed faith into his heart. He lifted the baby up, and as tears coursed down his cheeks and lodged in his beard, Simeon began to speak:

"Lord, may your servant now depart in peace, according to your word. For my eyes have seen your salvation, prepared in the presence of all the people—a light to enlighten the Gentiles, and the glory of your people Israel."

He turned and saw the young couple standing by silently, their eyes wide. "The blessing of Almighty God be upon you," Simeon murmured. "This child is destined for the falling and rising of many in Israel, and as a sign to be opposed. The inner thoughts of many will be revealed by him, and a sword will pierce your own heart as well."

The girl stared at him. She could not know, not at this moment, what the years to come held for her and her son. Perhaps it was just as well. God had promised that Simeon would live to see the Messiah face to face. That promise had now been fulfilled. But for some reason he only vaguely understood, Simeon hoped above all hope that the promise did *not* include living to watch the child's future unfold.

For a long time Simeon stood there, able to say no more, until a gentle tug at his sleeve brought him back to the present. He turned to see a withered old face looking over his shoulder.

It was Anna, the prophetess. Older than Simeon—if such a thing were possible—she had served in the temple for more than seventy years. She had been married once, long ago, but only for a few short

years, and ever after that had remained a widow. She stayed in the temple night and day. Most people thought her a little odd—she fasted and prayed and worshiped, and as far as he knew, had never set foot outside the temple doors. Simeon had never paid her much mind, but now, the expression in her eyes told him everything, She, too, had received a word from the Lord. And on this day, her promise also had been fulfilled.

She gazed first at the child, and then at Simeon. "He is the Promised One," she murmured. It was not a question.

Simeon nodded, placed the child in her arms, and stepped aside as Anna began to sing and worship God: "Hear O Jerusalem, sing and be glad. Redemption has come this day to the house of Israel . . ."

When the prophetess was finished, she handed the child back to his mother and wandered off into the temple. Simeon could hear her in the distance, speaking excitedly to everyone she passed, pointing back toward them and telling them that the Promise of the Ages had at long last been fulfilled. No one, it seemed, paid much attention to her words. She was just Anna, the crazy old woman who lived in the temple.

The young couple, still looking a bit dazed, took their son, received Simeon's blessing, and went to offer their sacrifice according to the law—a pair of turtle doves and two young pigeons. The poor man's offering.

> *The Promise of the Ages had at long last been fulfilled.*

All the way home, Simeon thought about what he had seen this day. An ordinary infant, to all appearances, whom the hand of God had touched. The Messiah. The Chosen One. God's Anointed. It had finally happened.

He went into his house, removed his cloak, and lay down. He had to admit that he didn't feel quite so old anymore. His joints seemed to work a little better on the walk home, and he wasn't as winded by the time he reached his door. But still, he was tired—that wonderful, relaxing kind of tired that comes at the end of a fulfilling day.

Never again would he pray, *Soon, Lord. Soon.* From this day forth his prayer would be, *Thank you, Lord. Thank you.*

"Master, may your servant now depart in peace," he murmured. "For my eyes have seen your salvation . . ."

And then, before he could finish his thought, Simeon fell asleep.

—PENELOPE STOKES
from *The Miracle of the Christmas Child*

Narrative of the Story in Luke:
Simeon and Anna Retold

When Jesus was six weeks old, Mary and Joseph brought Him to the Temple at Jerusalem to present Him to the Lord. They did this out of obedience to the law of God in the Scriptures that says all firstborn males are holy to the Lord and are to be set apart for a special purpose. Also, the forty days of Mary's purification were over, and she was required to offer a young lamb as a burnt offering. Because they were poor and could not afford a lamb, she was permitted to offer a pair of turtledoves instead. When that was completed, she and Joseph entered the Temple court to have the Baby dedicated.

> *"We've come to present our firstborn Child."*

"We are Mary and Joseph of Nazareth," explained Joseph to the priest. "We've come to present our firstborn Child."

Immediately, an elderly man called out from afar.

"Wait! Please wait!" he shouted as he ran up to Mary and Joseph as fast as his frail legs could carry him. He took the child out of Mary's arm.

"Praise be to God, I recognize Him," said the old man, looking at the face of Jesus. "He is the Holy One."

Tears filled the old man's eyes and spilled down his cheeks as he embraced the child and looked toward heaven.

"Lord, You are letting me die in peace just as You promised," he prayed. "Today my eyes have seen Your salvation which you have given to all people. This Child is a light to bring revelation to the Gentiles and glory to the people of Israel."

Joseph and Mary looked at each other in amazement over yet another prophetic confirmation of who this Child was.

"I'm sorry, let me introduce myself," the old man said to Joseph. "My name is Simeon. For years I have been waiting for the coming of the Messiah, the Consolation of Israel, the One who will save us. The Lord revealed to me that I would not die before I saw Him."

Turning to Mary, he looked her directly in the eyes. "This Child is destined for the fall and rising of many in Israel," he said to her. "Though a sword will pierce your soul, you have been entrusted with His care. Through Him hearts will be revealed, and men will speak against Him everywhere."

Mary looked at Joseph with grave concern, and he drew her close to him. This was another sign that there would be difficult times ahead.

"What my eyes have seen, the Spirit reveals to be the Child of the Promise of God," declared Simeon in a loud voice for all to hear. "Though this Promise seems small and fragile, He will be filled with the power of the Lord. Some will receive Him and some will reject Him, but He will never be ignored. He is the Lord."

Many people stopped what they were doing to listen. Mary and Joseph hung on Simeon's every word.

"This Child is the Light of the World, the Savior, Messiah and King," Simeon continued, his voice full, rich and warm. "Now I can depart in peace because of what my eyes have seen."

From across the courtyard the voice of an elderly woman rose up so strongly that it drew the attention of everyone standing around. "Lord, I have seen Your salvation," she declared. "Praise to You, O God, for this Blessed Child."

> *This Child is a light to bring revelation to the Gentiles.*

"This is Anna, a prophetess," explained Simeon as the woman made her way to them. "She has not left the Temple in many years. She prays and worships night and day, and you can trust that she hears from God."

Anna's advanced age, plus the depth of her experience and wisdom, were written on her kind and beautiful face. Some of Anna's family mem-

bers were Mary and Joseph's neighbors, people who were said to be blessed with joy, happiness, and strength. Anna clearly exhibited all three.

"This is the long-awaited Messiah!" Anna announced to everyone in the vicinity, and a crowd quickly gathered.

Anna knew the Scripture better than any woman, and she had been teaching younger women for years, showing them how to seek God and know His Word. A devoted woman of prayer, Anna strove to honor and serve the Lord in all she did. She had been married nearly seven years before her husband died, and had been a widow for decades. Now quite old, she lived at the Temple, dedicating her life to God. Every-

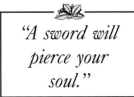

"A sword will pierce your soul."

one knew Anna and no one could deny the power of God upon her. She recognized that God's reward for her years of service had come in this one moment.

"What my eyes have seen, the Spirit reveals to be the long-awaited Son of God," she declared for all to hear. "He is the grand fulfillment of all prophecy. No longer just a silent dream, He has come here to redeem anyone who seeks to know Him." The people who had gathered around began to praise God boldly.

"He is the Light of the World, the Savior, Messiah, and King." Anna's voice rose above the noise of the crowd. "Now I can depart in peace because of what my eyes have seen."

The singing of praise, the shouts of joy, the unmistakable sense of God's presence in this very public declaration of who this Child was, all affected Mary deeply. The words Anna and Simeon spoke melted over her soul like a soothing balm.

Since that day in the Temple, Mary had not been able to forget Simeon's words. A sword will pierce your soul, she heard over and over in her mind.

"O God," she prayed out loud as she gazed at the contented face of her Son. "Protect Him from His enemies. Keep us all safe. Guide us as You always have."

—STORMIE OMARTIAN
from *Child of the Promise*

Advent

The sky is deep above the hill,
The silent stars, the frozen tree,
The world so still!

Builder of stars beyond our sight,
Touch our hearts that are so cold
With fire and light

That fire may leap from heart to heart
Across the reaches of the dark!
Shatter the night!

One master and one lasting home!
Awake and kindle, rise to praise!

The Lord will come!

—JANE T. CLEMENT
from *Behold the Star*

The Presentation in the Temple

Simeon the just and the devout
Who frequent in the fane
Had for the Savior waited long,
But waited still in vain.

Came Heaven-directed at the hour
When Mary held her Son;
He stretched forth his aged arms
While tears of gladness run:

With holy joy upon his face
The good old father smiled,
While fondly in his withered arm
He clasped the Promised Child.

'At last my arms embrace my Lord;
Not let their vigor cease;
At last my eyes my Saviour see,
Now let them close in peace;

'The star of glory in the land
Hath now begun to shine;
The morning that shall gild the globe
Breaks on these eyes of mine!'

      —MICHAEL BRUCE
        from Philip Law's *Saviour: The Life of*
        Christ in Words and Paintings

Hymn on Simeon

Das Knäblein nach acht Tagen
After eight days, the baby boy

Ward gen Jerusalem
was carried to Jerusalem,

Zum Gotteshaus getragen
to the house of God,

Vom Stall in Bethlehem.
from the stall in Bethlehem.

Da kommt ein Greis geschritten,
There comes striding an old man,

Der fromme Simeon,
the pious Simeon;

Er nimmt in Tempels Mitten
in the middle of the temple he takes

Vom Mutterarm den Sohn;
the son from his mother's arms.

Vom Angesicht des Alten
From the face of the old man

Ein Strahl der Freude bricht,
beams bright joy;

Er preiset Gottes Walten	he praises God's ways,
Weissagungsvoll und spricht:	full of prophecy, and says:
"Nun lässest du in Frieden,	"Now, permit your servant
Herr, deinen Diener gehn,	to depart in peace, Lord,
Da du mir noch beschieden,	for you have allowed
Den Heiland anzusehn,	me to see the Saviour,
Den du der Welt gesendet,	whom you sent into the world
Daß er dem Heidentum	to bestow upon the Gentiles
Des Lichtes Helle spendet	the brightness of your light,
Zu deines Volkes Ruhm!"	to the glory of your people!"
Mit froh erstaunten Sinnen	With happily astonished minds,
Vernimmt's der Eltern Paar,	the pair of parents listen,
Dann tragen sie von hinnen	then leave, carrying away
Das Knäblein wunderbar.	the wondrous infant boy.

—PETER CORNELIUS
Translations to English by
Emily Ezust

On the Character of Simeon

One of the devout witnesses to Jesus in the Lucan infancy account is Simeon. As an old man, he exemplified one who served the Lord and was content to be used by Him until the Lord took him home. Told that he would not see death until he beheld the Lord's Christ, Simeon offered praise to the child and predicted what the new born's career would be like. The prophet then was ready for the Lord to bring him to heaven, his watch completed with him having served God faithfully. He is the first person in Luke's Gospel to predict that Jesus would be a blessing to Gentiles, as well as Jews, even though he himself was awaiting the deliverance of Israel. He also was the first to predict Jesus' suffering, as he warned Mary of her pain at what Jesus would

experience. Simeon was a faithful servant of God who told what God was doing, but did so with compassion and openness to God's working broadly among all types of people.

—PAUL D. GARDNER
from *Encyclopedia of Bible Characters*

On the Character of Anna
(Hebrew = "grace")

When Anna was 84 years old (actually debated by scholars as to whether or not she was actually 84 years old or had been widowed for 84 years. The latter is the most widely accepted making her somewhere around age 104), an event occurred which adorned her with purpose. She was at the Temple during the presentation of the child Jesus: the long-awaited Messiah. Anna publicly gave thanks to God and proclaimed Good News about her Redeemer. The account of Anna and Simeon in the same passage reveal the existence of people who were trusting him to fulfill his promise of sending a Savior King.

—PAUL D. GARDNER
from *Encyclopedia of Bible Characters*

O Zion Open Wide your Gates

O Zion, open wide thy gates,
Let figures disappear;
A Priest and Victim, both in One,
The Truth Himself, is here.

No more the simple flock shall bleed;
Behold, the Father's Son
Himself to His own altar comes
For sinners to atone.

Conscious of hidden deity,
The lowly virgin brings
Her newborn Babe, with two young doves,
Her humble offerings.

The aged Simeon sees at last
His Lord, so long desired,
And Anna welcomes Israel's hope,
With holy rapture fired.

But silent knelt the mother blest
Of the yet silent Word,
And pondering all things in her heart,
With speechless praise adored.

All glory to the Father be,
All glory to the Son,
All glory, Holy Ghost, to Thee,
While endless ages run.

Simeon: "God Hears"

There was nothing special about Simeon that qualified him to take up the Christ child in his arms and bless Him. To our knowledge he was not an ordained religious leader and he had no credentials or special authority. He was simply a 'just and devout' man who had a close walk with the Holy Spirit.

Thus, Simeon, whose name means, "God hears", is an example of how God honors those who engage in lifetimes of quiet prayer and constant watchfulness. Simeon was a man of patient faith, yet his wait for the Messiah must have seemed interminable. He likely had many opportunities for doubt, as numerous would-be Messiahs sounded false alarms in the land.

Yet somehow he knew that the Redeemer would first come, not as

a great, heavenly champion wrapped in banners of nationalism, nor with a political agenda of violence, but as a baby carried in the arms of his parents. His kingdom would prove to be a stumbling block to some and the Rock of Salvation to others, both Jew and Gentile. Simeon also knew that the young couple standing before him would be hurt by the controversy that would eventually surround their Son.

—JACK MILES
from *Christ: A Crisis in the Life of God*

JACK MILES (1942–   )—Writer of the Pulitzer Prize winning, *God: A Biography,* Jack has written many pieces that have appeared in the *Atlantic Monthly,* the *New York Times,* and the *Boston Globe.* He has served for ten years as the literary editor and a member of the editorial board of the *Los Angeles Times.* He received a Ph.D. in Near Eastern languages from Harvard University, and he has served as a Regents Lecturer at the University of California, director of the Humanities Center at Claremont Graduate University, and visiting professor of humanities at the California Institute of Technology. Currently, he is the senior advisor to the president of the J. Paul Getty Trust, a foundation supporting art and scholarship. He and his wife and daughter now live in Southern California.

Our Days, Alas! Our Mortal Days

Our days, alas! our mortal days
Are short and wretched too;
Evil and few, the patriarch says,
And well the patriarch knew.

'Tis but at best a narrow bound
That Heaven allows to men,
And pains and sins run through the round
Of threescore years and ten.

Well, if ye must be sad and few,
Run on, my days, in haste.
Moments of sin, and months of woe,
Ye cannot fly too fast.

Let Heavenly Love prepare my soul
And call her to the skies,
Where years of long salvation roll,
And glory never dies.

The King of Glory sends his Son
To make his entrance on this earth;
Behold the midnight bright as noon,
And heavenly hosts declare his birth.

About the young Redeemer's head
What wonders and what glories meet!
An unknown star arose, and led
The eastern sages to his feet.

Simeon and Anna both conspire
The infant-Saviour to proclaim;
Inward they felt the sacred fire,
And blessed the babe, and owned his name.

Let Jews and Greeks blaspheme aloud,
And treat the holy child with scorn;
Our souls adore the eternal God
Who condescended to be born.

—ISAAC WATTS

The Story of Anna

The Prophet is old and stooped over, her face covered with wrinkles, like Mother Theresa. Her eyes are bright and clear, like a child's. She is beaming with excitement and obviously has something important to tell us. Her voice is quiet and peaceful, but also convinced and powerful. As she speaks she constantly looks up, searching for the next word which produced gaps in her speech, as age has produced gaps in her

teeth. The boundary between the present and eternity has long begun to dissolve for her.

ANNA THE PROPHET:

He's here!
What we're waiting for.

His parents came to the temple this morning!
Cutest little thing!

Every baby, we always wondered, is this the one?
Then we'd say, "Maybe the next one."

The Romans told us to stop.
They said, "We're it. Get used to it."

But all they had was soldiers, what could they do?
Make work for the gravediggers.
If that's all there is, why bother?
We don't need more dead bodies to bury.

We need people to pray.
It's the only thing that works.

I'm eighty-four years old.
People ask me why I don't give up.
I say, "I'm waiting."
They say, "What for?"
I say, "The same thing you are."

That's why you can't get on a train if you don't
have a ticket.
You wouldn't know when to get off.
People don't understand that.

They say, "What you see is what you get."
But what you see is what you're looking for.

Forget about the pie-in-the-sky-by-and-by stuff.
Dreams never turn out the way we think.

There's got to be real babies.
Somebody you can feel their heart beat.
Change their diapers.

People who pray understand.
The others mostly stand around and argue.

Whoever changed anything arguing?
The prayers, they're up to Yahweh,
Who knows what Yahweh can do?

That should make even the sourpusses happy.
Well, it's time for me to go now.
But you—you stay and have a party.

Sing a lot.
Kiss the girls,
Be happy.

It's gonna be a great time.

—Ivan J. Kauffman
from *He Was Here*

On Simeon and Anna

An unimpressive looking couple walked into a temple built for the very presence of God—and God had never been more present. No cloudy pillar. No consuming fire. The Word made flesh first entered the temple wrapped in a baby blanket. His earthly parents lifted Him to His Father and, in essence, purchased Him from heaven—for a while—for a lost world. One day that Baby would buy them from earth for the glory of heaven.

Two deeply discerning people were at the temple the day Jesus was presented . . . They both were watching and waiting for the Messiah. In a spiritual sense, the same principle is true for us. God constantly reveals His glory to us. The more we prepare ourselves through devotion, prayer, worship, watching, and expectantly waiting, the more likely we will be to see the glory of God.

God emphasized that the road to redemption would be costly and confrontational. Simeon didn't proclaim only the joy of Jesus as the Lord's Christ. He also spoke painful prophecy. Imagine all that Mary had experienced during the past year. How could she have understood that the infant Son of God would one day cause the piercing of her own soul? Surely the greatest callings of God are the gravest as well.

—BETH MOORE
from *Jesus, the One and Only*

O Come, O Come Emmanuel

O come, O come, Emmanuel,
And ransom captive Israel,
That mourns in lonely exile here
Until the Son of God appear.

Refrain
Rejoice! Rejoice!
Emmanuel shall come to thee, O Israel.

O come, Thou Wisdom from on high,
Who orderest all things mightily;
To us the path of knowledge show,
And teach us in her ways to go.

Refrain

O come, Thou Rod of Jesse, free
Thine own from Satan's tyranny;

From depths of hell Thy people save,
And give them victory over the grave.

Refrain

O come, Thou Day—spring, come and cheer
Our spirits by Thine advent here;
Disperse the gloomy clouds of night,
And death's dark shadows put to flight.

Refrain

O come, thou Key of David, come,
And open wide our heavenly home;
Make safe the way that leads on high,
And close the path to misery.

Refrain

O come, O come, great Lord of might,
Who to Thy tribes on Sinai's height
In ancient times once gave the law
In cloud and majesty and awe.

Refrain

O come, Thou Root of Jesse's tree,
An ensign of Thy people be;
Before Thee rulers silent fall;
All peoples on Thy mercy call.

Refrain

O come, Desire of Nations, bind
In one the hearts of all mankind;
Bid Thou our sad divisions cease,
And be Thyself our King of Peace.

Refrain

"O COME, O COME EMMANUEL"—One of the most ancient Christmas carols, the hymnal music was used in church services beginning in the 12th century. It was sung in a series of short stanzas (called "The Seven O's"), with each section praising the coming of the Savior by a different name (Wisdom, Lord, etc.) In the 18th century, the hymn was cut down to five stanzas, with an added refrain. In 1851, it was published in Dr. John Neale's *Medieval Hymnal* where he translated the Latin text. *Immanuel* is the name of the Messiah as prophesied by the Old Testament prophet, Isaiah.

The Wait

Epworth

Every Sunday for nearly three years Walter had a routine. Just before 10:00 AM he would open the doors to Epworth and prepare the church for worship. If the weather was cold, he would build a fire in the old wood stove. If it was hot, he would open all the windows and distribute the hand fans with a picture of Jesus on one side and an ad for a local funeral home on the other.

> *God had a divine purpose for his life.*

Next, Walter would open the Bible located on top of the wooden pulpit and read the selected scripture for that week. Then it would be time for prayer. Often there were folks in the community included on Walter's list. The latest national and world news would be mentioned. But always, Walter ended every prayer with a plea for God to remember and bless his beloved church.

Every Sunday, Walter had a routine but what makes this story so unique is that with very few exceptions, Walter began and ended the Sunday morning worship service . . . alone. Alone? Why? Many years ago, Epworth church was built on land donated by a neighboring farmer but if for any reason they stopped meeting regularly, if Walter stopped opening the church doors every Sunday the property would revert to the original owners . . . Epworth church would cease to exist.

So what is the big deal? If Walter is the only one bothering to attend, let him go somewhere else or stay at home. Why not face the

inevitable and allow Epworth to quietly disappear? What harm would it do? For Walter, it was a big deal. God had a divine purpose for his life and for the church he loved. But for now, Walter must be patient, be faithful . . . and wait? Wait for what?

"To wait" is not one of my favorite verbs. I define wait as "waste" . . . as in waste of time. I become frustrated just waiting in line at a grocery store. I bought a new computer because it claimed to be faster, with less waiting time. So, according to my definition of wait, Walter was wasting his time at Epworth, refusing to face reality by waiting for something to happen that would never happen.

> *Generations died never knowing the promised Messiah of God.*

Walter waited. Not me! I would move on. So would most of you. Yet, you and I, in our impatience and lack of faith would have missed the miracle of Epworth church!

In another time

For nearly eight hundred years, prophets foretold the coming of the Messiah.

"But you, O Bethlehem Ephrathah are only a small village in Judah. Yet a ruler of Israel will come from you . . ." (Micah 5:2)

"All right then, the Lord himself will choose the sign. Look! The virgin will conceive a child! She will give birth to a son and will call him Immanuel God is with us." (Isaiah 7:14)

"But he was wounded and crushed for our sins. He was beaten that we might have peace. He was whipped and we were healed!" (Isaiah 53:5)

But for eight hundred long years the people of God waited . . . and waited . . . and waited . . .

Generations were born, grew up, lived, and died never knowing or seeing the promised Messiah of God. What were they waiting for? No one really knew. Yet, to fully value the significance of Christmas we must understand why "waiting" is such a necessary part of serving God.

In Luke, a man named Simeon who is described as righteous and devout spent most of his time in the temple . . . waiting. "He was filled with the Holy Spirit and he eagerly expected the Messiah to come . . ." (2:25) Day after day, year after year, Simeon was faithful in his task. Why?

In the same part of Luke, there was also a prophet named Anna. She became a widow at an early age and spent most of her adult life waiting: "She was now eighty-four years old. She never left the Temple but stayed there day and night, worshipping God with fasting and prayer." (2:37)

What were Anna and Simeon waiting for?

Return to Epworth and Jerusalem

Every Sunday for three years Walter opened the doors to Epworth church and worshipped . . . alone. Why? Why not face the inevitable and allow Epworth to die? Well, God had a divine purpose for Walter and the church he loved. So for now, Walter must be patient, be faithful, and wait. Simeon and Anna from chapter two of Luke anticipated seeing the Messiah foretold by prophets for hundreds of years. Meanwhile, day after day and year after year they both waited.

> *Waiting on God is essentially an eventful time of preparation and anticipation.*

Maybe it would help us to understand what is meant by the word, "wait"? My tendency is to think of waiting as idle time doing nothing such as waiting for a movie to start. Actually, waiting is more like receiving word that an honored guest will soon be visiting. You busily clean and decorate your house, prepare special foods, take a shower and search through the closet for just the right outfit. In other words . . . waiting on God is essentially an eventful time of preparation and anticipation.

—"I waited patiently for the Lord to help me and he turned to me and heard my cry." (Psalm 40:1) Waiting is learning to trust in God's leadership and competence.

—*"But those who wait on the Lord will find new strength. They will fly high on wings like eagles. They will run and not grow weary."* (Isaiah 40:31) Waiting renews your strength.

—*"This time he (Christ) will bring salvation to all those who are eagerly waiting for him."* (Hebrews 9:28) Waiting is a sign of faith and faith in Christ is the source of our salvation.

Simeon waited, filled with the Holy Spirit, expecting an honoured guest, the Messiah, to appear at any time. Anna waited by staying busy in the Temple day and night, worshipping God with fasting and prayer.

> *"Lord, now I can die in peace!"*

Walter waited by faithfully preparing his beloved Epworth church for worship each and every Sunday morning. God responded to Simeon, Anna, and Walter with a miracle.

One afternoon a young couple named Joseph and Mary came to the temple to offer their eight-day-old baby for dedication to God. "Simeon was there. He took the child in his arms and praised God, saying, 'Lord, now I can die in peace! As you promised me, I have seen the Saviour you have given to all people. He is a light to reveal God to the nations . . .'" (Luke 2:28–32) Anna came along, "just as Simeon was talking with Mary and Joseph and she began praising God. She talked about Jesus to everyone who had been waiting for the promised King . . ." (2:38)

Simeon and Anna were among the first to witness the Christ child and proclaim Him as the Messiah. Every year they are remembered and celebrated as a part of Christmas.

One Sunday morning a young family, new to the area visited Epworth and after meeting Walter joined him in worship. They found something unique about this little church nestled among the trees and the old man who faithfully opened her doors. On the following Sunday they came back, and within a few weeks the children were bringing friends. At year's end a minister was hired.

Today, Epworth is a small family church situated between several farms and hidden among the trees. Every summer they offer Vacation Bible School for the neighbourhood and each Christmas is celebrated

with a pageant performed by the children. Many of the original family have died and some of the children have moved away, but the miracle of Epworth has never been forgotten.

On the first Sunday of August, people come from across the U.S. to visit the church of their youth and relive the miracle of the old man who refused to let his beloved church die. The worship service is followed by a picnic on the church grounds. While the children are playing and the adults are eating, you may notice a family wandering over to the nearby cemetery. If you listen carefully you'll hear a parent telling her child, "Let me tell you a story about Walter . . ."

The example of Simeon, Anna, and Walter are a reminder that we must express our faith in God through the power of . . . waiting!

So no matter how hard it may be as a leader for changes to take place, for growth to occur, and for God's Spirit to move, we have Simeon, Anna, and Walter to remind of the power behind faithfulness and . . . waiting!

—from *Just a Minute*

Words from an Old Spanish Carol

Shall I tell you who will come
To Bethlehem on Christmas morn,
Who will kneel them gently down
Before the Lord, new-born?

One small fish from the river,
With scales of red, red gold,
One wild bee from the heather,
One grey lamb from the fold,
One ox from the high pasture,
One black bull from the herd,
One goatling from the far hills,
One white, white bird.

And many children—God give them grace,
Bringing tall candles to light Mary's face.

Shall I tell you who will come
  To Bethlehem on Christmas morn,
Who will kneel them gently down
  Before the Lord, new-born?

—from *Behold that Star*

The Name of Jesus

Untethered by time, he sees us all. From the backwoods of Virginia to the business district of London; from the Vikings to the astronauts, from the cave-dwellers to the kings, from the hut-builders to the finger-pointers to the rock-stackers, he sees us. Vagabonds and ragamuffins all, he saw us before we were born.

> *In the end they called him Jesus, since that's what the angel said.*

And he loves what he sees. Flooded by emotion. Overcome by pride, the Starmaker turns to us, one by one, and says, "You are my child. I love you dearly. I'm aware that someday you'll turn from me and walk away. But I want you to know, I've already provided you a way back."

And to prove it, he did something extraordinary.

Stepping from the throne, he removed his robe of light and wrapped himself in skin: pigmented, human skin. The light of the universe entered a dark, wet womb. He who angels worship nestled himself in the placenta of a peasant, was birthed into the cold night, and then slept on cow's hay.

Mary didn't know whether to give him milk or give him praise, but she gave him both since he was, as near as she could figure, hungry and holy.

Joseph didn't know whether to call him Junior or Father. But in the end called him Jesus, since that's what the angel said and since he

didn't have the faintest idea what to name a God he could cradle in his arms.

Neither Mary nor Joseph said it as bluntly as my Sara, but don't you think their heads tilted and their minds wondered, "What in the world are you doing, God?" Or, better phrased, "God, what are you doing in the world?"

"Can anything make me stop loving you?" God asks. "Watch me speak your language, sleep on your earth, and feel your hurts. Behold the maker of sight and sound as he sneezes, coughs, and blows his nose. You wonder if I understand how you feel? Look into the dancing eyes of the kid in Nazareth; that's God walking to school. Ponder the toddler at Mary's table; that's God spilling his milk.

—MAX LUCADO
from *When God Whispers Your Name*

Acknowledgments

e have made every effort to locate the source for correct attribution to the publisher or writer. In the event that we did not provide the proper source, we welcome written documentation, and we will make corrections in future printings. If the material was not eligible for public domain, we selected quotations according to the generally accepted fair-use standards and practices. We greatly appreciate the publishers and authors who worked with us to create such a unique anthology about the birth of Christ. The following acknowledgments are offered for these contributions.

He Still Moves Stones, Max Lucado, 1999, W Publishing Group, Nashville, TN. All rights reserved.

Allen, Charles L. and Charles L. Wallis. *Christmas in Our Hearts.* Old Tappan: Fleming H. Revell Co., a division Baker Book House, 1977.

Beth Moore, JESUS, THE ONE AND ONLY (Lifeway Christian Resources 2000). All rights reserved. Used by permission.

When God Whispers Your Name, Max Lucado, 1999, W Publishing Group, Nashville, TN. All rights reserved.

Menashe. Samuel. "The Annunciation," in *The Niche Narrows: New and Selected Poems.* Chicago: Talisman Books, 2000. Used by permission of Samuel Menashe.

"The Annunciation," from AMAZING GRACE by Kathleen Norris, copyright © 1998 by Kathleen Norris. Used by permission of Riverhead Book, a division of Penguin Putnam, Inc.

Copyright © 1998 by Kathleen Norris. Original publication in *Amazing Grace.* Reprinted by permission of author.

From the book *The Lord* by Romano Guardini. Copyright © 1954 by Henry Regnery Publishing. All rights reserved. Reprinted by special permission of Regnery Publishing, Inc. Washington, D.C.

"The Miracle of the Christmas Child" by Penelope J. Stokes. Copyright 1999 by Penelope J. Stokes. Used by permission of J. Countryman, a division of Thomas Nelson, Inc.

"The Annunciation" from PARABLES AND PORTRAITS by STEPHEN MITCH-ELL. Copyright © 1990 by Stephen Mitchell. Reprinted by permission of HarperCollins Publishers Inc.

Craig, David. "Annunciation" in *A Widening Light: Poems of the Incarnation*, ed. Luci Shaw. Wheaton : Harold Shaw Publishers, 1984.

"Mary's Song" and "Made Flesh." Reprinted from *Polishing the Petoskey Stone.* Copyright © 1990 by Luci Shaw. Used by permission of Waterbrook Press, Colorado Springs, CO. All rights reserved.

Wiersbe, Warren. "Be Compassionate." © 1988 Cook Communications Ministries. *Discipline Them Love Them* by Betty Chase. Reprinted with permission. May not be further reproduced. All rights reserved.

Taken from WOMEN WHO MADE BIBLE HISTORY by HAROLD JOHN OCK-ENGA. Copyright © 1962 by Zondervan Publishing House. Used by permission of Zondervan.

"Vermeer" from PARABLES AND PORTRAITS by STEPHEN MITCHELL. Copyright © 1990 by Stephen Mitchell. Reprinted by permission of HarperCollins Publishers Inc.

Card, Michael (BW) and Scott Brasher (BW/ME). © 1993 Birdwing Music (ASCAP)/ Mole End Music (BW) (ASCAP). "The Love that I Bear."

"The Mother of God." Reprinted with the permission of Scribner, a Division of Simon & Schuster, Inc., from THE COLLECTED WORKS OF W. B. YEATS, Volume I: The Poems, Revised, edited by Richard J. Finneran. Copyright © 1933 by The Macmillan Company; copyright renewed 1961 by Bertha Georgie Yeats.

Yeats, W. B. "The Mother of God." Reprinted by permission of A. P. Watt Ltd. on behalf of Michael B. Yeats.

"Incarnation" and "Virgin Birth" from WISHFUL THINKING: A THEOLOGICAL ABC by FREDERICK BUECHNER. Copyright © 1973 by Frederick Buechner. Reprinted by permission of HarperCollins Publishers, Inc.

HOPE FOR EACH DAY by Billy Graham. Copyright © 2002 by Billy Graham. Used by permission of J. Countryman, a division of Thomas Nelson, Inc.

"The Nativity" from POEMS by C. S. Lewis, copyright © 1964 by the Executors of the Estate of C. S. Lewis and renewed 1992 by C. S. Lewis Pte. Ltd., reprinted by permission of Harcourt, Inc.

THE NATIVITY by C. S. Lewis copyright © Pte. Ltd. 1964. Extract reprinted by permission.

"The Maid-Servant at the Inn," from THE PORTABLE DOROTHY PARKER by Dorothy Parker, edited by Brendan Gill, copyright 1928, renewed © 1956 by Dorothy Parker. Used by permission of Viking Penguin, a division of Penguin Putnam Inc. Also by permission of Gerald Duckworth & Co. Ltd.

Finch, Rosalyn Hart. "Open My Heart" in *Guidepost's Prayers for Christmas*. Nashville, 2000. Used by permission of Rosalyn Hart Finch.

Cosmic Christmas, Max Lucado, 1997, W Publishing Group, Nashville, TN. All rights reserved.

From FOR THE TIME BEING by Annie Dillard, copyright © 1999 by Annie Dillard. Used by permission of Alfred A. Knopf, a division of Random House, Inc.

The Applause of Heaven, Max Lucado, 1999, W Publishing Group, Nashville, TN. All rights reserved.

Eckhart, Meister. *From Whom God Hid Nothing*. Franz Pfeiffer, trans. Boston: Shambala Publications. Copyright © 1954 by John M. Watkins.

The Tale of the Tardy Oxcart, Chuck Swindoll, 1998, W Publishing Group, Nashville, TN. All rights reserved.

Szymborska, Wislawa. SOUNDS, FEELINGS, THOUGHTS. Copyright © 1981 by Princeton University Press. Reprinted by permission of Princeton University Press.

"John I:14," translated by Willis Barnstone, copyright © 1999 by Maria Kodama; translation copyright © 1999 by Willis Barnstone, from SELECTED POEMS by Jorges Luis Borges, edited by Alexander Coleman. Used by permission of Viking Penguin, a division of Penguin Putnam.

Phillips, Ron. "Call Him Wonderful," in *The Spirit of Christmas*. Nashville: Thomas Nelson Publishers, 1999.

Tozer, A. W. *Christ the Eternal Son*. Pennsylvania: Christian Publications, Inc. 1991. Pages 14–16.

"Adoration of the Kings," by William Carlos Williams, from COLLECTED POEMS 1939–1962, VOLUME II, copyright © 1962 by William Carlos Williams. Reprinted by permission of New Directions Publishing Corp. Also by permission of Carcanet Press Limited.

"Journey of the Magi" from COLLECTED POEMS 1909–1962, by T. S. Eliot, copyright 1936 by Harcourt, Inc., copyright © 1964, 1963 by T. S. Eliot, reprinted by permission of the publisher.

"Star Song." Reprinted from *The Sighting*. Copyright © 1981 by Luci Shaw. Used by permission of Waterbrook Press, Colorado Springs, CO. All rights reserved.

"The Three Holy Kings: Legend" from THE BOOK OF IMAGES by Rainer Maria Rilke, translated by Edward Snow. Translation copyright © 1991 by Edward

Snow. Reprinted by permission of North Point Press, a division of Farrar, Straus, and Giroux, LLC.

Jennings, Elizabeth. "Words for the Magi" in *Consequently I Rejoice.* Published by Carcanet. Used by permission of David Higham Associates Limited.

Yeats, W. B. "The Magi." Reprinted by permission of A. P. Watt Ltd. on behalf of Michael B. Yeats.

From: *Home With A Heart,* By: James Dobson © 1996, Used by permission of Tyndale House Publishers, Inc. All rights reserved.

"The Gift" by William Carlos Williams, from COLLECTED POEMS 1939–1962, VOLUME II, copyright © 1962 by William Carlos Williams. Reprinted by permission of New Directions Publishing Corp. Also by permission of Carcanet Press Limited.

Excerpt from THE GOSPEL ACCORDING TO JESUS CHRIST, copyright © 1991 by Jose Saramago e Editorial Caminho S.A. Lisboa, English translation copyright © 1994 by Harcourt, Inc. reprinted by permission of Harcourt, Inc.

Taken from THE JESUS I NEVER KNEW by PHILIP D. YANCEY. Copyright © 1995 by Philip Yancey. Used by permission of Zondervan.

"A Song for Simeon" from COLLECTED POEMS 1909–1962, by T. S. Eliot, copyright 1963 by Harcourt, Inc., copyright © 1964, 1963 by T. S. Eliot, reprinted by permission of the publisher.

Taken from: *Child of the Promise,* Copyright © 2000 by Stormie Omartian, Published by Harvest House Publishers, Eugene, OR 97402, Used by permission.

Taken from *New International Encyclopedia of Bible Characters* by Paul D. Gardner. Copyright © 2001 by Paul D. Gardner. Used by permission of Zondervan.

Kauffman, Ivan J. "The Story of Anna" from *He Was There.* Grand Rapids: Baker Book House.

In the Grip of Grace, Max Lucado, 1996, W Publishing Group, Nashville, TN. All rights reserved.

"While the World Awaited," by R. Michael Cullinan. © 1996, Robert Cullinan.

"The Man Joseph," "Mother Mary," "Room In the Inn," "Wise Man," "Shepherd," by Sally Meyer. © 1997. All rights reserved. www.ofworth.com/ea/christmas_poems.htm

The Works of G. K. Chesterton, G. K. Chesterton, 1995. Reprinted by permission of Wordsworth Editions, Ltd., Hertfordshire, UK.

Hope For Each Day, Billy Graham, 2002. Excerpted from *Hope For Each Day, Unto the Hills,* and/or *Decision* magazine. W Publishing Group, Nashville, TN. All rights reserved.

Index of Authors

Alexander, Cecil F., 98, 172
Allen, Charles L, 9, 132, 161, 170, 186, 211, 253, 263
Ambrose of Milan, 130, 141
Anstice, Joseph, 118
Aquinas, St. Thomas, 137
Athanasius, 115

Barker, Elsa, 12
Barnett, Tommy, 165
Barth, Karl, 126
Blake, William, 139
Bonhoeffer, Dietrich, 76, 140
Borges, Jorge Luis, 134
Brasher, Scott, 74
Brooke, Rupert, 25
Browne, Sir Thomas, 155, 209
Bruce, Michael, 278
Buechner, Frederick, 76, 142
Byrom, John, 218

Card, Michael, 74
Chaucer, Geoffrey, 49
Chesterton, G. K., 7, 84, 116, 151, 184, 223
Clement, Jane T., 278
Coleridge, Samuel, 206
Cook, Joseph Simpson, 67
Cornelius, Peter, 279
Craig, David, 50

Crashaw, Richard, 210
Cullinan, R. Michael, 12

Dante, 27
Dickens, Charles, 147, 201, 247, 266
Dillard, Annie, 90
Dobson, James, 189
Dollar, Creflo A., 68
Donne, John, 20, 68, 87

Eckhart, Meister, 119
Eliot, T. S., 150, 269
Elliott, Emily E., 109

Farrar, Frederic, 241
Finch, Rosalyn Hart, 80

Gannett, William C., 72
Gardner, Paul D., 280, 281
Gerhardt, Paul, 110
Godolphin, Sydney, 148
Graham, Billy, 77, 256
Guardini, Romano, 33

Hagee, John, 29
Hardy, Thomas, 89
Hayford, Jack, 59
Herbert, George, 111, 169, 220
Hewitt, Eliza E., 213
Hopkins, Gerard Manley, 55, 146

Jennings, Elizabeth, 173
Jeremiah, David, 127
Jonson, Ben, 114

Kauffman, Ivan J., 284

Lewis, C. S., 78
Longfellow, Henry Wadsworth, 162, 204
Lucado, Max, 2, 16, 81, 113, 294
Luther, Martin, 54, 217

McCullough, Jackie, 47
McDonald, Mary M., 86
Menashe, Samuel, 19
Meyer, Sally, 11, 64, 82, 168, 215
Miles, Jack, 282
Milton, John, 99
Mitchell, Stephen, 42, 71
Moore, Beth, 14, 43, 286

Norris, Kathleen, 20

O. Henry, 193
Ockenga, Harold John, 65
Omartian, Stormie, 275

Parker, Dorothy, 80
Perry, Jean, 46
Phillips, Ron, 135
Prudentius, Aurelius, 227

Rahner, Karl, 138
Rilke, Rainer Maria, 13, 51, 61, 159, 202, 255
Robbins, Howard C., 93

Rossetti, Christina, 37, 109, 214
Rowe, George Stringer, 107

St. Germanus, 63
Saramago, Jose, 228
Sedulius, Caelius, 41
Sewall, Frank, 222
Shaw, Luci, 53, 143, 153
Skilton, A. L., 86
Southwell, Robert, 79, 131
Stevenson, Robert Louis, 221
Stokes, Penelope, 38, 250, 270
Suckling, Sir John, 97
Swindoll, Chuck, 125
Szymborska, Wislawa, 128

Tate, Nahum, 225
Tennyson, Alfred Lord, 126
Thring, Godfrey, 190
Toke, Emma L., 247
Tozer, A. W., 140

Van Dyke, Henry, 173
Vaughan, Henry, 94

Wallis, Charles L., 9, 132, 161, 170, 186, 211, 253, 263
Watts, Isaac, 201, 283
Wesley, Charles, 219
Wiersbe, Warren, 62
Williams, Theodore C., 211
Williams, William Carlos, 146, 192
Work, John W., 220
Wylie, Elinor, 258

Yancey, Philip, 259
Yeats, William Butler, 75, 189

Zwingli, Ulrich, 73

Index of Titles

Adoration of the Kings, The, 146, 192

Adoration of the Wise Men, The, 172

Advent (Clement), 278

Advent (Rossetti), 37, 109, 214

All Hail, Ye Little Martyr Flowers, 227

Ancients, The, 270

Angel Assured Mary That Nothing Is Impossible With God, The, 59

Angelic Encounter: Mary and Gabriel, The, 43

Annunciation (Craig), 50

Annunciation (Donne), 20, 68, 87

Annunciation (Norris), 20

Annunciation (Stokes), 38, 250, 270

Annunciation, The (Menashe), 19

Annunciation, The (Mitchell), 42, 71

Annunciation to Mary, 51

Annunciation to the Shepherds from Above, 202

As Shepherds Watched Their Flocks, 201

Be Compassionate, 62

Betrothal: A Commitment Remembered, 14, 43, 286

Birth of Christ, The, 126

Blessed Virgin Compared to the Air We Breathe, The, 55, 146

Born of Woman, 128

Burning Babe, The, 131

Child and the Shepherd, The, 222

Child in the Manger, 86

Christians, Awake, Salute the Happy Morn, 218

Christmas I, 111, 169, 220

Christmas II, 220

Christmas Carol, A (Coleridge), 206

Christmas Carol, A (Rossetti), 109

Christmas Is a Simple Story, 132

Christmas Memories, 189

Christmas Prayer, A, 221

Come Thou Redeemer of the Earth, 130, 141

Cradled in a Manger, Meanly, 107

Divine Comedy, The, 27

Divine Dawning, The, 138

Flight by Night, 253

From East to West, From Shore to Shore, 41

From the Eastern Mountains, 190

Gabriel's Questions, 16

Gentle Mary Laid Her Child, 67

Gift of the Magi, The, 193

Gift, The, 192

Glory to Thee, O Lord, 247
Go Tell It On the Mountain, 220
Good Tidings of Great Joy, 47
Great and Mighty Wonder, A, 63

Hark! The Herald Angels Sing, 219
Holy Mother, The, 33
Hymn, 148
Hymn on Simeon, 279
Hymn on the Nativity of My
  Saviour, A, 114

I Know of a Name, 46
Incarnation, 142
Incarnation Is No Compromise,
  The, 140
In the Lonely Midnight, 211

Jealousy of King Herod, The, 147,
  201, 247, 266
Jesus Is An Esteemed Name, 127
John 1:14 (1964), 134
Joseph, 7, 84, 116, 151, 184, 223
Joseph, Son of David, 9, 132, 161,
  170, 186, 211, 253, 263
Joseph's Prayer, 2, 16, 81, 113, 294
Joseph's Suspicion, 13, 51, 61, 159,
  202, 255
Journey of the Magi, 150, 269

Lamb, The, 139
Lauda Sion Salvatorem, 137
Love That I Bear, The, 74

Made Flesh, 143
Magi, The, 189
Maid-Servant at the Inn, The, 80
Making a Home in Nazareth, 266
Man Joseph, The, 11, 64, 82, 168,
  215
Mary and Gabriel, 25
Mary Model, The, 68
Mary's Song, 53, 143, 153

Mary's Visitation, 61
Massacre of the Innocents, The,
  228
Moonless Darkness, 146
Mother Mary, 64
Mother of God, The, 75, 189
Murder of the Innocents, The, 247

Name of a King, The, 135
Name of Jesus, The, 294
Narrative of the Story in Luke:
  Simeon and Anna Retold, 275
Nativity, The (Chesterton), 84
Nativity (Donne), 87
Nativity, The (Lewis), 78
Nativity, The (Vaughan), 94
New Prince, New Pomp, 79, 131
Night Flight into Egypt, 250
No Room at the Inn (Lucado), 81
No Room in the Inn (Skilton), 86
Now Yield We Thanks and Praise,
  93

O Come Redeemer of Mankind,
  141
O Jesus Christ, Thy Manger Is, 110
On Simeon and Anna, 286
On the Character of Anna, 281
On the Character of Simeon, 280,
  281
On the Favored One, the Virgin
  Mary, 65
On the Flight Into Egypt and the
  Massacre of the Innocents, 241
On the Incarnation (Barth), 126
On the Incarnation (Bonhoeffer),
  140
On the Incarnation of the Word,
  115
On the Morning of Christ's
  Nativity, 99

On the Mystery of God's Ways, 76, 140
On the Purity of Conception, 73
Once in Royal David's City, 98, 172
Open My Heart, 80
Other Wise Man, The, 173
Our Days, Alas! Our Mortal Days, 283
Oxen, The, 89

Peaceful the Wondrous Night, 213
Presentation in the Temple, The, 278
Putting Christ Back Into Christmas, 29

Rest on the Flight into Egypt, 255
Room for Jesus, 77, 256
Room in the Inn, 82

Satan Legend, 125
Second Nun's Tale, The, 49
Shepherd, 215
Shepherds at the Grange, 204
Shepherds Had an Angel, The, 214
Shepherds, Rejoice! Lift Up Your Eyes, 201, 283
Shepherd's Hymn, The, 210
Simeon: "God Hears," 282
Sleep, My Little Jesus, 72
Small Cathedral, A, 113
Song for Simeon, A, 269
Song of Gifts to God, A, 184
Star in the East, A, 186
Star Song, 153
Star, The, 169
Star Still Guides, The, 165

Story of Anna, The, 284
Suffering Servant, The, 256
There Came a Little Child to Earth, 109
There Came Wise Men From the East, 161
There Were Shepherds, 211
They Saw His Star, 170
Three Holy Kings, The, 159
Three Kings of Cologne, The, 155, 209
Three Kings, The, 162, 204
Three Poor Shepherds, The, 209
Truce of Christmas, The, 223
Twelfth Night, 258

Upon Christ His Birth, 97

Vermeer, 71
Vigil of Joseph, The, 12
Virgin Birth, 76, 142
Virgin Mary, The, 68
Visited Planet, The, 259
Visiting Bethlehem (Dillard), 90

We Have Christmas in Our Neighbor, 217
When Came in Flesh the Incarnate Word, 118
Where God Enters, 119
Where Shall We Find Him, 263
While Shepherds Watched Their Flocks, 225
While the World Awaited, 12
Wise Men, 168
Wise Men, The, 151
Wondrous Soul, The, 54, 217
Word, A, 116
Words for the Magi, 173